The Gun Digest® Book of
Firearms
Fakes
and Reproductions

Rick Sapp

©2008 Krause Publications
Published by

Gun Digest® Books
An imprint of F+W Publications
700 East State Street • Iola, WI 54990-0001
715-445-2214 • 888-457-2873
www.gundigestbooks.com

Our toll-free number to place an order or obtain
a free catalog is (800) 258-0929.

Library of Congress Control Number: 2008928406

ISBN-13: 978-0-89689-679-6
ISBN-10: 0-89689-679-X

Designed by Paul Birling
Edited by Dan Shideler

Printed in China

The Gun Digest® Book of
Firearms
Fakes
and Reproductions.

Rick Sapp

Other KP Firearms Titles

CONTENTS

Acknowledgments

Many people deserve to be thanked once again for their generous assistance in the preparation of this book. I would especially like to recognize Ted Bell, Marie Brown, Kevin Cherry, Richard Clauss, Joe Cornell, Ed Cox, Dean Dillabaugh, Jim Downing, Ralph Epifanio and family, Norm Flayderman, John Kopek, Sam Lisker, "Ragnar," Ken Ramage, Jim Rawls, Oliver Shapiro, Dan Shideler, Derrek Sigler, Jim Supica, Gabby Talkington and Nancy Worrell. Also David Arnold (Springfield Armory National Historic Site), Cristi Gates (Uberti), Mike Harvey and Rich Karras (Cimarron), Stefano Pedersoli (Davide-Pedersoli), Debra Satkowiak (ATF), Patrick Hogan and Judy Voss (Rock Island Auctions), Ken Van Hoose (Chaparral) and Chris Kortlander (Custer Battlefield Museum).

Introduction: Who We Are

Antiques and collectibles are fascinating subjects. Imagine having a hobby where you were paid to study "cold cases," unsolved mysteries from the past. Collecting is perfect for an amateur detective or someone interested in history or puzzles. So to have an opportunity to study and then to write about restorations, and replicas and fake guns...well, from the first moment my editor, Dan Shideler, mentioned this project it sounded like fun.

The subjects of the book are antique and collectible firearms: those that have been altered, those that have not, and factors in-

Reproduction guns such as this six-shooter from U.S. FireArms make brilliant gifts and shoot like a charm, as well. This magnificently engraved specimen was presented to actor Charlton "When they pry this gun from my cold dead hands" Heston for his service as president of the National Rifle Association from 1994-2003.

volved in recognizing the difference. In many an interview, we have danced around the subject of fakes and fraudulent practices by discussing restoration and bluing, trigger mechanisms and stock cleaning, but what we really wanted to learn are:

- Are there many fake firearms are in circulation?
- If so, how many and what kind?
- Why do people alter firearms?
- How do they go about making a fake?
- Are specific types or genres of guns usually selected for faking?
- And how does the average consumer or collector recognize and avoid buying a fake?

This book does not present every facet of this interesting problem, but it takes the discussion forward in a broad and, I believe, or-

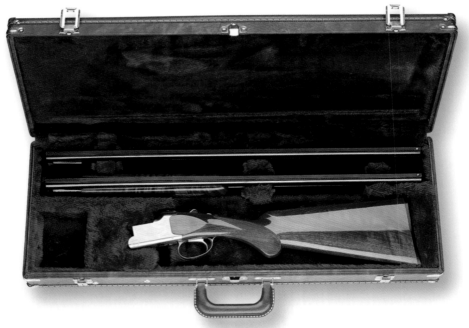

It is not only antique guns that become collectible firearms. Browning's Citori has been a popular design with enthusiasts of clay target games such as trap and skeet, and also with upland bird hunters, for nearly a quarter century. Formerly made in Belgium it is now manufactured by Miroku in Nangoku, Japan.

derly manner. Thus, in *The Gun Digest Book of Firearms Fakes and Reproductions* we will attempt to provide both specifics and "context." That is, we not only want to show examples of practices that could be considered fraudulent if not disclosed to potential buyers, and to mention ways to detect such practices, but to provide some background to the problem, to a bygone era, to the current uses and sometimes to the guns as well. Hence, we have dug into the archives for old advertisements, photographs from the mid 19th century, and then sought to balance the old with the newest and most exacting replicas or reproductions. These are guns so close to the originals that, if the current mark of Pedersoli or Cimarron or Dixie Gun Works were removed, the average gun enthusiast simply could not tell them apart.

And therein, of course, lies part of the problem.

Our objective has not been to turn out a handbook, a how-to book. Instead, our approach is to give readers and collectors (especially new collectors) a broad view of the hobby of gun collecting with specific attention to getting what we pay for – and avoiding that nagging, and sometimes infuriating, sense of buyer's remorse.

In researching this book, I quickly learned that the term "fake" caused people at every level in the gun business to shy away from a candid interview. No one wants to be associated with faking valuable firearms, thus cheating innocent collectors, or indeed with any other fraudulent practice. I am confident that the dozens of individuals I spoke with while gathering information for this book have never personally condoned faking or even telling some "little white lie" about a collectible firearm that would cause it to sell for more money. Their hands are clean. These are the good guys.

What I have learned is that viewpoints about slightly altered – or completely faked – firearms are all over the place. One authority believes that a very high percentage of the old Colt six shooters he sees have been worked on fairly recently by a gunsmith or a restoration specialist, some of them obviously restored, re-stamped or mechanically jiggered…while others are not so obvious.

The guns that are obviously altered or come with documentation – in the antique business a collectible's written, verifiable history is referred to as its "provenance" – are not the guns that trouble

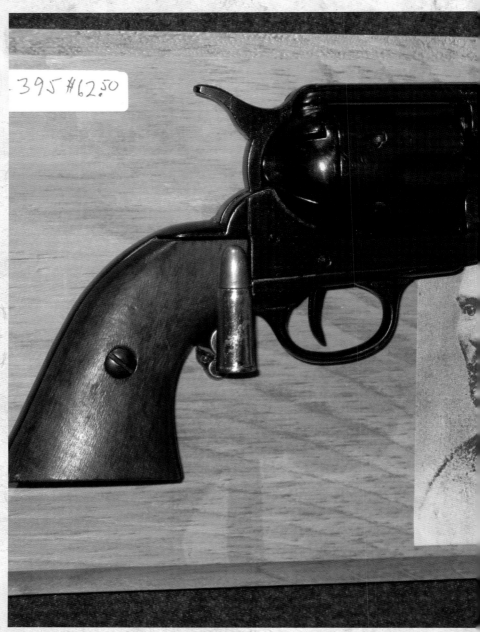

395 #62.50

The inscribed plate on this reproduction of a gun that Jesse James was supposed to have used says that the outlaw was "known as America's Robin Hood, giving stolen loot to weep-

JESSE (DINGUS) JAMES (1847-82)
GUERRILLA RAIDER, BANK/TRAIN ROBBER,
AND NOTORIOUS OUTLAW KNOWN AS
AMERICAN ROBIN HOOD,
GIVING STOLEN LOOT TO WEEPING WIDOWS.

ing widows." Phooey. At $62.50, it might be fun to hang this humorous bric-a-brac on the wall…just do not try to shoot it or sell it, and beware of such legends.

The fascination, even the romance of collecting can begin anywhere. A friend's father dug up this gun in their yard in Cañon City, Colorado, in the early '60s. The top strap over the cylinder – if the cylinder had survived – is clearly stamped "BULL DOG." F&W Editor Dan Shideler tentatively identified it as a "scarce long-barreled knockoff of a Webley, perhaps made by Forehand & Wadsworth, Iver Johnson, or Crescent." Who would have buried or lost such a gun? Was a gunfight involved? A murder? The possibilities are endless and we will probably never know the answers.

us, really. It is the ostensibly virgin guns, the ones that are presented innocently enough, but which leave us with a nagging shadow, a "Something is wrong here, but I can't quite put my finger on it" feeling, that throws the collecting field into turmoil.

Some appraisers and auctioneers believe that there is an epidemic of fakery sweeping through the gun shows, the auction houses and private collections. Others realize the problem exists but would

rather not speculate about its extent. "Of course," they respond, "there are a few rotten apples in every barrel – and I've known some of them – but only a few."

In an odd way, the few who do re-stamp serial numbers and stretch barrels and prematurely age a not-so-old gun do the rest of us a favor. They force us to study; keep us sharp; help us clarify the reasons we are part of this field.

People value antique and collectible firearms for all sorts of reasons. Some folks simply like to hold a thing of value and antiquity in their hands, know that they possess it; others feel the pride that comes with purchasing something rare and expensive, something desired by many others, but something that is – if truth be told – otherwise relatively useless.

Many people look at an old flintlock or percussion rifle hanging on their wall and imagine the world through the eyes of the original users; a hundred or three hundred years ago when the world seemed simpler, even though it may not have been so simple in reality.

Finally, I believe there is a significant category of people who collect because doing so affords them a fascinating life-long hobby, a never-ending opportunity to learn about our cultural and mechanical heritage. These are the collectors who sleuth through crumbling documents and enter on-line chat rooms to talk about old guns. They may not own the greatest number of or greatest value in guns, but these are the collectors who expand their own horizons – and sometimes ours as well – by devoting their leisure time to studying an arcane, sometimes mysterious field.

Collecting and learning about old guns is not altogether different than collecting other categories of "stuff" from years gone by: stamps or coins or porcelain dolls or Studebaker automobiles. The artifacts will collect dust, fade if exposed to sunlight, rust unless protected from humidity. The collector's knowledge, unless he writes it down and thereby passes it along for peer review, will evaporate.

In a larger sense, and despite television's momentary fascination with the program *Antique Road Show*, the world of antiques and collectibles generates experts in – and we say this with sincere respect – relatively worthless fields (unless one is a member, with the author, of that small, but earnest group that believes that history is important) and this is, paradoxically, what gives the study of old firearms (or old stamps or militaria or the like) its unique charm. The men and women who write extensively detailed monographs about some insignificant corner of the shooting universe, who know so much about so little – the "gun nerds," if you will – are frequently the ones who provide true building blocks to our understanding. It has been my great pleasure to climb up on their shoulders for a wider view.

Rick Sapp
Gainesville, Florida
March, 2008

Chapter One

Faking a Firearm

A guest took a gun to the traveling *Antiques Roadshow* production in Seattle.[1] His objective was "to learn more about a gun he had purchased a dozen years earlier because it appeared to be an Indian rifle."

The man handed the rifle to Bill Guthman, a well-known dealer in historical and military Americana of the colonial and federal periods based in Westport, Connecticut. With only a quick once-over, however, Guthman realized that the gun had originated with and been decorated in the "Indian fashion" by unscrupulous owners, not actual American Indians.

"You're a collector, you've been collecting a long time, and we all like to buy wonderful things," Guthman supposedly told the man. "But sometimes we don't buy wonderful things."

Forgers usually re-manufacture or copy older guns because their market value is greater to collectors than are newer guns. *(U.S. FireArms photo)*

Apparently, the metal butt plate, attached to protect the wooden butt of the musket, was added after the gun's construction and fit crudely – although these guns did not have a reputation for meticulous construction. The brass tacks were hammered in to the gun's stock to approximate a lightning bolt. "These tacks were aged to look old," Guthman said, "but you don't see any oxidation around them. The whole rifle has been made to deceive."

According to J. Christopher Mitchell, a nationally recognized militaria expert from Point Clear, Alabama who is also an occasional guest appraiser for *Antiques Roadshow*, it is not rare to discover faked antique firearms. Gun forgers only bother making fakes when their product can earn a substantial sum, he says. Thus, forgers usually copy only the more expensive guns in the marketplace – Colts, Winchesters and Kentucky rifles – or rare guns that have survived from the Revolutionary War or from the Civil War's Confederate Army.

Still, not all forgers go for the big score. Many faked guns or simply those that have been tampered with to increase their value sell for below $10,000 (the one Guthman reviewed in Seattle was bought for $250). A low price can be just large enough to make a nice profit, yet so small as to avoid the careful detective work that ordinarily accompanies the sale of an expensive gun.

Usually, forgers re-manufacture or copy older guns, because they are generally worth more. Authentic old guns corrode over time and show natural signs of aging. Mitchell believes that for spotting fakery nothing substitutes for experience: "After looking at a lot of guns you can tell what man has done and what nature has done," he says. "Nature applies the right patination. You can tell when it's artificially applied."

Less-than-honest handlers stain wood to mimic age and rub new metal with acidic chemicals to make it appear old. Often, a strong acidic odor clings to the metal and resists the application of a base substance to fool the nose.

Instead of manufacturing a brand new gun and making it look old, an expensive and time consuming proposition if one were to begin with a chunk of wood and an ingot of steel, forgers make their job easier by modifying an ordinary old gun or one of the marvelous new reproductions to make it seem more valuable. Additionally, numerous kit guns are now available through legitimate outlets that, carefully constructed, would fool most amateurs.

Deceitful sellers don't hesitate to alter a gun's basic marks, either – removing Pedersoli or Pietta proof marks and re-stamping with "Confederate" insignia. The resellers then artificially age the metal and pass the guns off as originals or with a shrug

Your Sharps rifle does not have a rear sight in the *Quigley Down Under* style? No problem, if you're a faker. Just boost its value with the careful attachment of a new Creedmore sight, adjustable for windage and elevation, from Davide Pedersoli and Traditions Firearms. A "properly aged" hundred-dollar add-on such as this could significantly increase your gun's value. Think that no one would do such a thing? Think again!

and a well-practiced deceit: "The guy who sold it to me didn't really say." It is relatively easy for a sophisticated machine shop to file off an original marking and add a new, but false or spurious mark to make it seem like a more expensive model.

Sometimes, Mitchell notes, the careful observer will see or even feel a slight dishing in the metal where it has been filed. Once forgers learned that antique appraisers were wise to this tactic, they began welding metal over the scooped shape. If this practice grew to great proportions and the forger's art became sufficiently refined, they might destroy the market altogether as almost no one would be able to differentiate between new and old, antique and modern, faked and original.

Another trick – occasionally seen on reproduction Henry repeaters or Sharps rifles – is to improve a gun's value with engraving. "They might have the name Wells Fargo put on a gun to imply it was owned by that company," Mitchell says. (Wells Fargo firearms were always rare and have been accounted for, so to find a genuine model at a gun show or under glass at a neighborhood retailer would be a Miracle.)

He notes that unscrupulous individuals have also been thought to connect an anonymous gun to a historical individual to boost its value. "They'll find a beat-up Colt and some Captain John Doe who was killed during the third day of the Battle of Gettysburg and engrave the gun, 'Presented to Captain John Doe as a token of esteem from the members of his company.' Now you don't have just a beat-up Colt anymore. You have a Colt with history." Unless the forger is careful to smooth the sharp edges of the engraving and darken the shiny silver, both relatively simple tasks, such inscriptions might reveal the gun's fictional provenance as a fraud.

Both Guthman and Mitchell have preached "being prepared" to prospective antique buyers. A solid education in old guns is especially necessary in the antique gun-collecting field because, unlike an oak table thought to be an antique, but only refinished the day before yesterday, an antique gun has little or no utilitarian value.

Guthman's advice was that people should "look at as many guns as they can in museums and dealer shops and familiarize themselves with what's real and what isn't."

One of the best ways to learn about collecting and wise purchasing is by getting to know a good local gun shop. Travis Guggenheim of Pickett Weaponry in Newberry, Florida displays a vintage Colt revolver left on consignment.

Mitchell recommends reading books, which are "the backbone of everything. Whether you want to be a mathematician or a gun collector, you're better off spending your first $2,000 doing research and building a library than buying $2,000 worth of old guns."

The Gun on the Cover

The revolver photographed for the cover of this book is an 1858 New Army Remington. This .44 caliber revolver has an eight-inch octagonal barrel and six-shot cylinder. The frame is blued and case hardened with walnut grips. The barrel is marked "Patented Sept. 14, 1858 E. Remington & Son's Ilion, New York, U.S.A. New Model." Approximately 132,000 were manufactured between 1863 and 1873 and according to the 2007 *Standard Catalog of Firearms* the gun is worth approximately $2,500 in only good condition. (A martially marked example is extremely rare and would be worth an additional 35 percent.) [2]

The gun is an absolute fake...but you cannot tell that just by looking at the photo, and perhaps not even then without investing an hour to be certain and using a powerful magnifying glass.

In truth, the Remington on the cover is a superb replica of that original .44 revolver. It is made by Pietta of Italy and F&W Editor Dan Shideler purchased it new from Cabela's for approximately $200. In the fall

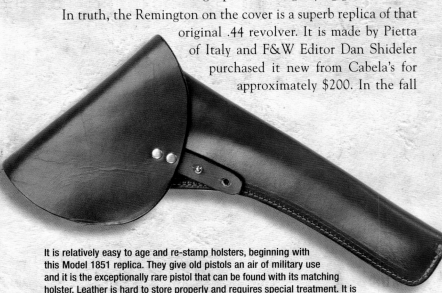

It is relatively easy to age and re-stamp holsters, beginning with this Model 1851 replica. They give old pistols an air of military use and it is the exceptionally rare pistol that can be found with its matching holster. Leather is hard to store properly and requires special treatment. It is prone to flaking and dryness.

The inscription on the barrel reads "N. Wise." The scrolling font is verifiable for the early 19th century and rust is embedded in the depth of the letters as well as on the surface. Probably genuine and, with enough effort and luck, the name might be traceable. *(Photo courtesy Rock Island Auctions)*

of 2007, Shideler worked with his favorite local gunsmith, Richard Clauss, of Garrett, Indiana, to determine what would be required to give this 100 percent new-in-the-box gun the look and feel of a firearm that was nearly 150 years old.

"It was the darndest job I ever had," Clauss says. "Dan gave me this beautiful, brand new Pietta 1858 Remington six-shooter and said, 'Here, Richard. Make this look 100 years old.' Well normally what I do is just the opposite. Guys bring me an old grody piece of crap and they want it restored; make it look like new, they say. So this was a reverse deal."

Clauss, who does a lot of work on Stevens guns ("They're well made for the working man and I admire them") says, "I've never done that [faked or antiqued a gun] before so I kinda had to scratch my head and think, 'Now how am I gonna pull that off?' Dan sent me pictures of some old guns from catalogs, kind of showed me the effect he wanted to achieve, and there were some dings and dents in them where guys had dropped them over the years. So my job was to make something just like in those pictures. You could tell the bluing was pretty well worn off, too just from being used and kind of exposed through the years."

The gunsmith mulled it over for several days and says an idea "gradually came to me. I disassembled the gun completely and plugged the barrel. Then I got a hot plate and put a pan of water on it with a screen across and laid out all the parts on top; all the parts except the grips, which were nice walnut.

"I put a clear Rubbermaid container over it all and steamed it for four days. Each day I would steel wool all the parts to take the rust off, steel wool them right down to bare metal…and then put them all back on top of the screen and do it again. I didn't have the water at a boil, just a simmer, so each day the metal would turn bright orange

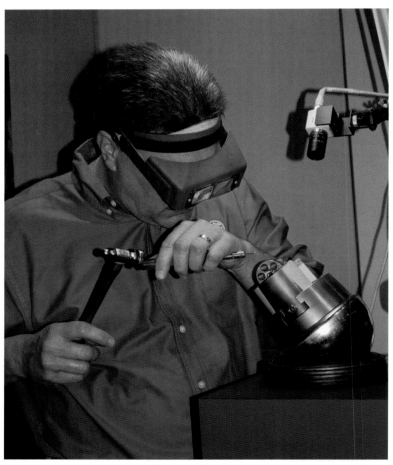

Gun engraving is a fine art. The patterns are intricate and change over time, and surfaces are almost never flat. Watch for sharp edges on old guns and "shine" from a cut that should be dull. Fine engraving enhances the quality of a gun, but add recent engraving to a certified antique and watch the collector value plummet.

with rust. I kept steel-wooling all of that off, not letting the rust get down into the metal. I didn't want it to get deep, and on the fifth day I put plumb brown on it while it was still hot – plumb brown gives the steel an antique-looking finish – and it honestly amazed me, that it turned out better than I thought."

He decided not to steam the internal parts, the parts that do not show in a photograph. "There was no sense ruining a beautiful bore like that," he said, "so mechanically, the gun is still perfect. It's just on the outside that it looks old."

Meanwhile, Clauss stripped the finish off the new walnut grips. He carried them to a lakeside beach and "stepped on them and kind of wiggled my foot around into the stones to make them look kind of dinged up. I was careful not to crack them by applying too much pressure, and just moved them around a little to make them scratched and dinged-up."

Clauss has an engraving machine that could be used to re-letter or re-number a gun that was being restored. If it had to be polished down to the barrel metal, he says, the gun would lose some of the original lettering. "I do restore original lettering if someone asks me to, but have never been asked to change a date or make something an imposter and I wouldn't do that."[3]

Gunsmith Richard Clauss helps with our cover photo.

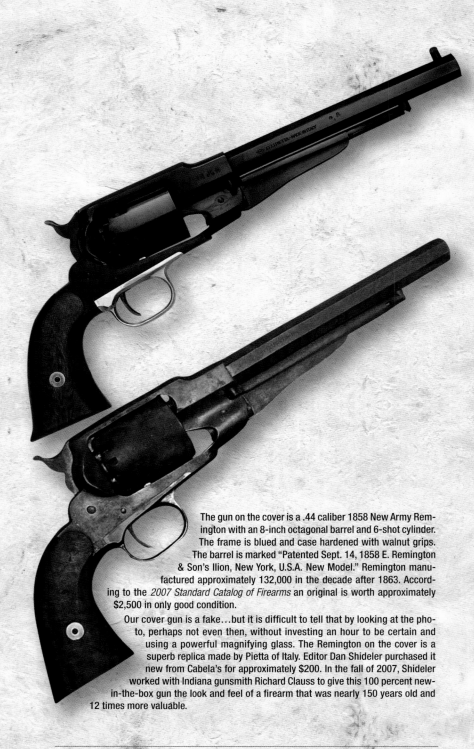

The gun on the cover is a .44 caliber 1858 New Army Remington with an 8-inch octagonal barrel and 6-shot cylinder. The frame is blued and case hardened with walnut grips. The barrel is marked "Patented Sept. 14, 1858 E. Remington & Son's Ilion, New York, U.S.A. New Model." Remington manufactured approximately 132,000 in the decade after 1863. According to the *2007 Standard Catalog of Firearms* an original is worth approximately $2,500 in only good condition.

Our cover gun is a fake...but it is difficult to tell that by looking at the photo, perhaps not even then, without investing an hour to be certain and using a powerful magnifying glass. The Remington on the cover is a superb replica made by Pietta of Italy. Editor Dan Shideler purchased it new from Cabela's for approximately $200. In the fall of 2007, Shideler worked with Indiana gunsmith Richard Clauss to give this 100 percent new-in-the-box gun the look and feel of a firearm that was nearly 150 years old and 12 times more valuable.

The Letter Of Authentication: Best Medicine For Fakery?

We know from personal testimony that even experts are fooled by gun fakery now and then. If this is the case, how can we, the average intelligent collector who has a job in something other than studying firearms day-in and day-out, who has read several of the gun monographs and is careful with our money, ever hope to ensure that our all-star purchase is legitimate? We hire an expert to double-check our purchase.

Such an expert, with years of experience in the narrow, but immensely popular field of Colt cavalry and artillery revolvers, is California's John Kopek. With many years of study and thousands of correct identifications, Kopek has established a quality reputation among knowledgeable collectors and auction services. Here is what he recently had to say about fakes, frauds and the people who perpetuate them in antique firearms:

RS: Are many faked Colts in circulation?

JK: Most of the SAAs (single action army revolvers) you see at

The Expert Speaks

Some thoughts on the value of provenance by John Kopec, noted authority on the Colt Single Action Army:

"We are pleased to offer this [authentication] service to the discriminating collector or dealer. Each authentication letter relates the subject revolver's serial number to the data in our survey, provides a historical analysis of its probable unit of issue/service, summarizes unique or noteworthy features and lists replacement parts – noting any attempts at 'faking.' We estimate that almost 90% of Colt SAA Cavalry & Artillery model revolvers currently being offered for sale – especially at shows – have been faked or 'helped' in some way. Don't you get fooled! Ask for money-back guarantee of authenticity – make sure all exceptions are disclosed and explained. Make provision of an authentication letter as condition of the sale. Protect your valuable investment – always get an authentication letter!"[4]

smaller gun shows have been altered in some way. It is a tremendous volume; it's horrible. There is a lot of fakery going on. I'm even working for some of the auction houses now because unless it comes with a lot of paperwork they're scared to put one on and describe it as original and then have it bounce back. That's embarrassing and expensive.

I've studied this field for a quarter century, first as a single-action gunsmith for 17 years. Then, I really got started when we published our first book, A *Study of the Colt Single Action Army Revolver*, in 1976.

RS: What causes someone to fake firearms?

JK: Greed and money. It's simple. They try to improve them; make them into something that they are not. Sometimes they alter something that – I've run into New York Militia revolvers for instance where mismatching serial numbers doesn't mean anything because usually the mismatched number corresponds with another New York Militia issue. So that wouldn't hurt the value among serious collectors.[5] But a number of these fakers have it in their mind that some of these guns have to be all matching and so they will re-stamp a mismatched part even though it is correct as is, even mismatched, and thereby they ruin the value of the revolver.

Back in the '70s and '80s, they used to stretch barrels. Now they don't stretch them, they just put a new barrel on with the old style rifling and the old style writing, the address and such. We wrote an article back in 2001 where we showed eight different facsimile addresses being used on just the early Colts.

They are welding over these old numbers just absolutely beautifully and re-stamping new digits. One of the fakers said he defied anybody to tell the digits he's stamping from the originals.

Here's an example. I had a gun the other day where I stated that the revolver was totally re-stamped. It really, really looked good. Well the owner didn't believe me and so he sent it to my co-author of the *Colt Book on Colt Calvary & Artillery Revolvers...A Continuing Study*, Sterling Fenn. Fenn looks at and says this gun looks right to him. The digits are 100 percent right all the way through. There's no problem. I said okay let's look at it again and I found that the backstrap had been artificially thinned. "Okay if there is that much metal missing from the backstrap and the serial number is clear as

For the type of gun you are considering, was it typical for the caliber to be stamped in multiple locations? Is this an extremely rare variation with a separate or test stamping performed at the factory or was this done by an unscrupulous gunsmith with access to stamps and tools? Is that a smudge of carbon/graphite powder around the stamp in the wood or simply the natural darkening of age? And why would one stamp note "44.CF" while the other noted "44 W?"

the morning sky, doesn't that indicate a problem? That means that all the other numbers are re-stamped." That gun was shiny as new and that's another tip-off, wear. You can't have a 120-year-old gun without some scratches or smudges.

RS: Who should get their guns authenticated?

JK: Well certainly old Colts and especially military guns. Most dealers now won't sell one without my letter. A buyer shouldn't buy one without a written money-back guarantee that if it doesn't prove to be exactly as the seller says they get their money back. I've seen lots of horror cases, especially at smaller regional gun shows.

Even at the national Colt show a friend of mine got carried away and he bought a .44-40 etched barrel and then brought it to me. I said, "This has a brand new barrel, new address, newly applied etching and I think the backstrap number has been re-stamped." He was very fortunate. He called the guy and he's getting his money back, but that was a $3,500 deal; not small by any means, but not huge, either.

The big international shows are in Louisville, Hartford, Las Vegas and Reno. It is the smaller shows that you have to be wary of, though, because a lot of fly-by-night dealers go to them and you hear the story over and over: "Well I bought this Colt, but I don't remember the name of the guy I bought it from." And a lot of times people just buy themselves a piece of junk.

Lugers and semi-automatics, Civil War stuff, too, are also heavily faked, but I don't know anything about those categories. The Winchester faking is almost as rampant as the Colts.

I try to keep one of everything so that I can compare the authentic with the phony. Also all the inspector and grip cartouches are being copied…and very well, I might add. A person getting into collecting has to proceed with caution and get help because they can really get burned. The new trend is to accept totally refinished or reworked guns in a separate category and I don't think the purist collector is interested in those. They're just pretty guns.

Wherever there is money there is larceny. Best to read and then deal with reputable dealers, not with some fly-by-night guy who has a hot deal or two. Most guns even in a big show like Reno are bad one way or the other.

RS: What about parts replacement? Does that affect gun value and if so, how?

JK: If it is internal, a mechanical part, I'd say no, if it is to make the gun functional in a manner that does not destroy the gun's value.

Parts-Are-Parts, Pieces-Is-Pieces

Parts may not be precisely interchangeable as-is between firearms of the same period, but with a slight bit of machining and attention to the detail of finishing and polishing, any name can be replaced or stamped on any part, such as these percussion locks from Davide-Pedersoli.

It takes very little searching to find trigger mechanisms, custom stocks, parts drawings and every other conceivable part needed to upgrade a collectible firearm.

Norm Flayderman estimates that a Spiller and Burr revolver from the Confederate States of America might bring $15,000 at auction in only fair condition. Similar to many Colts, Remingtons and other revolvers with octagonal barrels of the period this gun is now made in Italy, by Pietta.

Most of the time these old guns have had hammer notches that have been worn off because of improper cocking or stuff like that so to rebuild the hammer and make it functional does not destroy the value. But if they are doing outside or surface stuff like renumbering, putting a new barrel on or new grips, re-stamping inspector's cartouches and so on, that's considered faking.

Disclosure is really important. Then, if someone wants to buy it under those circumstances, well then it is their problem. But you always have a problem with some excuse or even the next guy down

the line. Those famous last words, "I don't intend to sell this gun. Just keep it in my collection and maybe pass it down to my son." Well, you know, four months later I get the same gun back for authentication...from someone else! Oh yeah. I have had lots of them back two and three times, because if you write a bad letter on them the letter somehow gets lost before the gun is sold again. Those guns are real moneymakers for me.

RS: How long does the authentication process take?

JK: I usually turn them out [authenticate a gun] in a day unless there is something special I have to do for the research. I have about 8,000 guns listed on my survey and I've got all the National Archives [the National Archives and Records Administration, www.archives. gov/] stuff and all the Colt factory stuff that lets me do all the back and forth research. There was nothing listed, for instance, by Colt for military guns under #3,600 unless they were returned as artillery guns later. It's the little stuff that helps you do good authentications.

The Factory or Archival Letter

One of the most collectible guns in the world, Colt Manufacturing offers an "Archival Letter" that is considered to be practically bulletproof in the world of antique firearms. If you are interested in old Colts, you will definitely want to be familiar with this service – what it says and what it does not say – and collectors of other types of guns undoubtedly wish that all other companies with history dating to the blackpowder era had the same service. In the best of all worlds, an Archival Letter will list the name of the original purchaser of the gun as shipped from the factory (usually a distributor or wholesaler, but

To rebuild or restore a gun – or to fake one if you are a scoundrel – it is only necessary to shop around with the various manufacturers to find new parts. Then, assisted either by a competent gunsmith or machine shop, one can re-invent a valuable collectible. Let the buyer beware!

sometimes an individual), the date it was shipped, the configuration of the gun (finish, barrel length, caliber and so on) and any special features. Sometimes, incomplete factory documentation means that one or more of these elements will be missing from the Letter.

Generally speaking, says firearms authority Jim Supica, the more information you provide in your initial request (and photos of both sides, the serial numbering – any spot there is a stamping – and so on are immensely helpful), the more likely the factory researchers can find something interesting...if there is something to be found. At a minimum, include positive identification of the mode, serial number, caliber, and any special features.

"Remember, like guns, documentation can be faked!" Supica says, as if the collector needed additional bad news. "Most factory letter sources will write a fresh letter on any gun that has already been lettered for a reduced fee in order to confirm the information in the previous letter. Also bear in mind that it is not unheard-of for serial numbers to be altered on guns to correspond to an historically attributed gun."

Colt Manufacturing says, "The Archive Letter is universally recognized as an unparalleled investment in firearms collecting. The Archive Department will search through Colt's vast archives to provide you with accurate and documented details confirming the original specifications and delivery of your particular Colt firearm. You will then receive a personal letter outlining all the fine points of your firearm, written on the Archive Department's distinctive stationery, embossed with the official seal and signature of the Colt Historian.

"Whether your Colt is a treasured family heirloom or a more

recent purchase, a Colt Archive Letter can provide fascinating and valuable information of historical or anecdotal importance. The collectability of the piece referred to in a Colt Archive Letter is significantly enhanced. The value of your Colt is often greatly enhanced when it is authenticated in this exceptional fashion.

"Colt Archive Letters can finally provide descriptive details about custom engraving and other special features that will ensure the value of the firearm for future generations to treasure."[6]

After recommending Factory Letters and Letters of Authentication from experts – when you get ready to sell, if your gun is at all valuable, they are worth their weight in gold – it is necessary to remind the reader once again that these, too, can be altered and faked. With the rapid development of software such as PhotoShop that allows for scanning, duplicating and altering documents in a very precise manner, it is always worthwhile, especially in a transaction of any magnitude, to verify a letter's authenticity. Whether such a letter turns out to be genuine or not, the effort and expense of double-checking is certainly worth the cost.

To Buy or Not to Buy: Seven Basic Principles

Getting just what you pay for is not always the easiest thing to determine. Did I do well when I bought an American car? Should I buy or invest in Colt Custom Shop Commemoratives? Are my children getting a good education at the state university or should I have taken a second job and sent them to a private school? The decision, of course, is ultimately weighed in the outcome; when you try to sell the car, will it hold its estimated value; will the 1961 125th Anniversary Colt SAA double or triple in price; when the kids graduate, will they be able to get good jobs?

Lacking a Letter of Authentication from the company or an accepted expert, how does one go about overcoming every hesitation

Turn a sow's ear into a silk purse? A good gunsmith is a high-quality craftsman. If in doubt about a gun, ask for a letter of authentication or a factory letter…and remember that these have also been faked!

and doubt and make the crucial buying decision? At that moment when the gun is in your hands and the seller holds out his hand for your credit card, what elements should go through your mind? Let us assume that you have "done your homework:" a fair share of reading and studying, talking with other collectors, following some of the online bidding and maybe even attended a local collector's meeting or a gun show that specializes in collectible firearms.

At this point in your accumulating/collecting career, probably, the more you learn the less convinced you are that you can make a proper decision by yourself. The amount of data is simply overwhelming and the abilities of the fakers are devious. This makes for many opportunities to screw up. Still, at some point, there is a time when one must make the leap, get into collecting or forget it. You could study until the proverbial "cows come home;" interview until you lose your voice; hesitate until there are no more guns to buy (there will always be guns to buy); but until you actually put money down, you are only a looker, not really a collector at all.

1) Caveat Emptor. According to Merriam-Webster online, the Latin phrase caveat emptor is "a principle in commerce: without a warranty the buyer takes the risk." Let the buyer beware. The friendliest, sweetest old gentleman who puts a price tag on a gun is there only to take your money. He may be entertaining and filled with gun data; he may deluge you with magazines and photocopies, but everything will be a smoke screen. You are not friends: he is a seller and you are a buyer. End of conversation.

2) Assume Every Transaction Is A Fraud. Perhaps the inexperienced collector should approach every transaction as if it involved an element of fraud. Not unfriendly, but cautious; your job is to suspect fraud and work to find it. To research the mismatched serial numbers (sometimes this suggests fraud, but often it does not); to verify that every element of the gun meets some standard for the period (the barrel has lost much of its blue, but the interior of the bore is 100 percent and spotless). Study everything you can about the gun you are considering. Take time to look it up in reference books – and if the seller says, as realtors often do when purchasing a house, that someone else is ready to make an offer – by all means let them do so.

Do not, under any circumstances, be panicked into a decision you may later regret!

3) Every Bad Purchase Is The Buyer's Fault. This is a variation on the principle of caveat emptor, which means that you are an adult and you are responsible for your decisions. Not every bad purchase is the fault of the seller. Every bad purchase is the fault of the buyer. Of course, some poor buying decisions are aided by illusion and fakery, fraudulent statements by the seller, but the owner must take responsibility because recourse is thin once you walk out of a crowded gun show with a collectible and a receipt in a box. You

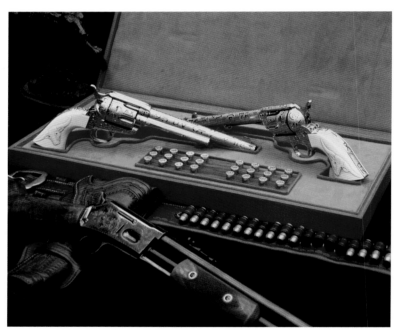

Living the dream...or bringing the dream to life. U.S. FireArms initiated its "Fine Art Gallery Program," with a pair of guns it dubbed "The Cattlebrands of Jackson Hole, Wyoming." According to USFA, only one was produced exclusively for show at the Legacy Gallery. "This 2-year project made its debut in July of 2006 and features a pair of one-of-a-kind cowboy masterpieces from the USFA 'The Legend Lives' gallery series. The two single action 45 caliber revolvers are consecutively numbered, JH1 and JH2, and have 7-½ inch barrels, carved ivory grips and ruby eye inlay. 100% high relief coverage engraving of famous Jackson Hole Brands including "JY", "MH" Moosehead and "W4" Walton ranches. A fitted case, which has cattlebrand motif embossed around the entire top without duplication, is included. Interior is French fit and includes cartridge block."

Numerous companies produce special editions for collectors. Smith & Wesson produced a .45 for "Rolling Thunder" which, ironically, was the name of the sustained bombing campaign of North Vietnam from 1965-1968. It is also an annual motorcycle rally staged to remember American POWs and MIAs.

The new S&W Thunder Ranch Model 22 is a fixed-sight "wheelgun" chambered for .45 ACP. The top front of the frame has been scalloped down much like the old S&W Outdoorsman model. Will this gun, because it has a special relationship to Thunder Ranch, a 2400-acre world-class firearms training facility in Oregon, have any special value in 25 or 100 years? Maybe, but probably not....

Whether one should buy a commemorative collectible is a question of personal interest and taste. Purchasing special-issue commemorative firearms as investments, however, is rarely a sound economic decision unless you're in it for the very long term.

Weighing 4 lb. 9 oz. the Walker is a massive revolver. Sam Colt's relationship with Captain Samuel H. Walker, a veteran of the frontier fighting with Mexico and the Comanche in Texas, attracted a flurry of attention and helped Colt get back on his feet after the Paterson venture collapsed. How difficult would it be to make modifications to this F. Pietta Walker, which comes already "antiqued," to pass it off as the real thing? Even in poor condition, the original gun has sold for more than $50,000 although the price varies – downwards – for other model Dragoons. Still, the incentive is there….

could complain to show management or even hire an attorney, but words begin to twist and change meaning in the "He said, she said" world of law, especially when only two people are involved in a transaction. A simple, "Well, that's what the former owner told me" can be sufficient to muddy most waters in court. If one enters a transaction with the realization that it is absolutely your mature decision, then in most cases you will be fine.

4) The Gun Should Speak For Itself. Curiously, the people who consistently ignore you when you ask to pick up and examine a firearm at a gun show may actually be your new best friends. You are not buying BS…and often the more objects a seller has on his table the less he knows about any particular one of them. Remember that you are exchanging your very hard-earned cash for an object of limited or doubtful value; an object that has value only because you and a few others have agreed so. Outside the narrow circle of collectors an old gun has little or no worth and indeed, as a decorative object,

Winchester Model 1885

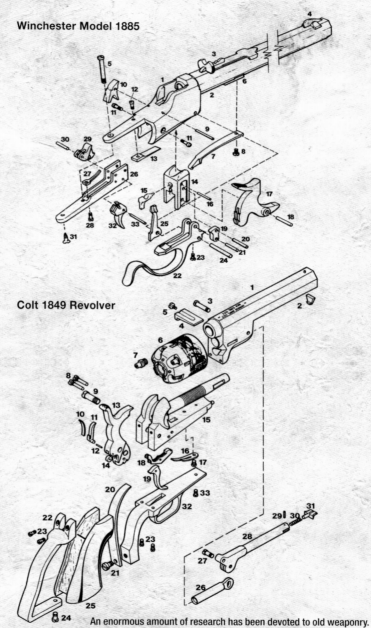

Colt 1849 Revolver

An enormous amount of research has been devoted to old weaponry. A person wishing to build a "new-tique" can readily find parts drawings (gun schematics) online. Using these with a little craftsmanship and the availability of only basic tools, it would be possible to re-manufacture almost any old gun.

the shiny fake is much to be preferred to the dull, rusty original. Thus, the gun must speak for itself. Before you lies a puzzle, and it is your challenge and opportunity to determine whether this artifact is worthy. Whatever condition or subtle restoration or trickery may

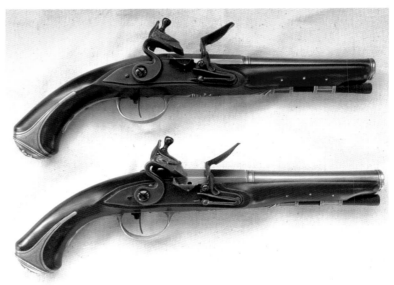

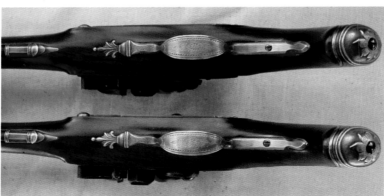

A matching pair of 20-gauge French pistols weighing about 20 ounces each and featuring English walnut, brass (bronze) barrels and brass furniture with a special aged look, which "makes them look old, but not distressed and beat up." Also note the bottom of the pistols showing the entry thimbles, trigger guard inletting, engraving and the raised flower treatment of butt caps. All visible screws are fire blued and timed. (Reproductions from Charles Caywood, Caywood Gunmakers, Berryville, Arkansas)

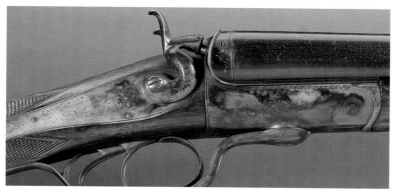

A manufacturer that you have never heard of? A Fred Wood (of Salisbury) percussion 12-gauge? It is one way to attempt fraud, but knowledgeable shotgun people would be all over it. "Very good plus as refurbished," note Rock Island Auctions which expects $1,500-$2,000 (Lot 428). "The barrels show almost all of the Damascus pattern."

be involved in its presentation cannot be fully concealed once it is lying open to the world under the glare of neon lights. Your thorough inspection – the application of everything you have learned – should now allow this gun to speak for itself, to reveal its history. The muzzle, exhibiting greater wear on one side than the other, the carefully cut down front sight and the ultra-light trigger may be signs that indeed, some gunslinger spent many an hour drawing it from his holster. The fanciful notches on the grip, however, may be (probably are) just that – some recent owner's desire to deceive.

5) If It Seems Too Good To Be True, It Probably Is. You have understood this since you were a kid, when you just knew that the sneaky Sunday School teacher's offer to let anyone who didn't want to learn the day's lesson go outside to play, simply had to have a catch…and, of course, it did. Nothing has changed. If the gun's price seems far lower than you would expect to pay, than the *Standard Catalog* suggests is about right for the gun's condition, you need to keep your hand off your wallet while you ask more questions. It might be comforting to know that expert collectors occasionally fall into this trap as readily as newcomers, and the bottom line is that we are all ready to find buried treasure, to win the lottery. Someone will win the lottery, but with respect, it will not be you or me. Some call this syndrome "greed," but others give it a positive spin, suggesting that

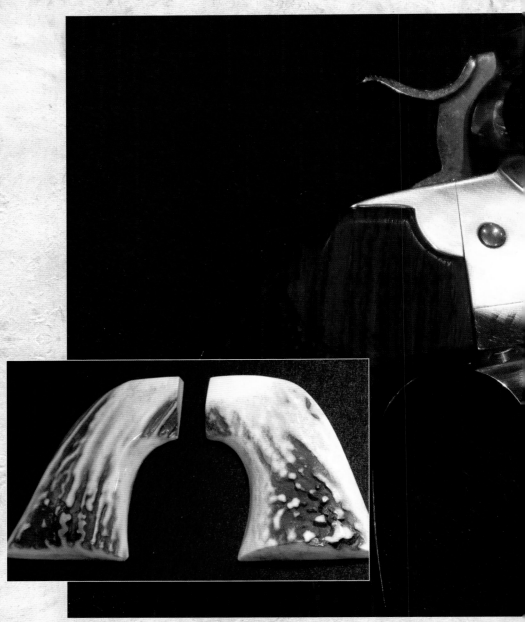

Your old gun is pretty beat-up. So what's wrong with adding beautiful new grips? These Pearlite and Sambar stag grips will not change the gun, just its appearance, giving it a dramatic and immediate upgrade. If you are careful not to scratch the grips or damage the head

of the old screw; and if you preserve the old grips; and if, when you sell the gun you inform a prospective buyer and give him or her the old grips...perhaps nothing is wrong with adding the new grips.

You may well want to display a fine collectible firearm in a new display case such as this one from Traditions Firearms, but beware the gun show firearm so displayed and any spiel from a vendor about "Grandma found this…."

the source is our American business "creed," simply a version of "buy low, sell high."

6) Never Buy A Collectible Without A Return Guarantee. Every old gun purchased from a vendor should come with a written guarantee that within three days or a week, if the buyer – for any reason whatsoever – decides not to follow through with the purchase, i.e. wants his money back, the gun can be returned and the buyer's money, less some appropriate and agreed-upon-in-advance charge for shipping, handling and paperwork, will be immediately refunded. The guarantee, which often specifies that the gun not be fired, should specify the mechanics of the return – sometimes, with larger companies one must call and obtain an RA, Return Authorization number

– and that of the refund as well. This written guarantee is not just to protect you, the buyer; it also protects the seller. Any high quality, reputable business will have such a guarantee in place. If they do not, ask for one and do not accept a verbal guarantee, because a simple "I didn't say that" versus "Oh, yes you did, too" will be enough to frustrate a jury. Don't accept the handshake and smile. We are far beyond the day when "gentlemen" did business that way. Today, gentlemen ask for a written guarantee.

7) Consider The Character Issue. You have made a purchase and now proudly display it in a case on the wall of your office, using cotton gloves to handle it. Then, someone points out an oddity: Sure, Wild Bill Hickok may have used this gun 150 years ago when he was an army scout, but why isn't there any evidence that the cylinder has ever been turned? Shouldn't there be a little "drag line" there from the cylinder stop? Your heart skips a beat. Your first impulse is grab the gun and club the bearer of bad news "right up aside his stupid head." Realizing immediately (now) that you have allowed yourself to be taken by an unscrupulous seller, you are presented with an array of choices. The path you choose speaks loudly for your character. Do you admit that you made a foolish decision and accept the loss of perhaps thousands of dollars with grace and humor? Do you quietly (and quickly) attempt to pass along the mis-represented piece to the next clueless buyer, thus saving your cash if not your conscience? No one is perfect, yet every now and then everyone is confronted with a perfect choice or decision; this is one of those times. Perhaps it helps to make the correct decision if you realize that you are not alone: "…rest assured that every gun trader, admit it or not, has misidentified a piece or two along the way, and then concluded that it was an altered 'something-else,'" George Knight writes.[7]

Footnotes

1 As reported by our friends at Lowe's Certified Guns in Sellersville, Pennsylvania (www.lowescertifiedguns.com), the original episode with photos can be viewed at http://www.pbs.org/wgbh/roadshow/tips/firearms.html. NOTE: In an article written for Antiques and the Arts Online (http://antiquesandthearts.com) and posted December 27, 2005, Laura Beach reported that Guthman himself gave a wonderful explanation of his collecting impulse, putting it into words as follows: "It boils down to the fact that I really collect early American history in objects and written words, in an attempt to acquire a complete picture of the period or periods...." Guthman passed away December 28, 2005.

2 Dan Shideler, Standard Cata;og of Firearms, Krause Publications, Iola, WI 2007 (page 911).

3 "By the way," Krause/F&W's Dan Shideler says, "It shoots like a champ and is now sitting on my mantle."

4 This quote is copied with permission from an online advertisement for John Kopek's authentication service on an Internet site owned by Nevada firearms collector Ed Cox www.coltparts.com/johnkopec.html. Kopek has co-authored a book titled A Study of the Colt Single Action Army Revolver (with Graham and Moore). The book and information about Kopek's authentication service is available from John Kopec Publications, 1366 Carla Circle, Redding, CA 96003 (530) 222-4440 [until 6:00 pm Pacific Time].

5 Joe Cornell, author, appraiser and longtime student of guns and other antiques in Denver recalls, "I have a particular fascination with Winchester Model 62s. Well, I found one at a gun show in Tulsa, a 62 that had a nickeled receiver, tang and butt plate. It had a curved butt plate that was numbered in the 62 range, and it was stamped Model 62, but it had the "W" logo on the top tang. Now that meant the receiver was an 1890 receiver.

"Well, I saw that and recognized it immediately as a factory 'parts gun' that was made at the beginning of the 62 in the real early 1930s, but the guys at the factory had gone to their parts bin...maybe because it was a special order for one of their expert shooters, who knows.

"The 62 for the most part replaced the 1890, but the frames were interchangeable. So for whatever reason, they went to the factory parts bin and picked out an 1890 frame and marked it 62 and serial numbered it as a 62 and sold it. I think it is the only nickeled 62 in existence.

"It was not up to the condition that I normally buy – I'm a condition collector – but I just couldn't resist because I have this special affection for 62s, you know. I cheat on my own standards some time."

6 For additional information about this valuable service, visit www.coltsmfg.com/cmci/historical.asp. This service is not free, however, so expect to pay $300. Prices vary by model and other listed considerations.
- Colt Historical Department, Kathleen Hoyt, PO Box 1868, Hartford, CT 06144
- Sturm Ruger, 10 Lacy Place, Southport, CT 06490
- Smith & Wesson, Roy Jinks, Factory Historian, PO Box 2208, Springfield, MA 01102
- U.S. Military Arms: Springfield Research Service, PO Box 4181, Silver Springs, MD 20904 (This service conducts ongoing research on military arms in government records and will research individual guns for fee.)
- Winchester, Marlin and L.C. Smith, c/o The Buffalo Bill Historical Center, PO Box 1000, Cody, WY 82414 (The museum has records for most early Winchesters after Model 1866 s/n #125000; for early Marlin lever action rifles; and for most L.C. Smith shotguns from 1890-1971.)

7 George Knight, *Successful Gun Trading*, Stoeger Publishing, Accokeek, MD 2006 (page 31).

Chapter Two

Spotting Fakes

*T*hree areas of collectibles are rife with opportunities for and have a reputation for passing off a sow's ear as a silk purse. These areas involve guns from the ever-fascinating Civil War era, guns from the Old West and military guns. In addition, any relatively rare issue with some special mechanical feature ("Well, I'm glad you asked, because this particular gun….") or guns with an interesting "provenance" ("You see this inscription here? This gun was presented to Sergeant….") are likely to be offered to new collectors as must-have or can't-wait buys. In this chapter, we will highlight the Civil War, Old West and military guns for special consideration.

The date stamp and inspector's cartouche are clear on the grip of a pistol offered for auction through Rock Island. Are they perhaps too clear, too evidently perfect – or are they exactly right for the wear and tear on the gun? Only a thorough inspection of the entire gun could answer that. *(Photo courtesy Rock Island Auctions)*

Do not be discouraged, however, or believe that we in the firearms field have some unorthodox curse. The problem of undisclosed alterations and even outright fakery is not solely the province of gun collecting. In his *Guide to Fake and Forged Marks* Mark Chervenka[1] writes:

"Several years ago, an advanced collector of cut glass I spoke with estimated as much as 30-40 percent of the signed cut glass he was offered had recently applied marks. Either there were new marks on new glass, new marks on genuinely old but originally unmarked glass or new marks that did not match the company known to have made a particular shape or pattern (a Libbey mark on a known Hawkes pattern, for example).

"The collector went on to say that almost all desirable old cut glass can fairly easily be attributed to specific companies by the pattern and shape of the blanks. 'About the only people interested in acid stamped marks,' he concluded, 'are beginning cut glass collectors or dealers that handle a general line. As long as someone is willing to pay extra for a marked piece, unethical people will fill that demand by applying forged marks.'"

U.S. Civil War

In his book about Civil War collectibles, John Adams-Graf notes the pros and cons of collecting era firearms and other articles of period militaria. Pistols and revolvers, he says, are plentiful, require little storage space, are eternally fascinating and relatively stable investments. The long arms, muskets and rifles, are similarly plenti-

ful, but are cumbersome to display. On the other hand, Civil War era guns attract thieves and those few guns with specific provenance proving use during the war are fairly rare and also quite expensive. "Provenance can add hundreds or thousands of dollars to the price of the most mediocre weapon," Graf says. And perhaps the most telling comment for the purposes of this book, "Rare models are often faked or pieced together from parts. High-end purchases should be left to advanced, knowledgeable collectors."[2]

No one knows precisely how many individual or small arms were present on the battlefields of the U.S. Civil War, although that number certainly is in the many millions. After all, battles took place not only in Virginia and Pennsylvania, but in Florida and Texas and California, as well. A generally agreed-upon number for total com-

Millions of weapons were built for use during the U.S. Civil War. Federal armies tended to standardize armament, but in the Confederate States where the naval blockade and Winfield Scott's Anaconda Plan of dismembering that temporary nation made procurement difficult, a variety of firearms were used.

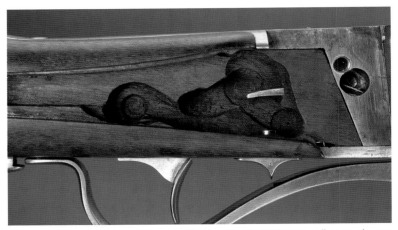

Often, repairs or restoration efforts made inside a gun will not interest collectors who are primarily concerned with external appearance. Still, inside is a place to look for valuable clues to firearms fraud. *(Photo courtesy Rock Island Auctions)*

batants of north and south, both soldiers and sailors, is 3.5 million. Perhaps half a million pistols and revolvers were issued to mounted troops. Assuming that each soldier was issued one and, during the course of the war, sometimes two weapons; other soldiers purchased weapons to supplement those issued; and during the war hundreds of thousands were destroyed and broken, captured or lost, and the eventual figure is perhaps well over 10 million guns, not even counting cannons, rifled artillery and mortars.

It is safe to assume that if you had ancestors in the United States during the war era, you had combatants on one side or the other – although members of peace parties such as the Copperheads in the north often refused to fight or purchased an exemption – and virtually everyone was involved in war industry in one way or another, including farmers. Thus, it is also safe to suggest that interest in the war and the weapons of this war – pistols and muskets, after all, represent the intensity of feeling on both sides – may never diminish and if that is the case, neither will the values assigned to collectible firearms of the era.

That very desirability, unfortunately, also means that Civil War collectibles are prone to reproduction and even outright fakery, from

Collectors typically hover around gun shows and haunt local expos and flea markets. Any place that something unexpected could turn up for sale is a place where you just might find a rare Butterfield U.S. Army Revolver ($6,000-$8,000) or a Confederate Richmond Rifle-Musket ($7,500-$10,000).

the relatively easy to produce bullet-in-the-belt-buckle – which every collector will have seen once or twice – to the recently "antiqued" handgun. Here is the temptation:

"*1851 Navy Brass Frame Revolver kit.* The brass frame 'Navy Type' revolvers are identified with the Confederate Griswold & Gunnison, and Leech & Rigdon revolver. Brass was used for the frames because of the scarcity of iron in the United States. 1 piece hardwood grips with brass frame. .36 caliber, blued 7-1/2" octagon barrel. 6 shot, .368 chamber diameter. Kit is left in white. The kit is not engraved. Skill level 1. Manufactured in Italy."

Serious about making an expensive gun buy? Study the inside as well as the outside. An old gun will not only have the correct roll-engraved cylinder scene, but the interior of the weapon will show signs of age as does this old Colt cylinder.

As a kit, this gun costs $157.00 from Dixie Gun Works. Add $12.95 for shipping and the total price of your new gun is $169.95 (www.dixiegun.com). At skill level #1, almost any able-bodied man or woman with even the most rudimentary tools can produce a working blackpowder firearm with this kit.

Case in Point: Griswold & Gunnison

Between July 1862, when they opened for business, and November 1864 when Federal cavalry destroyed their factory, the manufacturing team of Griswold and Gunnison built 3,606 revolvers based on the Colt pattern for the Confederate States. The brass frame is the distinguishing characteristic and both lettering and numbering are well established on the first model:

- Serial number on the frame, barrel lug and cylinder.
- Loading lever, trigger guard, back of frame, back strap, hammer, trigger and even the grips are secondarily marked.
- A "G" is stamped on the underside of the barrel and "II" on the back of the lug.
- Another "G" is stamped on the cylinder back and "GG" on the back strap, back of frame and trigger guard.

James D. Julia Auctioneers have sold authentic Griswold and Gunnison Confederate .36 caliber revolvers in reasonably good condition for up to $29,500.

If one could invest a few spare hours carefully converting a $169.95 kit into a $29,500 return – especially if the penalty for discovery was practically nonexistent – almost any of us would be willing to "give it a shot." If our math serves, at that sale price, our merchandise would be marked up a whopping 17,353 percent! And because this 150-year-old Confederate Colt is supposed to be in less-than-perfect condition, almost any careless handling error that we make while building the kit might actually help improve the gun's sellability!

Guns of the Old West

The American "Old West" with its iconic images of cowboys and Indians has an international reputation far larger than its le-

"USFA's new Gunslinger features a genuine 'browning' or patina process that gets better with use. This is not a wipe on/off finish or temporary acid treatment (gray appearance) such as the Italian imports. The Gunslinger antique finish is a process that involves the development of multiple patina layers, each building on the next, aging the surface without pitting the metal. Age and use will only enhance the character of this gun. The USFA Gunslinger - this is your great-great-grandfather's gun. Inherit yours today!

"Serial numbered from the Colt 1st generation beginning around 55,XXX or your special serial number {Birthday, special date, SASS Member #Etc }, fitted with our trademark aged hard rubber grip you'll swear Gunslinger has been around a long time and will become an instant heirloom."

gitimate place in history. With its image of wide horizons, plentiful game and the ever-present danger of attack by the natives – or by native wild animals – the Old West has come to represent freedom, self-reliance and unlimited opportunity. Apparently, this is a vision

The 1873 Springfield Trap-door carbine from Traditions Performance Firearms shoots as well as if not better than the original. And it certainly looks better than a gun that is 135 years old, even reconditioned.

that is shared by over-regulated, over-studied, over-fenced peoples around the world.

One proprietor of a prominent auction house has said that a high percentage of the highly sought-after Colt Single Action Army revolvers – the iconic gun of the Old West – that his company sees on a regular basis have been altered. Of course Colt firearms of the era are not the only ones that have seen the sly touch of restoration, but they are dominant in the imagination for "God created man, but Sam Colt made them all equal."

It thus behooves the collector to take special care when reviewing SAAs of that era for possible purchase. Colt's earlier Paterson,

A rare Model No. 3 Belt Paterson…or a fake. The original is valued at $75,000 in good condition and "only" $30,000 in fair condition. Before making such a purchase, one would need to personally inspect the gun and to have either a factory letter or a letter of authenticity from a certified firearms appraiser. *(Photo courtesy Rock Island Auctions)*

The easiest type of gun to fake might be the solidly built, but very basic and inexpensive six-shot single action. Millions were made and so they are relatively common and, depending upon the model, prices vary from precious to throwaway.

Walker and Dragoon revolvers are so rare, so expensive and so diligently studied that an alteration specialist would almost certainly risk immediate exposure were he to attempt to pass off a replica or re-manufactured gun as an original. This leaves the Civil War era Colts, and especially the Confederate Colts – spoken of earlier in the chapter – and those from the Old West as potentially lucrative fakes.

The interest in cowboy action shooting has brought several hundred thousand enthusiasts into the shooting family. While most were already pro-firearms, their hobby has boosted the sale of reproduction revolvers, rifles and shotguns – most, but not all, of which are built in Italy – that represent the 1800s cowboy era.

To protect against the fakes, alterations and frauds of firearms of this era, to at least make sure that any changes are disclosed to the buyer, most reputable auction firms give the guns they sell a cursory inspection before banging the gavel…or they inspect at a distance, meaning they are able to get an authoritative (or semi-authoritative) opinion based entirely on photos and descriptions provided by the seller.

It is worthwhile to take an extended look at a particular sale, this one online, because it demonstrates the state of the art for Internet auctions and sales. After all, with gasoline driving toward the $5 per gallon mark and airline service crashing, Internet sales and auctions for all types of goods and services are growing at an astonishing rate. The lesser of all evils might be paying for high speed Internet service and elevated shipping charges, which are based on oil selling for more than $100 per barrel. (Unfortunately, shopping via the Internet opens up a whole new world of fraudulent practices and the need to defend against them. These are not the subjects of this book, but they need to be mentioned here.)

So here is an example of an Old West gun offered for sale and subsequently evaluated online at GunBroker.com in February of 2008:

Colt Single Action Army

Seller's Description: I thought this was a Colt Single Action Army .38-40 (Serial #193426) but everything I have read says the Army was introduced in 1873 and the Patent Date on this gun is Sept. 19, 1871. I have no idea what generation it is. The barrel is 4-¾ inches and the action is good. The grips are wood and it has never had others that I know of. The Colt emblem is engraved next to the patent date. The gun has not been fired in over 20 years but I would have no hesitation using it and have ammunition. I even have a left handed western gun belt with cartridge loops.

Condition: The finish has not been re-blued to my knowledge and is worn/faded due to age and holstering. The only flaw that I know of (other than worn bluing) is that the flange on the ramrod has broken off. The action and cylinder are excellent.

Provenance: Don't know.

Appraiser's Comments

History of the Item: Up to 1890 there are quite a few different versions of the Single Action Army, such as the Flat Top, the Bisley, Sheriff's, Storekeeper's and the Frontier just to name a few, but after 1989 and until 1940, there are only two versions, the Standard Production Pre War Model 1899 – 1940 and the Long Fluted Cylinder Model of 1913 to 1915. The Colt Single Action Army was made in more than 20 different calibers, some simple improvements and some changes from the basic configuration. This is probably the most recognized and famous handgun ever made. It was first introduced in 1873 and is still in limited production today, 130 years of continuous production speaks to it popularity and the constant demand. The

1871 number you mention is an early patent date and would have nothing to do with the actual production date or Model name.

Appraiser Tips: Yours was made in 1890; serial numbers for the year started at 130000. The values seem to be always on the rise for the really good ones. There are people that have made a life's study on the SAA and there are literally thousands of books published on this gun, I would suggest that you pick up one of these books to see what a fine and historic gun you have. SAAs made before 1894 are considered of higher value because after 1894 there were some production changes, mostly internal, to compensate for the introduction of the new smokeless powder. The Single Action Army has been made in more than 20 calibers and barrel lengths from 4 inch to 10 inch, from plain looking to extensive engraving and detailing. The above production numbers and serial numbers are from the book *Colt, An American Legend, the Official History of Colt Firearms, 1836 to Present* by R.L. Wilson. From the pictures and the serial number, this would be a Standard Civilian Production model 1876 to 1898. This Model included numbers from 127000 to 162000.

Research Sources: Serial Number information is from the book *Colt, American Legend, the Official History of Colt Firearms, 1873 to Present* by R.L. Wilson. Values are averaged from a few sources: *The 24th Edition of the Blue Book of Gun Values, 2005 Standard Catalog of Firearms, Flayderman's Guide to Antique American Firearms, 8th Edition*, and *Classic Colt Peacemaker*.

There are a few drawbacks when appraising a gun of this type and age, first, you do not have the original box and papers. This is

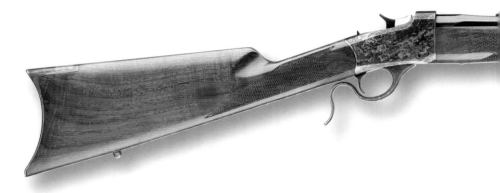

the biggest single drawback with values for the SAA. A Colt letter of authenticity would help to establish the early life of the gun. It shows the configuration of the gun at production and where the gun was initially shipped after production for sale, however, it would not show the buyer or where it went after that. Second, the gun has been used, this will usually cut the value by about one half right away, but its age and overall condition can usually mitigate that. Finally, there are a large number of these guns that have been inspected and certified as either New in Box or Excellent, meaning they have met the first two requirements and these are the ones that all of the others have to be judged against. The value below is for a Standard Civilian Production Model classed as "Good" based on the condition of the finish. Also, from the wear marks on the cylinder lugs and the finish fading at the front of the cylinder, this gun has seen an extremely extensive and active shooting life. Remember, there are more than 20 models of the SAA made up to the point of yours, some are definitely valued higher than others, possibly because of popularity, limited numbers or some special feature or caliber. I would suggest that you might want to contact an expert in the Colt SAA in your area and arrange for a physical appraisal, this would provide you with a lot more information than I can, simple because I am working from a basic description and pictures. Finally, the value is contingent on the physical appraisal simply because the gun deserves it. If the physical inspection warrants it, the value could quite easily increase.

Current Fair Market Value: $7,000 (Current Fair Market Value is the amount someone might receive when selling their item to a

The Model 1885 Winchester Low Wall, like the 1885 High Wall, has a long-standing reputation for accuracy. After firing, lowering the lever ejects the spent cartridge, while a convenient ejector/selector switch allows you to either extract or eject the spent case in any direction; perfect for both left- and right-handed shooters. The case-colored receiver, buttplate and lever, along with fine line checkering give it a classic look. Drilled and tapped for a scope. Old name, but new gun.

When you get stung by the collecting bug, an interest in antique firearms may take you in directions you never thought possible. Beware! Copies exist for everything from Colonial-era Betsy Ross flags to fraudulent autographs and photographs of famous people.

dealer or at auction. It is also the amount most government tax agencies (U.S. IRS, Revenue Canada, Inland Revenue, etc.) recognize as the tax deductible amount were the item donated to a charitable organization.)

Replacement Cost: $9,000 (Replacement Cost is the retail amount one might reasonably pay to purchase the item from a dealer, gallery, store, etc. It is also the amount for which one may want to insure an item.)

Note the prevalence of "I have no idea" and "that I know of" and "Don't know" in the seller's description. This is not to suggest that the seller is in any way bringing a fraudulent item to the market – although that possibility exists – simply that there are many unknown (or perhaps unrevealed) elements in the description and hence the "expert evaluation" cannot be anything but weak and incomplete. It is worthwhile and necessary to consider what additional questions one might ask after reading the online sales and appraisal certificates.

The seller does not give any indication of the facts of acquisition, either, which will almost certainly be key to understanding this

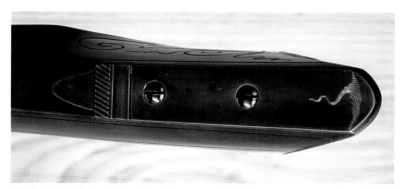

Finding a beautifully unscarred toe-plate on an old rifled musket would tell an experienced collector one of two things: A – that the gun was a reproduction or B – that the toe-plate had either been replaced or removed, polished and reattached with new screws.

particular gun. Did he buy it at a garage sale a gun show or dig it up intact in a buried chest or…is it perhaps an Italian reproduction that has been doctored? This lack of information would give tremendous pause to anyone who was not a certifiable expert and thinking of purchasing this firearm.

The appraiser says he is a member of the Canadian Personal Property Appraiser Association (CPPA) with an interest, among many other things, in guns. The information he gives regarding the Colt is straightforward from the books of gun historians (whom he properly cites). As far as it goes, it is harmless, but it is also – as we warned when one picks up a specimen at a crowded gun show and the dealer produces reams of interesting, but not precisely relevant paperwork – rather useless in evaluating the specific gun one is holding in hand.

Assuming the appraiser gave the best appraisal he could, given the circumstances and information, his commentary may actually be counterproductive because it gives the illusion of strength and veracity. If one were seriously considering purchasing this gun for anywhere near the $7,000 "current fair market value," it would be worthwhile to communicate directly with the seller and perhaps even travel to his home town to inspect the gun personally.

Unless one has recently won the PowerBall Lottery, from afar, the best advice is to be patient and cautious. Even if one has won that lottery, to rush into such a purchase would only encourage opportunistic sellers and thus cause the market in firearms antiquities and curios to collapse that much sooner.

In summary, to make a purchase – even to place a bid – on this gun based on the information available, without having a nationally recognized expert authenticate the gun and to have a factory letter, is probably going to be throwing a great deal of money away. You would have done a disservice to yourself and your family, and also to all those who might be tempted by the next such online offer. And finally, no one can do a complete and accurate authentication based on photographs on the internet. Can't be done. Period.

Militaria

Build it and they will come. Go to war with it and someone will begin collecting it as soon as the war is over. According to many sources, Civil War guns, bayonets, sabers and equipment begin selling as souvenirs the moment that war ended…those items the surviving participants had not themselves squirreled away. Militiamen, vigilantes and soldiers who overran Indian encampments typically stole everything that was not broken or had not taken root.[3] And everyone's Dad brought home abandoned detritus from World War II: Nazi flags, ceremonial daggers, pistols, helmets and so on.

Perhaps the thrill of militaria – guns to uniforms, unit patches, photographs and written orders – is the association with action. It is like being in the room with the Devil…without having to actually dance with Him (or Her). We may not have been present in Bastogne, fighting with the 101st Airborne or with the French Foreign Legion, surrounded at Dien Bien Phu, Vietnam, but when we handle a rifle or handgun from that war, we can nevertheless make an emotional connection.

Marie Brown is the owner of Chicken Coop Antiques at Effingham Falls on Route 153 North in Effingham, New Hampshire. She believes the world of militaria is endlessly fascinating, but warns that, "Reproductions and fakes run rampant in the military field. Some are obvious while others are so good that even the best of the best can be fooled. One thing to bear in mind is that no one person can possibly know everything, no matter how long they have been in this field. There is no one single way to tell reproductions and fakes from real items. My best advice is education. Reproduction items are not necessarily meant to deceive collectors. Reproductions are made for reenactments and as commemorative items. Fakes on the other hand are purposely made to deceive collectors. Reproductions and fakes are not pleasant things to have to deal with, but they do exist."[4]

Two of the most collected groups are memorabilia from the Nazi and Communist eras, especially the famous Mauser C-96 Model 1898 machine pistol and the Luger P08 semi-automatic. (Realize that there

This is a mid-1943 production Parkerized Colt M1911A1 .45 built by Remington Rand that has been non-arsenal-accurized as a national match pistol. The left side of the frame has ordnance inspector initials "G.H.D." for Major Guy H. Drewry with the "P" proof below the magazine release button. The right side of the frame has "UNITED STATES PROPERTY" over the serial number with the M1911A1 markings forward on the frame, and the Ordnance Corps escutcheon behind the right grip. It still has the WWII-style brown checkered plastic grips with the interior reinforcing ribs and mold marks. Rated very good overall, Rock Island Auction expected an enthusiastic 1911 collector to pay $800-$1,200 (Lot 644).

were numerous versions of each of these pistols and that they were manufactured over a number of years so that a specific generalization can be misleading.)

The Mauser

The Mauser pistol we are most familiar with, the 1898 "Broom-handle" Mauser was sold commercially worldwide in 7.63x25mm Mauser (.30 Mauser) and also in 9x19mm Luger/Parabellum and 9x25mm Mauser (rare). Winston Churchill is said to have favored this gun, and used one at the Battle of Omdurman in the Sudan and during the Second Boer War in South Africa. These pistols saw service in various colonial wars, World War I, the Spanish Civil War, the Chaco War (in which Paraguay enlisted trained guinea pigs to carry messages through the Bolivian lines) and World War II. It may only have been an authorized and issued military pistol, however, in China and many imports of the old guns originate in that country even though, through films and the popular imagination, they are associated primarily with Nazi SS officers and Soviet spies.

According to Ian Hogg and John Walter, writing in *Pistols of the World*, "Thousands of C/96-type guns were made in China by the Taku Naval Dockyard and Shansei Asenal, and near-copies were made in quantity in Spain by gunmakers such as Unceta y Cia (Astra) and Zulaica (Royal). The Chinese-made guns were essentially similar to the Mausers, but the material was inferior, the finish was far poorer

The famous Broomhandle Mauser

and the ideographs that appear on the frame are easy to recognize. The Spanish-made guns offer far better quality and also a variety of design differences – including a rate-reducing mechanism in the grip

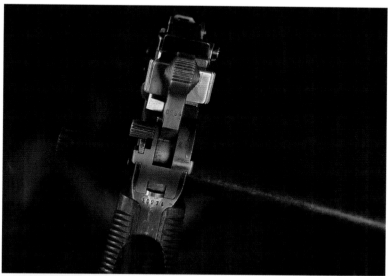

Many authorities in militaria believe that the Broomhandle Mauser is, after more than a century, still the most desirable and numerous foreign gun collectible in America. Thus, it lends itself to unscrupulous fakery, bizarre stories and guns with wonderful provenance. The first successful prototype was dated 15th March 1895 and numerous countries were granted licenses. Thus, there are many different stampings; serial numbers sometimes conflict and factories skipped entire serial number blocks.

of some Astra machine pistols."[5] Subsequent changes were made to the gun's designation, its chamber, configuration and action, making varieties of this gun almost endlessly collectible…and thus endlessly altered for sale to collectors who must own one of each variation.

A recent sale on GunBroker.com advertised this listing: "I have four Mauser [C-96] pistols for sale. They come with 3 stocks, 200 rounds of new 30 Mauser ammo, 2 sets of extra grips and 5 stripper clips. The ones numbered #3 and #4 have relined barrels. The other two have rough barrels. All have import marks. I will separate this collection. Feel free to ask any questions. Will ship to FFL or C&R. I have not shot any of these pistols, but all seem to be in functioning condition. Pistol #1 has number on top of bolt mismatched and a rough bore in .30 Mauser; Pistol #2 is commercial and does not have

A rare six-shot New Model No. 3 top-break, automatic ejector Smith & Wesson .44-Russian built under contract to the Japanese Navy! Note the unusual script proof mark. It is not an error, a stutter by the machine, or an attempt to confuse and fake this revolver. The serial number is marked on the rear face of the cylinder, the top strap latch and the butt which is followed by the Japanese Navy anchor. Rock Island Auctions rated this gun excellent: "The revolver retains approximately 95 percent of the original finish with some thinning on the barrel, high edge wear, some light spotting on the grip frame and overall minor dings and scratches. Strong original case colors remain on the hammer. The grips are fine with a few minor dents and dings and crisp checkering. The markings are clear with some fading of the anchor marking. Mechanically functions, but does not lock up." The auction asked between $2,750 and $4,250 (Lot 259).

numbered parts and rough bore in .30 Mauser; Pistol #3 has 3 different number on parts in .30 Mauser with relined barrel, and Pistol #4 is has matching numbers, relined barrel in 9mm Luger."

The four guns with holsters and boxes of ammo sold for a reported $3,500. Other Broomhandle Mausers generally sell via GunsAmerica.com for between $1,000 and $2,000 although prices, after all this time, still do not seem to have stabilized. Then, there is this from Simpson Limited in Galesburg, Illinois:

"Mauser C-96; 7.63 mm; 90% blue, 90% straw, very good bore, excellent grips, 5.5-inch barrel, antique, System Mauser marked step barrel, matching except follower which is #227. This gun was pictured in Dunlap & Belford's C-96 book in 1969. One of very few surviving examples of a "System Mauser". Includes an original leather belt holster., s/n 3xx. [Asking $39,995 www.simpsonltd.com.]

The Luger

Germany popularized the Luger during both World Wars of the 20th century…or perhaps it only exposed the sleek pistol to the "Greatest Generation," allowing hundreds of subsequent movies, books and television shows to popularize it as, for the next half-century and more, that generation continuously re-fought the war of its youth. Allied soldiers valued the Luger highly during both World Wars and thousands were captured and taken home; most are still in circulation and still eminently shootable today. Though the Luger pistol was first introduced in 7.65x22mm Parabellum, it is notable for being the pistol for which the 9x19mm Parabellum cartridge was developed.

Collectors prize old Pistole 08 Lugers because of the gun's connection to Imperial and Nazi Germany. Sleek in design and recognized for superlative accuracy, the pistol is otherwise obsolete in numerous mechanical ways. Limited production by its original manufacturer resumed when Mauser refurbished a quantity of them in 1999 for the pistol's centenary.

While there was even an Abercrombie and Fitch Luger – yes, the people with advertisements featuring scantily clad teens – made in Switzerland (approximately 100), the Luger seems to have been one of the most popular handguns ever produced. More recently, Krieghoff announced the continuation of its Parabellum Model 08 line with 200 samples initially priced to sell at $15,950 each:[6]

Caliber: 9mm (9x19)

Action: Toggle Lock Action

Overall Length: 220mm (approx 8 2/3 inches)

Sight Radius: 184mm (approx 7 ¼ inches)

Barrel Length: 102mm (approximately 4 inches)

Weight: 870 grams (1.9 pounds)

Magazine Capacity: 8

Krieghoff says that between 1934 and 1945, their factory in Suhl, Germany, produced 13,850 Model 08 Pistols. A small number, perhaps 1,650 were manufactured as civilian pistols which "contained additional features and details omitted on the military version." It is perhaps fitting that the German reproduction of this collector's item would reverse the usual trend whereby the original sells for many times the price of the replica.

With a showroom that includes more than 400 Lugers at any one time, Simpson Ltd. Collector's Firearms features models that sell for as little as a thousand dollars to this model with significant provenance that would appeal especially to nostalgic sons and daughters of the World War II generation:

"DWM 1918 Artillery; 9 mm; 94% blue, 95% straw, excellent bore, excellent grips. Historical firearm – this Luger is a war trophy taken by Major Richard D. Winters, E Company, 506th Regiment, 101st Airborne (*Band of Brothers* fame). All matching numbers, with non-matching wood bottom magazine, with Certificate of Authenticity, s/n 15xxa, Catalog Number OK-05." [Asking $15,000.][7]

So – What To Do?

Denver appraiser Joe Cornell (www.weappraiseguns.com, (303) 455-1717) says he sees fakes and frauds all the time and his comments go to the heart of collecting, investing and enjoying collectible firearms. With 18 years of appraising, dealing, trading and study, his comments also illustrate the complexity of the issue of fake firearms.

"I know of six dealers who I can think of right now and that's all they deal in. They buy guns and have ability to modify them, through their contacts, in such a way as to make them look original.

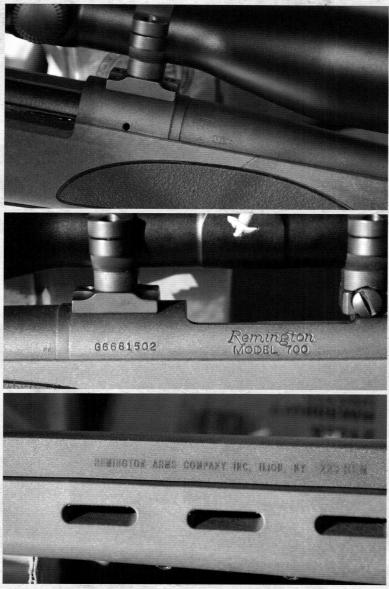

Certainly gun styles, materials and even calibers change over the years. What does not change, however, is that all guns have "fingerprints" and these are often stamped on the barrel or on other metal parts: proof marks, inspector stamps, manufacturer, patent information and so on. When none of these are obvious, the collector may have to carefully disassemble a gun to search for clues on the inside.

If you go to big gun shows, you know who those guys are because you see them. At one time or another they have all been here in Denver for the show in May.

"What made me interested in this, made me snap to the fact that these guns were around in somewhat abundance, was…there was a very famous gun dealer who was considered to be a gentleman and I got to know him in the '70s who dealt mostly in high dollar Winchester guns: Model 21s, 12s and 42s, some 1890s.

"If you remember in the mid-50s, Winchester would send guns in the white to Simmons in Kansas to have Simmons ventilated ribs put on. Simmons would put ribs on and send them back to Winchester who would proof them and finish them and sell them. For Model 12 and Model 22 collectors, those vent rib guns are worth more than plain barrel or solid rib guns. I suppose this all happened pre-1964.

"Well, this guy had a roll stamp and the proof mark on the Model 12 plain barrel is on top where the rib would go. So Winchester moved the proof mark to the left of the rib on vent rib guns when Simmons sent barrels back.

"This is the way that collectors could identify guns that Winchester sent to Simmons. So if you picked up a gun with a Simmons rib and left-side proof mark, a collector considered that ample evidence that it was a Winchester-approved rib – an original factory alteration.

"But a lot of guys sent their guns directly to Simmons and he would put a rib on for them, but his rib covered the proof mark on

Allow your fingers to feel their way gently along the barrel above the stamped type to feel for "dishing." Also look for any sign that metal has been removed and subsequently added. All Sharps rifles are not the same and some are worth much more than others. Note that the condition of the lettering and markings should mirror that of the gun itself. Sharp lettering on a worn gun can be a sign of trouble, as can too-perfect nickel plating. *(Photo courtesy Rock Island Auctions)*

A good machine shop or a gunsmith with sufficient hands-on training can take a new gun and, with a little time and ingenuity, can "antique it" so well that it will fool experts. On the other hand, the same group can give advice on re-stamping and re-storing or simply conserving – saving the gun in its present state without altering a thing.

top of the barrel. So those guns are considered altered and are not very valuable compared to guns with a proof mark on the left side.

"Well, this guy showed me that he had a proof mark and would put the stamp on the left side and this would increase the value of a gun dramatically – could triple or quadruple the value or even more – because the value of ventilated rib guns was very high.

"Also with Winchesters, a company used to advertise its solid red butt pad for shotguns. They advertised in *Shotgun News* and manufactured these pads with the Winchester name on them. If you encountered a gun where someone had changed the pad, they could order one of these as a replacement and make it look like the gun was original. The red pad was standard on Magnum Model 12s and was available by Special Order on any gun. It was standard on other models as well as on special order guns and high-end guns."

So this was "kind of where it all got started," Cornell says. "People bought these pads and stuck them on guns that had been altered and would then bring a changed gun back to quasi-original standards

In the war between collectible buyers and sellers, local gun shop retailers should not be overlooked. They often take guns on consignment, and they see and talk guns and related products all day. If a gun comes in that is a hot collectible deal, make sure they know you and can contact you…and if a gun comes in that questionable, they can alert you.

– at least people could argue that it was original. I got interested and learned how to distinguish between Winchester red and this other company's red pads.

"At the same time a welder in Chicago could turn the surface of a gun to liquid and then could do whatever his customers wanted. His process could take all the pitting out and could take an extremely old and rare firearm and make it look wonderful.

"Then, in the early '80s there was a big national dealer who deals in Winchester shotguns and some Brownings, and his guns started appearing in boxes and even with hangtags. Well, I have a large collection of Winchesters and so I studied the boxes I had and began asking questions. That same guy I was talking about with the roll stamp said, 'Hell, yeah. You can get new boxes for anything you want and hang tags, too. Tell me the serial number of the gun and we'll put the serial number on the box for you.'

"Apparently, this dealer was printing 'new, original' Colt boxes – black single action – and the Smith & Wesson red box. Cornell "was horrified. So I started looking at this aspect of fakery, too.

"There are two or three dealers I can think of who display everything on their table at 99 percent or better. They always have the rarest and the strangest variations you can name, and they are all in almost new condition and in the original box." I'd see these guys at gun shows and they would never ask me to put the guns down, but I would look very closely at their guns.

"There are thousands of these stories I could tell you. Fraudulent guns are everywhere at gun shows. A fraudulent gun is one that has been altered or helped in some way but is being sold as an original. There are a huge number out there. I used to be able to go to a gun show and never see one and now I don't think I can go to any gun show and not see one.

"Anything that is very valuable, that is worthwhile will be faked. Think of the Winchester boxes, for instance. They didn't box Henrys [in the 19th century] or '95 Winchesters or '86s, but they were boxing guns from 1930-1964. I could buy these 'new, original' boxes and hangtags today. I could buy you a truckload of them, along with a truckload of red butt pads."

Footnotes

1   Mark Chervenka, *Guide to Fake and Forged Marks*, Krause Publishing, Iola, WI 2007

2   John F. Adams-Graf, *Warman's Civil War Collectibles, 2nd Edition,* Krause Publications, Iola, WI 2006

3   Although we may not want to admit it, there is a subtle difference between souvenir hunting, collecting, scavenging and theft especially when, which- ever motive we ascribe to our actions, affects the poor, the defeated and the helpless: "Gone were his bow, arrows and otterskin quiver; his harpoon and firedrill; his knives, flakers and chisels; most of the kitchen and household utensils and all of the food. He looked for Tushi's raccoon and mountain lion cape, for the bearskin blanket, for Mother's feather cape, for the mended and ragged rabbitskin blankets. There was nothing." Theodora Kroeber, *Ishi: Last of his Tribe* (Parnassus Press, Oakland, CA 1964, page 132)

4   As we discussed her interest in women's militaria, antique shop owner Marie Brown mentioned two specific issues that we have not dealt with in the book, but which speaks to an important issue:

a.   "If you do buy a piece and question its authenticity, talk to the person you bought it from before you discredit their reputation."

b.   "Keeping an inventory from the beginning is important. Buy a spiral bound notebook and record what you bought, where you bought it, who you bought it from and how much you paid. I know this probably seems silly if you are just starting out, but once your collection begins to grow it is hard to remem- ber each piece. Inventorying a large collection is a monotonous job that is extremely time consuming. The big reason for doing this is for insurance pur- poses in the future. Most insurance companies will add a fine arts rider to your policy; however, you have to furnish an inventory of your collection. When you have three or four thousand pieces, it is not easy if you have not kept a record. Premiums vary from company to company, some collecting organizations of- fer policies also, so you have to shop around."

5   Ian V. Hogg and John Walter, *Pistols of the World: A Comprehensive Illus- trated Encyclopedia of the World's Pistols and Revolvers from 1870 to the Present Day* (Krause/F&W, Iola, WI 2004).

6   "Back from the Past, the Krieghoff Parabellum. For over 100 years, the Luger pistol has been one of the most well-known firearms throughout the world. Several versions of the Luger were developed for both military and civilian use. Celebrating this long standing history of the Model 08 pistol as it was also called, Krieghoff is producing the 2006 Limited Edition Model 08 Parabel- lum. Only 200 pistols will be offered, serial numbered 18001 – 18200, continu- ing the production halted in 1945 when the last Krieghoff Parabellums were made for U.S. military officers.

   "The Parabellum civilian model, containing features not found on the military version existed in very limited quantities during 1934 – 1945. Now this coveted collector's item is available once again, not as a replica, but as an authentic continuation of the original Parabellum Model 08 line." (www.krieghoff.com/ pages/8/pages/8.html)

7   The 2001 television mini-series *Band of Brothers* is the story of Easy Com- pany, 101st Airborne Division and their missions in World War II Europe from Operation Overlord (the Normandy invasion) through V-J Day. Actor Damian Lewis portrayed Major Winters. The mini-series is based on the Stephen Am- brose book *Band of Brothers: E Company, 506th Regiment, 101st Airborne From Normandy to Hitler's Eagle's Nest* (Pocket Books/Simon & Schuster, New York, 1992).

Chapter Three

What is a Fake Firearm?

The president of an established and reputable auction house once said that a high percentage of old Colt firearms his firm was asked to sell had been significantly altered in such a way that they could no longer be considered original. Without full and complete disclosure of the alterations by the seller, and few sellers mention anything of the kind, these guns, as presented are outright frauds.

So, just what is a "fake firearm?" Let's take a walk on the wild side and consider some of the possibilities, beginning out in left field:

Is a fake firearm one that will not shoot, but looks like one that

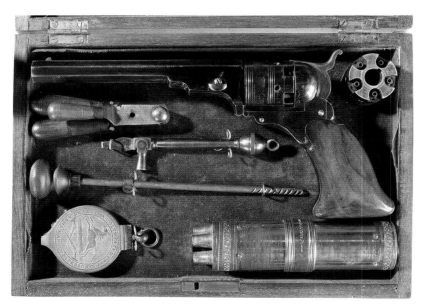

A Texas Paterson almost new in the box with loading gear. Also known as the "holster model," this is the physically largest and most sought-after of the Paterson Colt revolvers. A verified military model would be worth a great deal more than a standard model, so qualified appraisal is essential prior to a purchase…especially since this set could easily run into the six figures. *(Photo courtesy Rock Island Auctions)*

will? In that case, the guns sold for instance by Louisiana's Stage-Props-Blanks-Guns.com are fake guns. "None of our replica or blank guns can be converted or modified to fire real ammunition," says the company's Internet site. Obviously these are fake guns, but intentional fakes and therefore…not fakes? Such "guns" are ideal for some movie scenes, theatre presentations and reenacting scenarios, or as curiosities on hooks over the fireplace.[1]

Perhaps paintball "markers" or soft-air (one also hears "air-soft") guns fall into the category of "fake guns." Still they actually do fire a projectile down and out their barrel – paintball markers[2] shoot .68-caliber, dye-filled gelatin balls while soft-air guns shoot small 12- or 20-gram plastic 6mm BBs – using either compressed air, "green gas," CO_2 or a cocked spring that relies on a battery for propulsion energy. In fact, because soft-air "guns" (not markers) are usually made as exact replicas of the "real thing," some police forces prefer them for

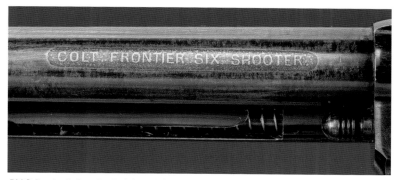

Did Colt actually inscribe their barrels in such a manner: "Colt Frontier Six Shooter?" Certainly this is a toy gun, a fake designed to sell a customer on the romance of the Old West...or is it? It's genuine; this is the "etched" style of barrel marking on an original specimen. *(Photo courtesy Rock Island Auctions)*

realistic training scenarios. It is both dangerous and illegal to remove or paint over their required orange plastic muzzle.[3]

Seeing the M4 3181 AEG Electric Airsoft Rifle with M203 Spring Grenade Launcher ($79 at www.hobbytron.com) on the street without its orange tip would be alarming. Still, regardless of the public reaction is it a gun...or a fake gun?

What about a restored gun? We will discuss this at greater length later in the book for there a host of points of view on this subject, but let's say you purchase a field grade M1 Garand built by Springfield Armory from the Civilian Marksmanship Program in Ohio or Alabama (www.odcmp.com) for $495. The gun has been used and is showing its age with normal dings and scratches, so you send it to a restoration specialist such as Dean's Gun Restorations (www.dgrguns.com) in Tennessee for an overhaul. As of 2008, Dean has been restoring guns for 20 years and has a solid reputation for quality workmanship.

Dean's motto is "Life's too short to shoot an ugly gun," and that sounds good. You purchase DGR's "Complete M1 Package Deal with Standard Grade Walnut," which includes: a new .30-06 barrel, new stock and fore-arm sanded to 600-grit with a hand rubbed oil finish. The gun is completely stripped, all metal Parkerized (except the stainless gas cylinder which receives a baked-on lacquer finish), new

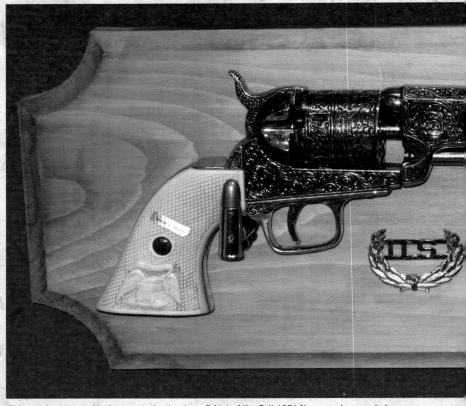

This gun is supposed to be a reproduction (non-firing) of the Colt 1851 Navy revolver carried by James Butler "Wild Bill" Hickok (1837-76). Made in Spain, it can be found on-line for $99 from various sources. Hickok was an army scout, stagecoach driver, lawman and gambler; it is reasonable to assume that he could never have afforded such a finely engraved pistol and that his were plain working guns.

springs, letters and numbers "highlighted," bore sighted and a guarantee that the rifle will function. At the end of this $845 process, your M1 looks stunning – as good as new.

Before they return it to you, however, Dean's mentions that they have ¾" or ½" stamps that can be applied to your new wood to authenticate that your rifle was re-built by DGR. According to DGR, these stamps are applied only at the customer's request. What do you do? You have already spent $1,340, a lot of money for an old M1. Applying the stamp (at no charge by DGR) could actually diminish this

WILD BILL HICKOK, (1837-76) INDIAN FIGHTER,
UNION SCOUT AND DEAD SHOT,
KNOWN FOR HIS LIGHTNING- QUICK DRAW
OF HIS 1851 NAVY PERCUSSION REVOLVER

Wild Bill Hickok, 1873.

OMNI-POTENT SIX SHOOTER

27-335 $7⁰⁰

U.S. FireArms has resurrected the name "Omnipotent" for a single-action .45 styled
after the Model 1878. In only good condition, an authentic original might bring $6,000 at auc-
tion; from the U.S. FireArms factory, a fully operational reproduction is $1,625.

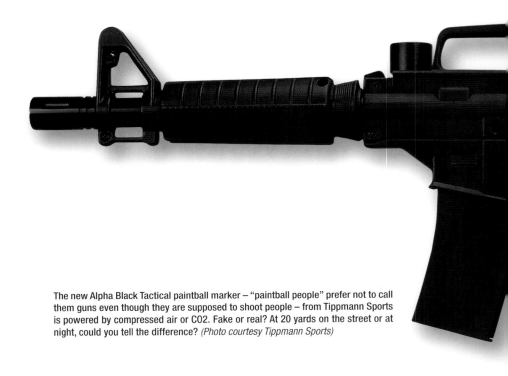

The new Alpha Black Tactical paintball marker – "paintball people" prefer not to call them guns even though they are supposed to shoot people – from Tippmann Sports is powered by compressed air or CO2. Fake or real? At 20 yards on the street or at night, could you tell the difference? *(Photo courtesy Tippmann Sports)*

M1's eventual value to a collector, meaning you might not get your money back when you sell it, whereas by not applying the stamp you could perhaps sell the gun as in original condition. Is this gun now an original or have you, by sending it to a specialist for complete restoration, faked its condition? Is it actually a new and different gun? Indeed its condition is veritably factory new and the gun is ready to be shot in competition or taken to a gun show for sale at a premium price…except to serious collectors.

To a collector, refurbishing causes confusion reflective of that expressed in the following advertisement for an M1 that was submitted for sale on-line in early 2008. The owner lived in Alaska and asked $1,000 OBO, or best offer. He would also trade the rifle for a Motorola satellite phone.

"It is a Springfield with the serial number 931273 which means it was made around October 1942. I have no idea about the stock. I was told it was refinished (it looks like it) and I can find no mark-

A BLACK ★

Is it real or is it…air-soft. If the weapons used by the camo-clad troopers in this converted dune buggy were real, these men would be a formidable fast-reaction team, although while inside the buggy they are easy prey. Both the machine gun and the pistol are air-soft and shoot small plastic pellets. Goggles that protect the face, ears and neck are required on supervised air-soft venues.

The Russian rifle known as the "Rifle Model 1891/30" *(vintovka obrazets 1891/30 goda)* is the Mosin-Nagant 1891/30 rifle. It was adopted by the Soviet Army in 1930, but this rifle might be an antique! Check the receiver for date of manufacture.

ings on it. The barrel I was told was replaced with a new one so it could be used in the matches. The bbl numbers are SA 8535448 1 67 MD88 M. The barrel looks great. Very good rifling and very shiny. The bolt is also new. The numbers are D28287 1 WRA. It is also in great shape. There is only one area that has what I'd call a blemish other than what would be expected and that is on the left side of the receiver. The rifle also has match front sights with 6 different sight types and the original front sight. It also comes with 17 standard 8-round en-bloc clips and 3 5-round en-blocs. The original oilers in the stock and the sling are also like brand new."

At this point, your beautifully restored M1 is practically in mint condition and a weapon to be proud of, whether or not you take it to a range and fire it or hang it carefully on the wall next to your dad's framed Combat Infantry Badge. It is that next step, however, when you decide to sell it, that critical decisions must be made...and your integrity is on the line. Having a visible gunsmith's restoration stamp applied is proof positive – unless some owner removes it in the future, an act over which you have no control – that this rifle, no matter how good it looks, will always be in something other than

LET'S GO GET 'EM !

U.S. MARINES

Beck Engraving Co., Phila., Pa., Regn.—469-1943, 7-11-42, 50M.

In a highly stylized, highly romanticized recruiting poster, U.S. Marines hunt for the enemy in the jungles of the Pacific during World War II. With such fanciful images, our fathers were lured into service as young men; the same images project the lure of collecting World War II artifacts such as the M1 Garand pictured in Marine Corps Captain Guinness' poster. (Captain Guinness, USMC, Library of Congress Digital ID #cph 3g09891)

To the true collector of the M1 carbine, the original G.I. model (bottom) is worth two to three times as much as a sporterized, rebuilt civilian model (top).

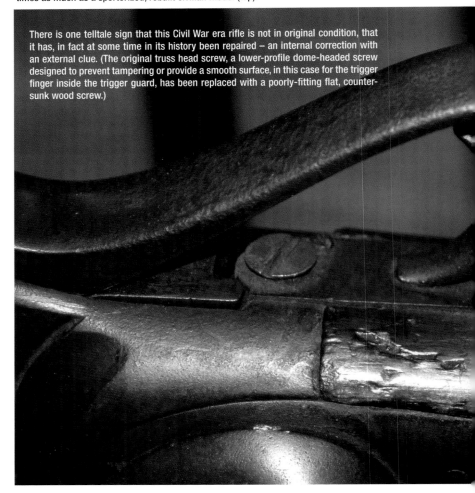

There is one telltale sign that this Civil War era rifle is not in original condition, that it has, in fact at some time in its history been repaired – an internal correction with an external clue. (The original truss head screw, a lower-profile dome-headed screw designed to prevent tampering or provide a smooth surface, in this case for the trigger finger inside the trigger guard, has been replaced with a poorly-fitting flat, counter-sunk wood screw.)

original condition. However, if you have chosen not to apply the stamp for whatever personal reason, you have a choice of selling it with the restoration known…or concealed.

This is precisely the point where a gun may become a fake or a fraud. It is your intention and the action you take based on your intention that could stain this beautiful gun (not to mention your reputation) forever.

Firearms specialist Jim Supica (www.armchairgunshow.com)

has written several specialty gun books[4] and is a recognized authority in collecting and valuing both antique and modern guns. He says, "The majority opinion seems to be that so long as the restoration or alteration is disclosed at the time of sale, restoration is an acceptable practice. It's easy to project, though, that the 'disclosure' may well not accompany the piece the third or fourth time it changes hands.

Denver appraiser Joe Cornell, CMA, ASA, ISA examines a 5-screw early S&W Model 17 in .22 caliber in excellent condition. Cornell, who has been buying, selling and trading guns for half-a-century and appraising since 1972, is a certified appraiser.

"Also there seems to be, perhaps unfortunately, a Clinton-style military policy ethic among certain gun swappers, a 'Don't ask, don't tell' style of morality Thus, if the buyer doesn't specifically ask, 'Oh, by the way, is this gun refinished or restored or does it contain replaced parts?' there is no obligation [from this point of view] to mention it.

"Equally common, and equally regrettable, are the well worn evasions such as 'Well, it looks old to me' or 'That's just the way I got it.'

"Now that is fraud!"

The $16,000 Story

"I have a special affection for single action Colts," says Denver appraiser Joe Cornell.[5] "Not long ago I was called by a guy who bought a gun that was made-up from parts. He lost $16,000!

"I did a rough appraisal over the telephone – never saw the gun – after listening to the facts and the guy's description. It was supposed to be particularly rare Colt revolver, but it did not have the correct serial number for what it was supposed to be. That was ultimately the issue. Single action serial numbers are totally researched now and there are plenty of books on single action Colts. This guy bought the gun without knowing jack about single actions."

And over the telephone, I could hear Joe Cornell shake his head in dismay.

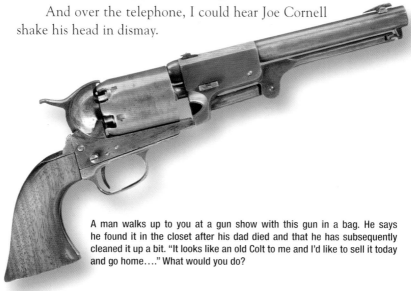

A man walks up to you at a gun show with this gun in a bag. He says he found it in the closet after his dad died and that he has subsequently cleaned it up a bit. "It looks like an old Colt to me and I'd like to sell it today and go home...." What would you do?

From the Collector's Point of View

Ed Cox, an inveterate collector of antique Colts and other guns of the Old West, has this to say about faked guns: "To take a gun like a new Uberti and remark it and stamp it like a Colt and then sell it for an authentic Colt instead of a Uberti is faking.

"If I bought a Uberti for say $300 – and the real Colt sells for more than $1,000 – if I do some stamping on that gun (I don't have any stamping, by the way) and made it look like an authentic Colt and took it to a gun show and walked around like some poor old farmer...and some guy comes up and says, 'What have you got there?' and I say, 'I found this in the desk and I want to get rid of it What'll you give me for it?'

"Well a guy will naturally try to buy it as cheaply as possible. If it's a Colt and he knows it's a $1,200 gun he might say he would give $700 or $800...and then that 'poor old farmer' has made $500 profit.

"But it's not only that. Let's say you take some Colt and fix up the side where the ejector housing is and put a different barrel on and texture it and color it and what-have-you and you say 'Here's a Sheriff's Model.' Someone at a gun show might look at it and want it, but there's no way to get it sent off for a letter of authenticity right away – and you're talking about a $5,000 gun – and they buy it for say $2,000 to $3,000 right there on the show floor.

"A lot of time I find that people who wind up getting stuck with the fakes are people who are trying to get something for nothing. Those are usually the guys who wind up with that kind of stuff. I'm not saying other people don't, I'm just saying that someone who thinks, 'Well, I'm going to steal this one. I'm going to buy this for $1,000 and can sell it for $10,000.' is going to get stuck sooner or later.

"But there are other kinds of fakes. Take an old Colt, for instance – as long as we're talking about Colts – and just stamp it to look like a military gun. Military (as opposed to civilian) guns are high dollar value. Then if you take it back out there and try to sell it as a real military gun and it's not...just a civilian gun that someone doctored to make look like a military gun...and I have seen that before, that's an out-and-out fake."[6]

Why Would Someone Fake A Firearm?

The story of King Midas[7] is instructive. For a good deed, Midas was awarded one wish by the god Dionysus. Without thinking, Midas blurted out a wish that everything he touched would turn to gold.

It only took a few days for Midas to realize his mistake, but not before he had turned the delicate roses in his famous gardens to cold,

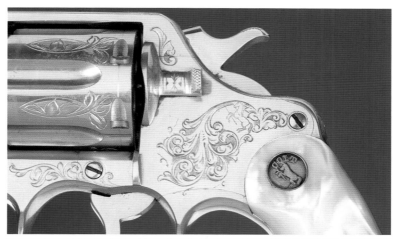

Midas would be proud. Not every gun is built to be a working-man's six shooter, blued with a plain walnut grip. Plenty of fancy guns were produced by Colt and other firearms companies for sale to the public and as special gifts to friends and influential people. Just because a gun is in marvelous condition and is stunningly engraved with mother-of-pearl grips does not necessarily imply that it is in any way faked. *(Photos courtesy Rock Island Auctions)*

Under close inspection, there appears to be a serial number shadow on this old Colt, as if the number has been re-stamped. Perhaps this is an instance where the machinery stuttered, hesitated, applied a partial stamp before an inspector caught the error; perhaps it is a case of intentional fraud; or perhaps it is an illusion of the camera lens. Only personal inspection under strong lighting and with a magnifying glass will allow you to know the truth. *(Photo courtesy Rock Island Auctions)*

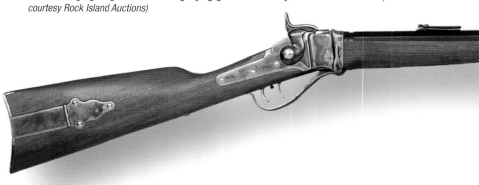

if brilliant, gold. At a touch, his wine and his food turned to inedible gold. In the most terrible irony, he turned his loving daughter to a solid gold statuette.

Almost overnight, Midas became immensely rich. On the other hand, that wealth did the starving and forlorn man no good at all. Locating Dionysus, he begged the god to reverse his former wish, to turn everything that he had touched back to the way it had been and to take away his golden curse. The god took pity on him, it is said, and soon Midas, though much less wealthy, realized that he was rich in the things that really mattered.

Why does such an old myth belong in a firearms book? Midas' unfortunate story illustrates the perpetual human interest in maximizing our return while minimizing our investment. King Midas may have been an intensely avaricious individual willing to sacrifice everyone and everything around him to his insatiable desire for wealth. If so, he was certainly a man of huge appetites, a flawed, but mythic and horribly greedy figure, indeed. Probably, however, he was simply one of us, a man who was presented with an opportunity and spoke or acted without thinking, without considering the consequences. Not greedy, just a little bit careless.

This applies to us personally when we reply to the gunsmith's question of whether we want him to apply his shop's restoration stamp. On the shooting line, a refinished stock will make no difference at all, but in a hall of collectors or even simple "accumulators" when a potential purchaser stands before your refinished M1, the difference in cash can be a car payment or, in some cases, a house payment!

Not a fake. This is a faithful reproduction, not a fake. Working with Italy's Pedersoli, Cimarron says, "We recreated Matthew Quigley's [Sharps] rifle for the adventurous souls desiring single shot rifles capable of the accuracy depicted in the epic film *Quigley Down Under*."

Types of Fakes

Looked at from the point of view of firearms collectors, both buyers and sellers, there are two types of fakes – intentional and unintentional or unknown – and while they may have similar consequences at some point, the origins are obviously different.

• Intentional: An owner scrubs out a true serial number and, with a gunsmith or friend in a machine shop, stamps a new number in its place – a new number, but one certainly earlier in the known production run for that model gun. (This almost certainly has happened with the Winchester Model 1894 that you will read about in a later chapter.) As a general rule, collectors pay more for older guns with lower serial numbers, so this is fraud. Someone purchasing a new Sharps Model 1859 Berdan manufactured by Italy's IAB ("assembled and finished just as they were over 100 years ago. They are perfect recreations of the original [which was used in the U.S. Civil War] in every respect including stocks made from select European walnut and quality rifling made with precision broaching equipment.")[8] who after adding a few minor scratches to the stock, a scuff mark (which can easily be polished away) to the receiver, firing and cleaning it once and perhaps ageing the barrel with a touch of rust then passes it off as a genuine 150-year-old antique is guilty of fraud.

The inspector's cartouche has nearly been worn away on this 19th century firearm. It could have been intentional – and the stock re-stained to cover the fraud – or perhaps a result of natural wear and tear from more than 100 years of use. *(Photo courtesy Rock Island Auctions)*

• On the other hand, many antique firearms and many valuable, collectible firearms that are not antiques, such as General George Patton's Colt Single Action Army .45s, for example, have been worked on and altered in various ways since their original manufacture that would not be considered fake or fraudulent.

For instance, called a "heartless, cold-blooded murderer, whose killings were frequently motivated by racism and a vitriolic hatred of Yankees" John Wesley Hardin carried an ivory-handled Colt .45 missing an ejector rod. Author Doc O'Meara wonders whether Hardin could have removed it to make it lighter and faster to handle, or was it merely lost at some time during its history? The left side of the barrel

By the time John Wesley Hardin went to prison in 1878, he claimed to have killed 44 men. Hardin carried an ivory-handled Colt .45 missing an ejector rod. Although his gun was certainly altered from factory condition, the fact that the notorious outlaw either did this himself or had it done for him makes this gun even more valuable. *(Photo courtesy National Archives and Records Administration)*

at the muzzle end, he notes, is worn nearly flat, indicating long hours of practice drawing it from his holster.[9] In this case, because the gun (which now resides in the Autry National Center[10]) has "provenance," a known chain of custody so there is no doubt about its originality, the alteration and wear on the handgun make it even more valuable because they are visible, physical corroboration of the Hardin legend.

• And what about the famous case of the Civil War "Coffee-Mill" Sharps, a .52 caliber breech loaded single shot Sharps with a grinder in its stock. Apparently, the idea was to issue one of these to each company of Federal raiders probably for the purposes of grind-

This grouping of Civil War weapons at an historical re-enactment site is an interesting mix of modern reproductions and genuine originals. Can you tell the difference?

Many of today's avid collectors (including the author) are in 50-years-and-up age brackets. As kids we would have "given our eye teeth" to find a 1909 S-VDB penny in the bottom of mom's purse. While the mintage of 484,000 seems high compared to other American rarities, one must understand that millions of people collect Lincoln Head Cents. There are simply not enough 1909-S VDB pennies to satisfy collector demand.

ing foraged corn or other grain and perhaps coffee as well, although coffee was a luxury in the field. Raiders presumably had to travel fast and light, thus the stock grinder replaced the patch box. Lt. Colonel Walter King of Missouri devised the modification, but a board of officers ultimately decided that it was impractical; especially since the recently adopted Spencer repeating carbine's seven-shot magazine ran through the center of the stock. This rifle was certainly modified from its basic design and thus, is it original? If one were to consider restoring it, would an accurate restoration require a new stock? Based on the value of the "Coffee-Mill" Sharps variation, which Flayderman's *Guide* lists at about $35,000 for a gun in fine condition, collectors must not have difficulty accepting this particular alteration or re-design.[11]

• If, however, a gun were presumed by a seller to have been restocked or thought to have had new parts substituted at some time in the past – even if he was not certain, did not do the work himself or have it done, or even if the replaced parts were broken, thus causing the gun to be inoperable – and did not pass along this information to a buyer, the sale would carry a taint of fraud and the gun – no matter how valuable or what its provenance might otherwise be – would be suspect and this would detract from its sales price among knowledgeable collectors. Such a scenario can take place inadvertently, especially with new collectors, but once those newbies gain experience – this kind of experience coming sometimes and unfortunately at a very high price – there is no excuse for ignorance, for not studying the books and articles available and then asking the hard questions before putting down one's money.

Again – From the Collector's Point of View

"Years ago," recalls Ed Cox of Fernley, Nevada, "I collected coins. I bought a 1909 S-VDB penny and sent it off to a numismatic association to have it graded and checked. Well, turns out that somebody had added the S-VDB, probably with some kind of tool. They took a VDB penny and add the 'S' and it was bogus.[12]

"It all gets down to the reason they fake a gun is to make money. 'Take it and fake it.'

There is a bottom line to the question of gun fakery and it is simply greed. Selling and buying in a small fraternity involves considerable trust. It is a buyer's responsibility to ask about any alteration to the state of a gun since its manufacture; and it is the seller's responsibility to disclose anything he or she may know or suspect.

"I bought a fake gun one time. I'm notorious for buying the 1889 double action Colts. It was the first swing-out cylinder revolver the factory made. The gun had long fluted cylinders and no notches on the cylinder for a stop.

"One time I was real busy at a show and a guy came by with a not-very-good one and he said – as I was talking to others – 'Do you want to buy this.' And there, on the spot, I gave him $200 for it.

"When I got it home and looked at it under a good magnifying glass it turned out that he'd actually just taken a '92 gun worth about $50 and stuck the proper cylinder style in it. I realized I was taken. I just didn't look at it close enough.

"So getting stuck with a fake happens when you're trying to do something and you go too fast. I guess it shows that anybody can get caught on a fake gun if you don't stop and look it over real well."

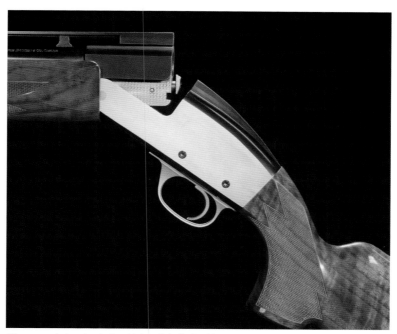

Give your shotgun's stock a high polish, fit it with an adjustable rib and re-stamp it in the Bruce Bowen Custom Gun style, and if you find a real pigeon – an eager, but innocent buyer – you could perhaps triple your money turning this admittedly delightful sow's ear into the fortune of a silk purse of ill-gotten profit.

The orange tip on the muzzle of this Daisy ASAX1 air-soft gun identifies it as a toy: even though the legal warnings begin, "Caution: Not a Toy to be Used by Children." Isn't it a shame that fake collectibles cannot come with a similar identifier and warning!

So...It's Your Call

The kind of fake firearm we are considering in this book is not the blank .38 used in cop movies or the plastic soft-air Uzi that is both so much fun to shoot and so dangerous when used incorrectly.[13] We are discussing the firearm that has been altered in some manner – almost any manner – and then presented as being "unaltered."

So when it is our turn to decide whether or not to have the refinishing stamp applied, how will we choose? Will we be part of the problem or part of the solution?

Footnotes

1 For background and for fun, I recommend Robert H. "Doc" O'Meara's *The Guns of the Gunfighters: Lawmen, Outlaws & Hollywood Cowboys* published by Krause/F&W (Iola, WI) in 2003. O'Meara profiles famous lawmen such as Bill Tilghman and his .38-40 Colt sixgun; famous actors like John Wayne and his .300 Weatherby Magnum; and notorious bad men of the Old West, such as John Wesley Hardin and his "self-improved" ivory-handled Colt .45.

2 The paintball industry – from manufacturers to the media – prefers not to use the term "guns." The heart of paintball is shooting opposing players and the reaction of a minority of the public has made that, in some quarters, politically indefensible. Besides, outlandish stories circulate occasionally about terrorist cells practicing with paintball gear, and other urban legends proliferate.

3 Numerous overblown incidents such as the following from a story filed by Neco Cockburn at Ottawa(Canada)Citizen.com February 23, 2008 have been reported as the use of soft-air guns and ammo has increased.
"Police and university at 'zero tolerance' in wake of Dawson College shootings." Alexander Bayus, 22, a fourth-year University of Ottawa law student, was "charged with pointing an air gun while on campus the day after the Dawson College shootings, said yesterday that the incident was a regrettable 'bad joke' between friends.

"There was no malicious intent or anything," said Bayus. "It was just a distasteful joke between me and a friend who was at school. There was never any intent to hurt or even scare anybody."
Arrested off campus, Bayus was charged with "careless use of a firearm, pointing a firearm, possession of a weapon for dangerous purpose and mischief." The gun used was a soft-air gun. "You can shoot yourself with it and it doesn't do much."

A humorless "police spokeswoman," bureaucrat constable Isabelle Lemieux, said the incident was "serious, regardless of the intent or firearm used."
In a true show of leadership and vision, University of Ottawa President Gilles Patry sent an Email to students yesterday calling for university community members to *"remain vigilant"* [author supplied highlight] and to continue to ensure that we demonstrate zero tolerance for such behavior.

Bayus, by the way, was scheduled to appear in court in October 2008. He was banned from campus and (at this date, spring 2008) may be expelled.

4 His most recent book (with Richard Nahas) is *Standard Catalog of Smith & Wesson, 3dr Edition* (Krause Publications, Iola, WI 2006)

5 Joe Cornell, CMA (Certified Master Appraiser), ASA (Accredited Senior Appraiser), ISA (International Society of Appraisers), says that he appraises "lots of stuff besides guns: farm and ranch equipment, guns, glassware, Japanese swords…. I owned an antique store in Denver – a large and prestigious store – with a lady friend who passed away from cancer [in April 2005]. We were together 18 years and did this virtually every day.

"In some circles I'm very well known. I've been buying and selling and trading guns for more than 50 years. Started when I was 6 years old with my father.

"I'm a condition collector. Almost everything I have is 98 percent or better. I buy only 8s, 9s and 10s – at least that's what I tell myself, though it's not always true.

"'Excellent' in NRA can be as low as an 80 percent gun. I don't know that I own an 80 percent gun – well, I do as I have a particular fascination with '66 Winchesters.

"But I've been appraising since July 27, 1972. Decided I'd be better off if I recognized and studied this stuff."
Joe Cornell's web site is www.weappraiseguns.com.

6   Personal communication. Nevada's Ed Cox does business in part through www.antiquegunlist.com and www.coltparts.com.

7   To read more about the Midas myth – it is highly entertaining – go to http://en.wikipedia.org/wiki/Midas or even to www.hipark.austin.isd.tenet.edu/mythology/midas.html.

8   I.A.B. srl can be found at www.iabarms.com/index.htm. "Broaching" is a method of manufacturing a rifled barrel. According to Clint McKee of Fulton Armory (www.fulton-armory.com), "All M14 G.I. contract NM M14 barrels were produced by the broach cut method. Many consider these barrels to be the finest ever made, in their given contour. Broach cut rifling is a fine way to make a barrel and a reasonably cost efficient method. In the DCM Service Rifle category, many believe that the broach cut barrels won more points and championships, than any other. But then, they have been around longer than any other, too. Broaching is a very efficient way to cut the barrel bore, as it does so, normally, in one pass."

9   O'Meara, page 41

10 The Autry National Center was formerly the Autry Museum of Western Heritage. www.autry-museum.org. The Center is located in Griffith Park, Los Angeles.

11 Reference David H. Arnold's article "Mr. Fuller's Most Peculiar Firearm" from the National Park Service's Cultural Resource Management magazine reprinted on line at http://crm.cr.nps.gov/archive/22-7/22-07-2.pdf. Norm Flayderman's *Flayderman's Guide to Antique American Firearms...and their values, 8th Edition,* is quoted throughout as the primary source for firearms values.

12 Coin values, like those of firearms, are subject to condition, demand and scarcity. The 1909 U.S. penny was made in two configurations. In very fine condition, a 1909 penny from the Philadelphia mint, which has no mint stamp, is valued at $2; the same penny from the smaller San Francisco mint with a tiny "S" stamped on the face is valued at $70. That year, a new design from sculptor and engraver Victor David Brenner, with Lincoln's image on the front and sheaves of wheat encircling the reverse, began rolling out of the mints. These new pennies were stamped at the six o'clock position on the reverse with tiny "VDB" lettering. Thus, 1909 VDB pennies from Philadelphia, again in very fine condition, are valued at $3 while the rare 1909 VDB pennies from the San Francisco mint are valued at $500. (source http://sammler.com/coins/wheat_pennies.htm)

13 See http://airsoftsafetyassociation.com/ for recommendations on face, ear and neck shields.

Chapter Four

Antiques vs. Curios & Relics,
Legally Speaking

*N*ow that we've discussed the faking of antique firearms, perhaps we should take a moment and discuss how various types of collectible firearms are legally defined.

What's What: Definitions

Antique firearm

(a) Any firearm (including any firearm with a matchlock, flint-lock, percussion cap, or similar type of ignition system) manufactured in or before 1898; and (b) any replica of any firearm [described in paragraph (a) of this definition] if such replica (1) is not designed or redesigned for using rimfire or conventional centerfire fixed ammunition, or (2) uses rimfire or conventional centerfire fixed ammunition which is no longer manufactured in the United States and which is not readily available in the ordinary channels of commercial trade.

Curios or Relics (C&R)

Firearms which are of special interest to collectors by reason of some quality other than is associated with firearms intended for sporting use or as offensive or defensive weapons. According to the Bureau of Alcohol, Tobacco, Firearms and Explosives (BATFE), the controlling Federal authority for firearms importation and sales, to be recognized as curios or relics, firearms must fall within one of the following categories:

(a) Firearms which were manufactured at least 50 years prior to the current date, but not including replicas thereof (Many collectors believe that as long as the receiver is more than 50 years old the firearm qualifies as a curio and relic, but according to BATFE

Cleaning the attic of "the old family place" you come upon a small chest. You carefully open it and discover an original Colt Paterson revolver. If you choose to sell it to your Cousin Eddy, it is okay to take his personal check for $50,000…but wait for it to clear the bank before you hand over this box. Should you discover that this magnificent set was recently manufactured by Uberti, take Cousin Eddy's check for $500. If it is the real thing, you can send it directly to him via the U.S. Postal Service.

It is a muzzleloader, but one accesses the break action of the Knight Shadow muzzleloader by pushing a button on the front of the trigger guard; the barrel then detaches from the receiver. Its removable breech plug accepts a bare 209 primer. This new-style muzzle-loading black-powder rifle must be purchased through an FFL holder.

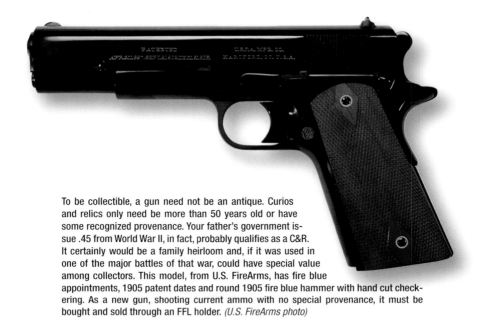

To be collectible, a gun need not be an antique. Curios and relics only need be more than 50 years old or have some recognized provenance. Your father's government issue .45 from World War II, in fact, probably qualifies as a C&R. It certainly would be a family heirloom and, if it was used in one of the major battles of that war, could have special value among collectors. This model, from U.S. FireArms, has fire blue appointments, 1905 patent dates and round 1905 fire blue hammer with hand cut checkering. As a new gun, shooting current ammo with no special provenance, it must be bought and sold through an FFL holder. *(U.S. FireArms photo)*

this is incorrect. Curios and relic firearms must be in their original condition. "Sporterized" military firearms are not C&R unless they were modified more than 50 years ago, then the resulting new firearm would be a C&R by age.);

(b) Firearms which are certified by the curator of a municipal, State, or Federal museum (and approved by the BATFE Firearms Technology Branch) which exhibits firearms to be curios or relics of museum interest; and

(c) Any other firearms which derive a substantial part of their monetary value from the fact that they are novel, rare, bizarre, or because of their association with some historical figure, period, or event. Proof of qualification of a particular firearm under this category may be established by evidence of present value and evidence that like firearms are not available except as collector's items, or that the value of like firearms available in ordinary commercial channels is substantially less. Note: When a firearm reaches its 50th "birthday," it is automatically classified as a C&R. A 50-year-old firearm does not have to be verified by BATFE.

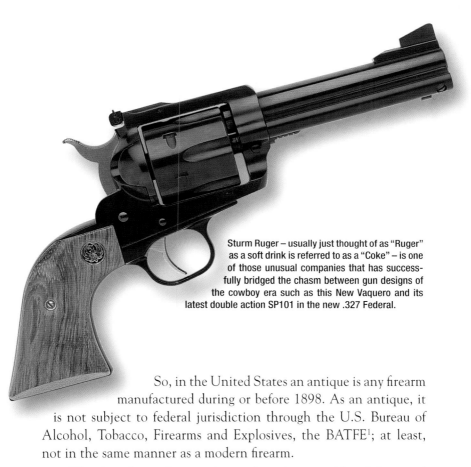

Sturm Ruger – usually just thought of as "Ruger" as a soft drink is referred to as a "Coke" – is one of those unusual companies that has successfully bridged the chasm between gun designs of the cowboy era such as this New Vaquero and its latest double action SP101 in the new .327 Federal.

So, in the United States an antique is any firearm manufactured during or before 1898. As an antique, it is not subject to federal jurisdiction through the U.S. Bureau of Alcohol, Tobacco, Firearms and Explosives, the BATFE[1]; at least, not in the same manner as a modern firearm.

Thus purchase of an antique takes place outside of the usual FFL requirements that exist when one purchases a current gun. Muzzleloaders or muzzleloading replicas, for instance, do not fall within BATFE regulation, either, and are classified the same as antique firearms.[2] Replicas of cartridge firing guns, your new .357 Ruger Vaquero[3], for instance, are not antiques and must be purchased with the assistance of a licensed FFL holder.

A true antique rifle manufactured before 1899 and firing the same cartridge as the replica is legal for sale without an FFL transfer. Not only that, but any rifle re-built on a receiver or frame that was manufactured prior to 1899 and is unaltered is classified as an antique, even if every other part has been replaced.

There are only two exceptions to the above rule:

1) Automatic firing machine guns such as the multiple-barrel Gatling gun (hand-cranked Gatlings or Gardners are not machineguns), which Colt produced for Richard Gatling (patented in 1862), or the single-barrel Maxim Gun, invented by the American-born Briton Hiram Maxim in 1884; and

2) Antique cartridge rifles with barrels shorter than 16 inches; shotguns with barrels shorter than 18 inches; or either gun with an overall length less than 26 inches. These guns are separately classified as "short barreled."

The original Gatling gun was a black powder field weapon. It used multiple rotating barrels turned by a hand crank, and fired loose (no links or belt) metal cartridge ammunition using gravity feed from a hopper. The Union Army first used it on an extremely limited and experimental basis during the Civil War. It won't hurt to check with ATF before purchasing one of these as a curio and relic!

The act that specifies the 1898-99 date is The Gun Control Act of 1968 (P.L. 90-618 as amended[4]). Earlier relevant legislation in the U.S. was the National Firearms Act of 1934. If this all seems clear as mud, just keep the basic rule in mind: a gun built before 1899 is an antique and can be personally transferred (i.e., bought, sold or traded) without Federal paperwork.

Shipping and Transfer

The novice can easily be confused by the laws that govern the shipping of collectioble firearms. To wit:

Example #1

You are a historical re-enactor who is also interested in old American guns, especially those used on the frontier in Texas, but originals are both tremendously expensive and incredibly hard to find.

The Crockett Legacy

Caywood Gunmakers of Berryville, Arkansas (www.caywoodguns.com) builds replicas of Davy Crockett's first gun. "The present owner, Mr. Joe Swann of Maryville, TN., has graciously consented to allow our company to recreate this beautiful piece of Americana in numbered, limited edition form. The gun was originally built in .48 caliber and we will produce 100 guns. The owner's name will be engraved on a sterling plate precisely fitted at the bottom of the patchbox recess. The plate will also carry the edition number."

Preserving the name and the tradition are perhaps as important than preserving the actual instrument purchased by the 17-year-old Crockett, his first rifle.

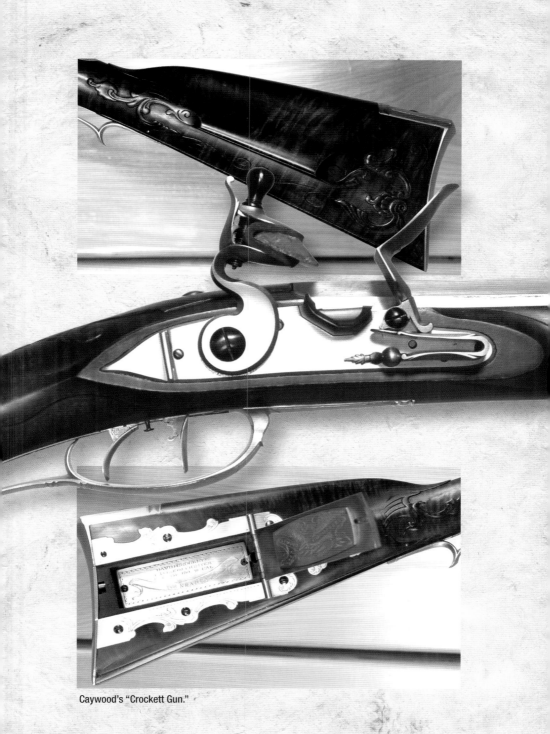

Caywood's "Crockett Gun."

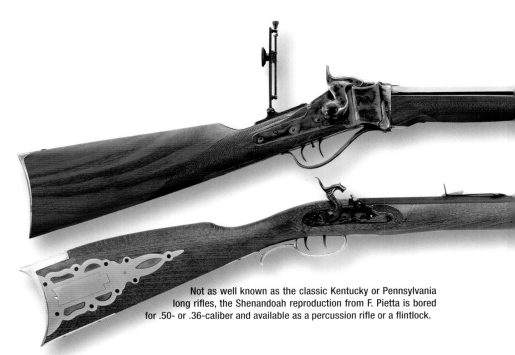

Not as well known as the classic Kentucky or Pennsylvania long rifles, the Shenandoah reproduction from F. Pietta is bored for .50- or .36-caliber and available as a percussion rifle or a flintlock.

Through Cherry's Fine Guns (www.cherrys.com) in Greensboro, North Carolina, you notice that a high quality flintlock reproduction of the historical rifle used by the Texans during the battle of the Alamo in 1836 is now available. (At the Alamo, 186 Texan patriots stalled 4,000 Mexican troops for 13 days. The patriots were all killed and became Texas martyrs.) This working reproduction is made by Davide-Pedersoli (www.davide-pedersoli.com) in Italy with adjustable double set trigger and rear sight, blue finished 36-inch octagonal barrel and a walnut stock; it weighs 7 ½ pounds. Shown on the patch box are two scenes from the U.S. War of Independence.

If you purchase this reproduction flintlock (.32-, .45- or .50-caliber) for $625 plus $30 s&h, Cherry's will ship it to your home address via UPS Ground because, although newly-manufactured, it is a muzzleloading gun and therefore can be shipped directly to the buyer.

Note: according to Norm Flayderman[5], a Jacob Dickert Pennsylvania flintlock such as the one on display in the long barracks museum at the Alamo and in fine condition would be valued at about $3,500. (The state of Pennsylvania contracted with Dickert and Matthew Llewellin for 1,000 flintlock rifles in 1797.) An origi-

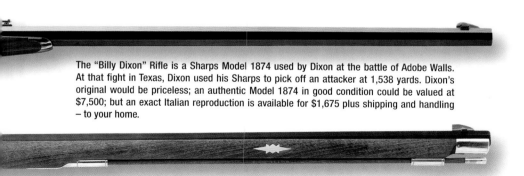

The "Billy Dixon" Rifle is a Sharps Model 1874 used by Dixon at the battle of Adobe Walls. At that fight in Texas, Dixon used his Sharps to pick off an attacker at 1,538 yards. Dixon's original would be priceless; an authentic Model 1874 in good condition could be valued at $7,500; but an exact Italian reproduction is available for $1,675 plus shipping and handling – to your home.

nal flintlock used at the Alamo, however, even if it did not belong to Davey Crockett, would be priceless.

Example #2

At the same site (Cherry's), you notice a Pedersoli reproduction of the "Billy Dixon" Rifle, a Sharps Model 1874. This percussion rifle is named for the young scout who shot a Kiowa warrior with his Sharps Sporting from an amazing distance of 1,538 yards on June 27, 1874, at Adobe Walls, Texas. (There, Dixon and 27 other buffalo hunters were surrounded by 500 Kiowa and Comanche warriors. The Indians were spurred forward by a medicine man who convinced them they were invulnerable to the white men's shots. In actual fact, they were not.) Pedersoli produces the Billy Dixon with a 32-inch octagonal conical barrel in .45/70 caliber, choice walnut for its stock and forearm with a German silver cap, checkered and oil finished "following the old system." It weighs almost 11 pounds.

You can buy this replica Sharps $1,675 plus $30 s&h, Cherry's will ship this gun, which is classified as a modern firearm because it fires a readily available cartridge, to your local FFL holder where you can pick it up (after paying a small handling and paperwork fee).

Note: Norm Flayderman's *Guide* says that a Sharps Model 1874 Sporting in fine condition would be valued at about $7,500. Produced from 1871-81 the total production was 6,500. Billy Dixon's gun itself would surely command a six-figure sale price.

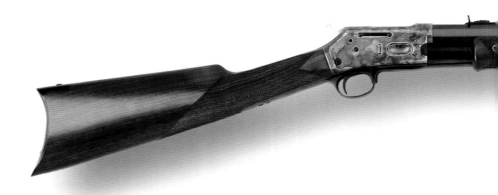

Example #3

For cowboy shooting, Cherry's has a Pedersoli Colt Lightning Standard pump rifle. It is a reproduction of one of the most famous rifles used during the late 1800s by cowboys and settlers on the Texas frontier. Today, cowboy action shooters, hunters and collectors find it desirable. "To the original American model, we made important modifications to the mechanical parts to make the rifle more safe and reliable," says the Italian manufacturer. "With great care, we retained the fascination, beauty and appearance of the original rifle while making subtle changes to design out the weaknesses of the original and give today's shooters an accurate and reliable rifle." The Lightning is available in a Standard version with 26-inch round or octagonal barrel, blued finish and walnut stock. It weighs 7-1/4 pounds. (Italics supplied.)

Available in a multitude of calibers this reproduction costs $1,250 (round barrel) or $1,330 (octagonal barrel) plus $30 s&h to a local FFL holder of your choosing. FFL holders usually charge either a set fee (often $20) or a percentage of the price (sometimes 5 percent – in this case $82.50) for their service which includes the FFL paperwork. Although a replica of a pre-1898 rifle, the Pedersoli Lightning fires readily-available ammunition and is therefore considered a modern firearm.

Note: Flayderman's *Guide* suggests that a Colt Lightning slide action large frame standard pump in excellent condition would be

Another instance where an original Colt Lightning in good condition would certainly cost $3,000, but where an exact Italian reproduction is only about $1,300 through Cimarron Firearms. The Lightning slide-action rifle was designed to be the companion for a single action revolver of the same caliber: .32-20, .38-40 or .44-40.

valued at about $3,250. Produced in several versions from 1887-94 the total production was 89,777 for the medium frame, 89,912 for the small frame and 6,496 for the large frame. (The large frame Lightning rifle is considered extremely desirable today. Shootable examples, especially those chambered for the "Express" type cartridge, command higher prices than the small and medium frame guns.)

The Curiosity

Production of a number of cartridge firearms, such as the famous Winchester Model 1894 lever action rifle (known as the Model 94 after 1927) took place both before and after December 31, 1898, the date that separates antique from modern status. That rifle was manufactured in several calibers although the most popular version was .30-30, and it is believed to be the first firearm to sell more than one million units. (To date, in excess of three million '94s have been produced.)

Thus, collectors rely on references such as Flayerman's famous *Guide* (which, along with the *Standard Catalog of Firearms*, we will frequently refer to as our primary sources of current firearms values) to determine whether a particular gun's serial number qualifies it as an antique.

For the Model 1894, for example, with serial number 147,684 – marked on the bottom outside of the frame at the forward end – we

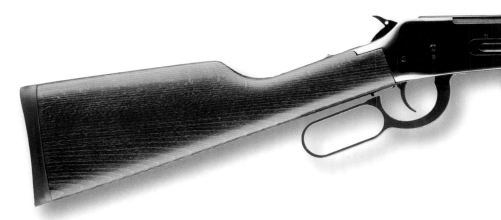

can probably trust that its receiver was built in December 1898 and it would hence be classified as an antique.

Note, however, that a Model 1894 with serial number 147,686 probably had a frame that was built in January 1899 and it is hence classified as "modern" and would be regulated by the BATFE.

In practical terms this means a significant difference in price asked for a particular gun. Collectors generally prefer pre-1898 examples and are willing to pay a premium for them. Here are a few illustrative prices:

• In January 2008 DeWing's Fly & Gun Shop in West Palm Beach, Florida was selling a Winchester Model 1894 that was produced in about 1934 and chambered for .32 Winchester Special. It had a 19-inch barrel and a 13-inch length of pull. The asking price was $995, but the serial number was not mentioned. (http://gunroom. shootingsportsman.com)

• That same month a private collector in Connecticut advertised a Winchester Model 1894 Deluxe Takedown in the Cabela's Gun Room. It had been built in about 1894 and chambered for .25-35 with a 26-inch barrel and a 13-inch length of pull. The serial number was #12xxx. This gun came with a factory letter and was rated overall as Very Good as the receiver had 80 to 85 percent of the original blue. "The fore-end has two professionally-filled holes with the trace outline of a base for a palm rest. This is a fairly professional job as the plug in the checkering has been checkered to match. It

John M. Browning designed the Model 94 to accept smokeless powder cartridges. It was a first for Winchester, which – in its multiple corporate configurations – has sold millions of the lever action rifle…in dozens of configurations including the carbine shown here. The collector should thoroughly research and inspect a '94 prior to a sale.

carries numerous nicks and dings that you would expect from a rifle of this age. Mechanics are crisp, bore is good with just some scattered light pitting. Asking price $9,999." (http://www.cabelas.com)

The Date on the Receiver

Since it is the date (presumably of manufacture) stamped on the receiver that is relevant to classifying a gun as either antique or modern, it is possible to have a weapon with date marks after 1898 but still be considered an antique.

An example cited by survival and gun writer James Wesley Rawles involves a number of Finnish M39 rifles (this Finnish rifle is a varia-

An interesting anomaly in U.S. law says that any rifle re-built on a receiver or frame that was manufactured prior to 1899 is classified as an antique…even if every other part has been replaced!

Agents from the Bureau of Alcohol, Tobacco, Firearms and Explosives (BATFE) are charged by congress with enforcement of America's gun laws, including regulation of the "curios and relics" that interest many collectors. *(Courtesy of BATFE)*

tion of the original Russian Mosin-Nagant). Those with hexagonal profile receivers are considered antique because some of them were built on receivers dated pre-1899, even though the rifle itself was only adopted in 1939. Until as late as the 1970s these guns were assembled using a mix of older round or hexagonal receivers. To be correctly evaluated, however, Mosin-Nagants that have been re-barreled need to be disassembled to check the date stamps on their tangs.[6]

Our Canadian Neighbors

In Canada, antique guns are defined under P.C. 1998-1664. A minor source of confusion for antique gun collectors as well as for dealers is that in Canada, the threshold for antique status is one year earlier than in the U.S. In the U.S. guns made before 1899 are "antique", but in Canada, they are defined as guns made before 1898. (www.panda.com/canadaguns/)

In Great Britain, antique guns are exempt from most police controls, but the definition of antique in Section 58(2) of the Firearms

As the nation becomes increasingly complex, expect that views of and for the future will clash: those that clamor for greater access to guns and those who insist on regulating firearms. Such a clash makes retailing, trading and collecting more insecure, especially if one moves between legal jurisdictions.

Act of 1968 is pedantically ambiguous and interpretation of the law is often left up to local police. This means that enforcement, even answering questions, will vary between jurisdictions. The Home Office in paragraph 2.7 of the Firearms Law, as amended, issued additional leadership as Guidance to the Police in 1989, suggesting that a range of vintage firearms might be considered for antique status. "Vintage" for those purposes meant manufactured prior to 1939. (www.nra-ila.org)

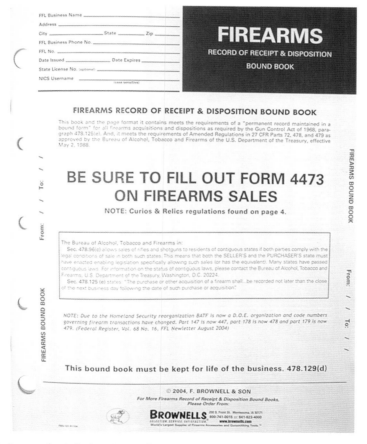

Most gun enthusiasts do not appreciate the strenuous record-keeping hurdles that their elected representatives have imposed and tend to blame the agencies of government – agencies charged with carrying out laws passed and signed – for any difficulty in purchasing or maintaining firearms. *(Photo courtesy Brownells)*

Condition Standards for Antique Firearms

Throughout this book, we will refer to the physical condition of antique firearms by grade or condition because that estimation is a major factor in establishing value. Other important considerations – sometimes overriding considerations – would be the general desirability among the collecting public; the gun's relative scarcity; any evidence of re-work and whether that was performed at the factory; the gun's provenance or chain of custody since it was built; any famous or infamous owners and whether the gun was used in a conflict as establishing military provenance usually boosts a gun's sale price. (These standards are adapted from the National Rifle Association's standards for antique firearms, which can be found online at www.nationalfirearmsmuseum.org/collector/condition.asp.)

Factory New – all original parts; 100 percent original finish; in perfect condition in every respect, inside and out.

Excellent – all original parts; more than 80 percent original finish; sharp lettering, numerals and design on metal and wood; unmarred wood, fine bore.

Fine – all original parts; more than 30 percent original finish; sharp lettering, numerals and design on metal and wood, minor marks in wood; good bore.

Very Good – all original parts; none to 30 percent of the original finish; original metal surfaces smooth with all edges sharp; clear lettering, numerals and design on metal; wood slightly scratched or bruised; bore disregarded for collectors firearms.

Good – some minor replacement parts; metal smoothly rusted or lightly pitted in places, cleaned or re-blued, principal lettering, numerals and design on metal legible; wood refinished, scratched, bruised or minor cracks repaired; in good working order.

Fair – some major parts replaced; minor replacement parts may be required; metal rusted, may be lightly pitted all over, vigorously cleaned or re-blued; rounded edges of metal and wood; principal lettering, numerals and design on metal partly obliterated; wood scratched, bruised, cracked or repaired where broken; in fair working order or can be easily repaired and placed in working order.

Poor – major and minor parts replaced; major replacement parts required and extensive restoration needed; metal deeply pitted; principal lettering, numerals and design obliterated, wood badly scratched, bruised, cracked or broken; mechanically inoperative; generally undesirable as a collector's firearm.

Readers should understand that determination of a particular firearm's condition for collection and sale according to this grading standard is not as objective as it may appear. Often, it requires study by an expert to resolve a gun's proper grade: whether screws have been replaced, or when a new grip was fitted or even what percentage of the original blue remains on the gun. (Bluing can be a particularly thorny issue.) While a panel of non-involved independent experts might clearly express a preference for one grade or another, they may not…and certainly, one ought to expect that even an absolutely honest purchaser would tend to evaluate an antique down in grade. Thus, when dollars and reputations are on the line, one really must exercise caution and not be afraid to ask for factory letters or independent, authoritative evaluations.

Footnotes:

1   Holding a Federal Firearms License (FFL) enables an individual or a company to engage in the interstate and intrastate manufacturing and/or sale of modern firearms. Dealing in modern firearms has required an FFL since 1968. Licensing is administered by the BATFE. There are currently nine types of licenses, including a "curio and relics" collector's license. A license is valid for three years, and is non-transferable.

The C&R ("curio and relic") license is available to individual collectors. A C&R license should not be used to conduct business as a firearms dealer. It is a license for collectors to enhance their collection. An individual must receive a Type 01 dealer's license to engage in the business of buying and selling C&R firearms.

Some automatic weapons have been designated as C&R firearms, and although a C&R FFL can be used to acquire these as well, they are also subject to controls imposed by the National Firearms Act of 1934. BATFE maintains a current list of approved C&R firearms on its website (for a current list go to www.atf.gov/firearms/curios/), but BATFE does not provide a service to date C&R firearms for the public. Contact the NRA or a reputable firearms historian. Individuals who have a C&R FFL may acquire C&R firearms in interstate commerce via mail or telephone order, over the Internet or in person. Licensed collectors are not considered to be FFL dealers, per se, however, and have no special privileges concerning non-C&R firearms. The purpose of the C&R license is to enable a collector to acquire C&R firearms for his or her personal collection; not to become a firearms dealer.

2   Muzzleloading blackpowder shotguns are not subject to the short-barreled National Firearms Act of 1934 restrictions.

3   Ruger's fixed-sight single action New Vaquero family includes "color-case" blued, stainless steel and engraved models in .357 Magnum and .45 Colt calibers (a $640 suggested retail price; see www.ruger.com), with barrel lengths of 4 5/8, 5 ½ and 7 ½ inches. Ruger's proprietary color case finish replicates the mottled case hardening pattern found on older guns and resulting from the process of hardening their softer steels; this is not necessary with modern steels. Stainless New Vaqueros feature a high-gloss finish, simulating the attractive, but relatively fragile, nickel-plating found on many original revolvers. The New Vaquero closely resembles the look and feel of classic single action revolvers of the 1800's. New guns are built with modern internal mechanisms, however. The Ruger Vaquero is popular among cowboy action competitors.

4   http://www.atf.gov/pub/fire-explo_pub/gca.htm

5   *Flayderman's Guide to Antique American Firearms…and Their Values*, 8th Edition by Norm Flayderman A Gun Digest Book an Imprint of F&W Publications, Iola, WI 2001.

6   James Wesley Rawles (http://en.wikipedia.org/wiki/Antique_guns and www.survivalblog.com). An M39 for sale from Florida Gun Works in Miami recently listed this additional information: "The M.39 is the very best Mosin-Nagant type rifle ever produced. It was manufactured by several contractors during World War II. Finland used captured Russian Mosin-Nagant M.91 actions and produced new barrels, stocks and hardware. The M.39 was the result." Listed as "very nice, good condition," this rifle was priced at $269.00 plus s&h. (www.floridagunworks.com)

7   About bluing steel: Bluing is a "passivation process" in which steel is partially protected against rust. Named after the blue-black appearance of the resulting protective finish, bluing is an electrochemical conversion coating resulting from an oxidizing chemical reaction with iron on the surface selectively forming magnetite (Fe_3O_4), the black oxide of iron, which occupies the same volume as normal iron. Black oxide provides minimal protection against corrosion, unless also treated with a water-displacing oil to reduce wetting and galvanic action.

In contrast, rust, the red oxide of iron (Fe_2O_3), does not occupy the same volume as iron, thereby causing the typical reddish rusting away of iron.

Both "cold" and "hot" oxidizing processes are called bluing, but only the "hot" process provides significant rust and corrosion resistance, and then only when also treated with an oiled coating.

In the context of corrosion, passivation is the spontaneous formation of a hard non-reactive surface film that inhibits further corrosion. This layer is usually an oxide or nitride that is a few atoms thick.

Bluing improves the cosmetic appearance of a gun and provides limited resistance against rust. Blued parts still need to be properly oiled to prevent rust. Bluing, being a chemical conversion coating, is not as robust against wear and corrosion resistance as plated coatings, and is typically no thicker than 0.0001 inch (2.5 micrometers). Thus, it is considered not to add any appreciable thickness to precisely machined gun parts.

New guns are typically available in blued finish options offered as the least-expensive finish, and this finish is also the least effective at providing rust resistance, relative to other finishes such as Parkerizing or hard chrome plating.

Bluing is often a hobbyist endeavor, and there are many methods of bluing and continuing debates about the relative efficacy of each method.

Chapter Five

Preservation and Conservation

*T*here is a continuing battle inside the world of antiques and collectibles, and it rages quite as vigorously in furniture and art and architecture as it does in firearms. The battle centers around the act or process of restoration. Should one restore an old collectible and if so, what should be done? At what stage of deterioration should an old gun or a bureau be refinished or a coin polished; should an old camera be returned to working order with precisely-made but new parts or even from parts scavenged from other, similar cameras that are too far gone to ever repair or to ever sell; to what

state or era in its history should an artifact be returned; how should it then be marked or presented; and – the ultimate question – if it is refinished, how should it then be valued?

A warning is in order before proceeding with this chapter and the next: the stakeholders take sides – professionals call names. Everyone who has something to gain or to lose in the antiques business, from avid collectors to gunsmiths to auction houses to those who simply write about collecting, hold strong and often inflexible opinions about the subject of restoration. These individuals are called "stakeholders" – they are not disinterested bystanders.

Perhaps in the beginning it would be helpful (and less argumentative) if we simply were more precise in our terminology.

What Is Preservation?

Preservation is intended to prevent further deterioration, to hold something "as is" for the future. We preserve wild lands, for example, so that in the future people can, at least for a brief period, experience solitude...and perhaps for other type of flora and fauna as we creep toward the understanding that we are not the only species of value on earth. We preserve works of art because genius is unevenly distributed through the human condition and what may provoke one generation to greatness may only cause the next to yawn.

If we owned an old Colt SAA that our great-great grandfather had carried when he fought Indians and homesteaded California in the 19th century, we would want to preserve that gun in the very best condition possible for our children or perhaps for sale at a later date. If we had a letter from great-great grandpa sending that same gun to a family member and then could trace ownership to the present day, we would want to preserve that as well. It would mean handling the gun rarely; storing it with the papers in a dark, humidity-controlled safe; and taking steps to ensure that we de-acidify the papers, slip

U.S. Fire Arms, one of America's foremost manufacturers of replica firearms, operates beneath the famous Colt blue dome in Hartford, Connecticut. Their display replicates the original Colt revolver display made famous by Samuel Colt more than 150 years ago. USFA guns are so faithful to the original Colts that an unscrupulous person with a newly-made roll die could pass one of as an original 19th-century Colt. Buyer Beware!

them into preservation sleeves, monitor for insect and UV damage and handle only with gloves because our hands contain oils that will stain old paper and cause it to deteriorate.

For the important paperwork (which may be just as valuable as the gun), the Library of Congress suggests, "Store paper materials in dark, cool, relatively dry locations. Aim for 35% relative humidity and below 72° F. Avoid light, heat and dampness. Maintaining steady temperature and relative humidity is preferable over conditions that cycle up and down."

David Arnold, Springfield Armory National Historic Site

David Arnold, the conservator at the Springfield Armory National Historic Site Museum in Springfield, Massachusetts says there are a few simple guidelines to help care for an antique gun (or a collection).

In the wider scope of collectibles and shooting, re-manufacturing exact replicas of early U.S. guns such as Lightning rifles is an integral part of the preservation and conservation process. Many Old West rifles were lever action, says U.S. FireArms. Thus the "anchor arm" breaks its hold to work the lever, which causes the shooter to lose barrel/target relationship. The benefit of the Lightning is the ability to hold the anchor arm steady and remain focused and ready on target. Many replica Lightnings are on the market, but the most eagerly sought-after Lightning, the large-frame "Express" rifle, has not been reproduced, so any example of one you might find is almost certainly an original. The small-frame rimfire Lightnings have not been reproduced, either, so the same holds true. *(U.S. FireArms photo)*

"This represents the safest, most conservative advice I can give without thoroughly examining a specific collection," he says. "Methods recommended here may not be the most efficient, but there are many more treatment options available to me which I cannot share in a public forum. What may work beautifully in one situation can be a disaster in another. I treat every gun as a unique object and the treatments I perform can vary considerably.

"You have to remember that my advice is limited in scope and can't cover every possible situation. It is based on my training and experiences as a conservator, and my experience working (so far) mainly with military firearms made during the last three centuries. I learn more with every treatment I do, so as a consequence, these guidelines are a work-in-progress. Feel free to contact me through the Springfield Armory site at www.nps.gov/spar/ with questions or concerns. By doing so you will perhaps contribute to the improvement of these guidelines."

To restore or not to restore? A bungled attempt at restoring this antique Starr revolver could reduce its value by thousands of dollars.

HARRY BECKWITH
USED
PRUSSION
FLINT CONV.
MUSKET
$1,100.00

CONFEDERATE CIVAL WAR
NSN, NO 4473
BLACK POWDER

Classified as a percussion/flint conversion musket with a Confederate Civil War heritage, this old rifle showed an age to match its purported military provenance: rust, obvious signs of wear and a seriously weathered, beaten-up surface. If you owned it, would you clean it? Restore it? Or would you choose to preserve it "as is?" (And of course, perhaps you noted from the photo of the trigger and trigger guard on pages 86-87 that at least one screw has also been replaced.)

Preventive Care

Environment

Avoid dramatic swings in relative humidity (RH). Try to keep the humidity stable and between 40 and 50 percent. Consistency is more important than precise maintenance of a specific RH reading, though RH control is critical because of an unusual physical property of wood called anisotropy. Wood cells expand or contract very differently in response to changes in relative humidity – depending on their specific grain orientation (axial, transverse or radial) in the log from which they came. Large swings in RH can result in cracks caused by compression-set shrinkage.

If the humidity remains fairly constant, changes in temperature make little difference to either metal or wood. A rapid rise in temperature, though, can pull the moisture out of the environment (including your artifact), causing a sudden drop in RH. Cell shrinkage and cracking or splitting can then occur.

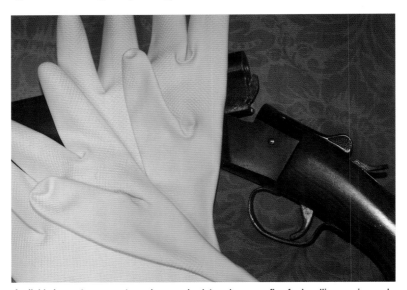

Available in most grocery stores, inexpensive latex gloves are fine for handling precious collectible firearms. However, the protein in latex causes irritation and an allergic reaction in a significant number of people. Nitrile gloves, used by your personal physician during examinations, are made of synthetic latex and contain no latex proteins. They are available inexpensively at medical supply stores or via Internet vendors.

Handling

Wear gloves when handling your collection. No protective coating can stand up for long against repeated barehanded handling. Best to always wear gloves and I recommend Nitrile examination gloves[1] when cleaning and coating your collection. Once an item has been coated, wear plain cotton gloves.

Housekeeping

Keep your firearms dust-free. Dust can trap moisture increasing the likelihood of corrosion occurring. Don't use commercial dust cloths, though. They often leave an oil film behind which traps dust and dust traps water vapor from the air. When dusting, use either a vacumn with a soft brush or a soft cotton cloth very lightly dampened with water. Without moisture, dust merely gets shoved around and will not be picked up. Dry the gun immediately with a clean cloth.

Don't use alcohol of any kind when dusting or cleaning a firearm stock. It can skin or strip an historic finish. Never use liquid or spray dusting products, either, because most of them leave mineral oil behind, which traps dust. Remember that dust traps and collects moisture.

Storage/Display

Narrow hooks or loops of wire should not be used to support collection pieces either in storage, transport or on display. The weight of most long arms on such devices is sufficient to cause indentations in their stock at the points of contact. Instead, use broad, padded supports. We

Narrow hooks or loops of wire should not be used to support collection pieces either in storage, transport or on display, says David Arnold, Springfield Armory National Historic Site. The weight of most long arms on such devices is sufficient to cause indentations in their stock at the points of contact. Instead, use broad, padded supports.

use thin sheets of a closed-cell polyethylene foam material[2] to pad our display fixtures.

To avoid mold and mildew during long-term storage, avoid at least two of the three conditions known to promote bloom outbreaks: elevated temperature, still air and elevated humidity.

Cleaning and Coating

Cleaning Wood Stocks

First, separate the wooden parts from the metal parts. They are

When handling collectible firearms, the first rule of thumb is that whatever you do will be questioned by half the people you tell. Even cleaning a collectible involves considerable anguish in some quarters.

cleaned and coated differently. Unless it should become absolutely necessary, leave the unfinished interior wooden surfaces alone.

Clean the exterior of the stock by placing a few drops of a mild detergent[3] in a gallon of warm distilled water. Apply with a slightly damp soft cloth and rinse with clean cloths dampened with distilled water. Dry with soft cloths immediately after rinsing.

Clean again with mineral spirits, using a soft cloth to apply. Be sure to work in fresh air or a well-ventilated area. Avoid using "oil soaps" as they can be caustic and may damage an historic oiled surface.

Replica firearms used for cowboy action shooting or for hunting need regular scrubbing and strong solvents to remove black powder residue, but a true collectible firearm should never experience cleaning with a wire bore brush. *(Photos courtesy Traditions)*

Cleaning Barrels and Other Metal Parts

[Please note: I believe that it is essential to practice any new technique on a sacrificial piece first, before applying it to something irreplaceable.]

Use nylon or animal-bristle bore brushes.[4] Avoid using brass or steel brushes because such hard materials can scratch, but also might (under certain conditions) cause galvanic (bi-metallic) corrosion (specifically when using a copper-alloy brush on ferrous metals) by leaving a slight metallic smear behind.

Use mineral spirits to soften accretions. Work in fresh air or a well-ventilated area. (Are there other solvents that are stronger? Yes, but they are difficult to work with safely.) Swab clean with a cloth patch.

Use only extremely fine abrasives such as oil-free 0000 steel wool.[5] Use only if absolutely necessary to remove stubborn rust or other accretions. Work slowly and watch constantly for any changes to the surface. There is always an element of risk in such work. If you are at all uncertain, hire a conservator or qualified gunsmith before causing irreversible damage.

When cleaning brass parts, never use products that contain ammonia. Ammonia can damage old copper alloy materials by corroding them from the inside out. In addition, such products may include abrasives, which may prove too harsh. Elbow grease and mineral spirits should be tried first. If something slightly stronger is needed, try applying small amounts of wet tooth powder with a cotton swab and rinse with water.

So – a general comment about commercial rust removers. To date, I have not found a rust-removal product that is entirely safe to use on historic metal surfaces. The problem is that most rust removers can't tell the difference between iron oxide and iron metal, and will leave an etched surface even where there is no rust. Some products do seem to come close, though. Often they require extremely close attention and precision – too much for most of us operating on a home workbench. In short, there are no magic solutions that are risk-free and I advise against their use on anything you value.

Most surface rust can be removed by first lubricating the area with a light penetrating oil[6] and cleaving it off with a sharp scalpel held at a very low angle to the metal. It requires close attention, a steady hand, and some patience, but if you are careful, you will probably get most – if not all – of the surface rust off without leaving a scratch. When done, remove any remaining oil with mineral spirits.

Disassembly and Reassembly

If you are organized and systematic you should be able to safely disassemble and reassemble most firearms successfully.

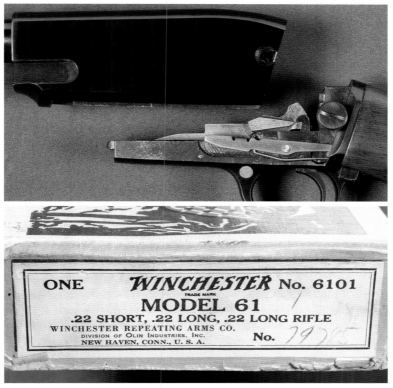

There is probably no better collectible – strictly as far as collectibles go – than to find a desirable New In The Box firearm. This Winchester Model 61 with 24-inch round barrel was manufactured in 1947 with a dovetail front sight and adjustable sporting rear sight: ¾-length magazine tube and standard barrel markings. A 17-groove flat bottom forearm with a plain pistol grip stock and checkered black hard rubber buttplate. Complete in its original Winchester picture box with a light colored background, red lettering and blue colored field scene. Only the slightest handling marks. The rifle appears to have never been assembled with no scratches or marks on the receiver. The value at Rock Island Auctions was estimated at $4,000-$6,000 (Lot1). Having an original box that is correct for the gun is a strong, but not infallible, indicator of originality.

First, probe the floor of every external screw slot with a sharp point held at a very low angle. It's amazing how much dirt can be packed into a clean-looking slot. All foreign matter must be removed for the screwdriver to do its best, safest work.[7]

A good selection of screwdrivers is a must. Their tips must be matched perfectly to each slot in order to maximize the area of mechanical contact. Taking this precaution will minimize slippage and the scratching and scarring that can result. The internal shapes of screw slots have changed a lot since their invention[8] and screwdriver tips often have to be ground or filed in order to get a good match. Keep this in mind when regrinding a screwdriver's tip.

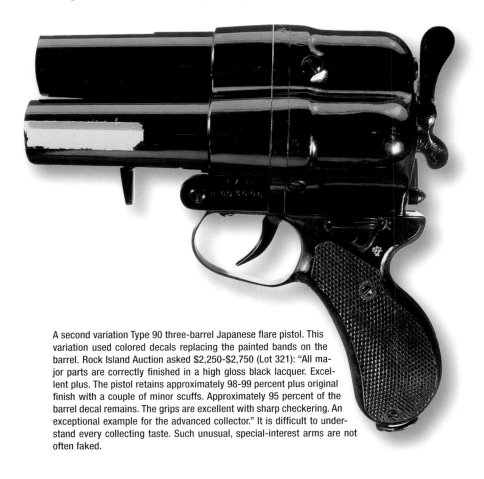

A second variation Type 90 three-barrel Japanese flare pistol. This variation used colored decals replacing the painted bands on the barrel. Rock Island Auction asked $2,250-$2,750 (Lot 321): "All major parts are correctly finished in a high gloss black lacquer. Excellent plus. The pistol retains approximately 98-99 percent plus original finish with a couple of minor scuffs. Approximately 95 percent of the barrel decal remains. The grips are excellent with sharp checkering. An exceptional example for the advanced collector." It is difficult to understand every collecting taste. Such unusual, special-interest arms are not often faked.

There are many publications that offer exploded drawings and disassembly/reassembly tips[9]. There is also a brilliant web site that illustrates with moving images how various types of firearms work[10].

Coating Stocks

Wood is neither thirsty nor hungry. It is usually covered by a finish that may have become corrupted in some way, thus making it look "dry." The wood beneath the finish does not need to be "fed," despite what wood-care product commercials may claim. So never put oil of any kind on an historic finish. There may well be unintended but permanently damaging consequences to ignoring this advice.

A cautionary word about linseed oil. Linseed oil takes forever to dry, will trap dust and will not stop water penetration, either. When linseed oil oxidizes, its molecules cross-link with one another, making it increasingly more difficult to remove as time passes. Oxidized linseed oil (linoleic acid) eventually becomes linoxin, better-known commercially as linoleum! Repeated, or seasonal, applications eventually develop into a surface that can look like very dark brown alligator skin, and can become almost impossible to remove.

Applying a modern finish over an equivalent historic finish can forever confuse the finish "history" of a stock by making it difficult, if not impossible, to tell what (if anything) is original, and what is a restoration material – even with an analytical microscope. Therefore, you would not want to touch up, say, a shellac finish with shellac.

An address stamped into a crease in the steel, perhaps between barrels, should still be sharp and legible after more than a century. On the other hand, if the lettering has burrs indicating that it was stamped without being completely finished, beware of a suspect gun. *(Photo courtesy Rock Island Auctions)*

Use paste waxes only. I prefer carnauba-based furniture waxes such as Kiwi Bois, Mohawk or Behlen, or Black Bison on wood stocks.[11] I also recommend using pigmented paste waxes. "Clear" waxes can collect in pores and appear as white specks against a dark wood background.

As much as we love bees and honey, avoid wax mixtures that include a high percentage of bee's wax when preserving wooden firearm parts. These wax mixtures are not especially harmful, but the are relatively soft (fingerprint easily) and can be slightly acidic.

Coating Metals

(Note: this advice is strictly for guns which have been "retired" from use and will never be fired.)

Avoid using oils. Oil is not the best material for long-term protection of collection pieces because it traps dust and dirt, eventually breaks down and has to be periodically replaced. A high quality light oil is fine for maintaining a gun you still shoot.

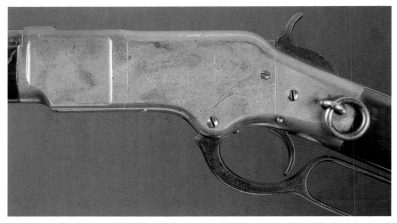

Close-up of Winchester M1866 "Yellow Boy" carbine, the Fourth Model manufactured in 1884 with a 20-inch round barrel and full tubular magazine. The frame is brass with a saddle ring attached to the left side. Graded at very good plus from Rock Island Auction which expected it to sell for $4,750-$6,500 (Lot 1001). "The barrel and magazine tube have a grayish patina with some spotting on the barrel and minor pitting on the magazine. The buttplate has a dark patina with some minor pitting. The receiver has an aged patina with a couple minor dings. The buttstock is very fine. The very good forearm has a few minor gouges on the left side and overall there are scattered minor dents, dings and scratches. The markings are readable." Note that there are several imported replicas of this gun that can be artificially aged to imitate the real thing. Don't be fooled!

Use a microcrystalline wax, such as Renaissance Wax[12] as a protective coating. Such a wax is practically inert, remaining stable for a very long time. Apply and buff out with a soft cloth or brush. I coat all parts this way, inside and out. [13]

Brass parts can also be coated with wax. I prefer to use Incralac[14] acrylic spray lacquer because it is easily removed with solvents but bonds especially well to copper-alloy metals, and will withstand more abuse and last longer than wax.

Minor Stock Repairs

If a split or detached piece of a stock must be repaired, use an adhesive that is both strong and reversible (i.e., can be safely removed at any time in the future). There is only one: traditional hide glue.[15]

Do not proceed if there is evidence that the damaged site has been previously repaired. In this case, if the gun has any value at all, I recommend that you consult a conservator.

Unless you work with hide glue every day, make it up fresh in small amounts as needed. It doesn't take long to prepare and it will do a better job than using old glue. Hot hide glue is preferable to liquid hide glue as it is less affected by humidity.

Dampen the area to be glued with hot water. Blot the area and wait a few minutes. Then apply hot glue to both surfaces with a brush and clamp immediately. An appropriate clamp can be as simple as a few pieces of masking tape, rubber bands, bicycle tire strips or small padded weights. Use the least force needed to do the job.

Clamps can usually be removed in a few hours, but it takes at least 24 hours for the repair to fully harden.

Excess glue can be removed with a lint-free cloth dampened with hot water. The best time to do this is usually right after removing clamps.

If you still need help

Seek the services of a professional conservator. Contact me or the American Institute for Conservation of Historic & Artistic Works (http://aic.stanford.edu/)[16] for a referral.

There are few, if any, conservators who treat nothing but firearms. Look for an "Objects" Conservator with experience working with metal and the other materials (wood, celluloid, leather, etc.) that are part of your artifact.

What Is Conservation?

The recommendations given by David Arnold, conservator at the Springfield Armory National Historic Site, may be precisely the formulation for taking care of antique firearms…in a museum. Parts of his advice may also suit those valuable weapons we want to take care of but which we do fire on occasion – dad's old double barrel J.C. Higgins box-lock shotgun with double triggers, for example, which we at last learned was purchased from Sears, Roebuck…and is not a fine old American gun

Rifle with Provenance and Paper!

This gun, ostensibly a standard .45-75 1876 Winchester manufactured in 1882, has "William Bros" scratched into the bottom of the elevator and there is a "V" filed into it as well.

The rifle is accompanied by a Winchester Gun Museum letter dated May 20, 1971 (see next page) and addressed to Arnold Charnoff stating that the museum had decided to thin out their collection. They offered him the first opportunity to purchase this so-called "Bob Ford" rifle. The letter further states that the rifle was originally shipped to Barnes Hardware, St. Joseph, Missouri on January 16, 1882. According to the letter, the museum purchased this rifle from the Williams Brothers of Boulder Colorado in 1920. The rifle was returned to the factory for repair on December 7, 1889 and after it was repaired it was shipped to Bob Ford, c/o Palace Hotel, Denver, Colorado on January 10, 1890.

Known as "the man who shot Jesse James," Ford ultimately earned his living posing for photographs. He later moved to Colorado where at age 32 on June 8, 1892 while in his tent saloon in Walsenburg, Colorado one Ed O'Kelley approached him from the back. O'Kelley said "Hello Bob," and as Ford turned O'Kelley let loose with both barrels of a sawed off shotgun killing Ford instantly. Ford is buried in Richmond, Missouri; his gravestone reads "The man who shot Jesse James."

Despite various dings and scratches, the rifle is graded very good. "This is not some 'Ripley's Believe it or Not' gun," notes Rock Island Auction, which expects to sell it for $35,000 to $65,000 (Lot 1024). "This is an indisputably documented Winchester Lever Action 1876 Rifle shipped to Jesse James' assassin."

GUN MUSEUM
275 WINCHESTER AVENUE, NEW HAVEN, CONNECTICUT 06504
WINCHESTER®

May 20, 1971

Dear

In answer to your inquiry about the possibility of our selling surplus arms from the museum, we have decided to thin out our collection over a period of time. Because you have been such a great help to us in the past, we are offering you the first opportunity to purchase these arms.

Our first offering to you will be Bob Ford's rifle you expressed interest in.

The 1876 Winchester rifle, serial number 24724, was shipped to Barnes Hardware, St. Joseph Missouri, January 16, 1882. It was listed as a standard 45-75 rifle with a 28 inch barrel. We have record of this gun being returned to the factory for repair December 7, 1889. When repaired, it was shipped to Bob Ford, c/o Palace Hotel, Denver Colorado, January 10, 1890.

The rifle was purchased from the Williams Brothers of Boulder Colorado in 1920 by the museum. We have no idea how they acquired the gun.

Let us **hear from you as** soon as possible. If you are interested, we will negotiate a price.

Respectfully,

Thomas E. Hall
Firearms Historian

TEH/bs

O L I N   C O R P O R A T I O N

like a Parker…and is valued on the open market at between $100 and $150. To us, a priceless heirloom…to anyone else, a truck gun.

Conservation is a word that we hunters, shooters and collectors are familiar with because it reminds us of our outdoor heritage. Theodore Roosevelt was instrumental in promoting the "conservation movement" in the U.S., a movement that has brought dozens of birds and mammals back from the brink of extinction often because of a huge commitment by men and women who hunt and fish, who actively use those resources.

The word "conservation" also denotes a profession that is devoted to the preservation of a cultural heritage for the future. And thus, it is similar to "preservation," but goes much further than the acts described by David Arnold earlier for caring for a particular firearm.

According to core documents of The American Institute for Conservation of Historic & Artistic Works, conservation activities include examination, documentation, treatment and preventive care, supported by research and education.

Stabilization

Preventive conservation should be important to a collector. Having acquired a valuable antique, a firearm that represents some part of our cultural and mechanical heritage, it now becomes the collector's responsibility create and maintain a protective environment for that firearm. As a general rule, the principal goal should be what is known as stabilization or preventing any deterioration from the current state.

Worth the effort?
This antique, early 19th century six-barrel pepperbox pistol (with close-up photos opposite) is in superb condition, but the demand for such pistols is unfortunately rather low. It would probably not be worth the time and effort of even a master con artist to alter these beautiful guns in any substantial manner. *(Photos courtesy Rock Island Auctions)*

Stabilization begins with the gun "as is." As much as we would like, we cannot go back in time for one second and thus there are both active and passive stabilization decisions. So the carefully de-termined – and irreversible, once it has taken place – decision to fire the antique gun, just one time, might cause irreversible damage.

If we begin with the end in mind, we take no action that might cause further deterioration to the firearm's state of being and we will take immediate steps to find the proper storage – safe from dust, fluc-tuations in humidity and temperature and from theft. Unfortunately, it is usually only the last of the above that concerns many casual collectors. Finding that place for storage or display that is environmentally controlled is always the greatest step in stabilization.

Documentation

Next, all conservation procedures should be backed up with documentation and the purchase of an antique may or may not come with relevant paperwork.

It is not uncommon at gun shows, to find sellers who have photocopied or printed thick stacks of documents relating to firearms. Let us say, for example, that you become interested in an Allen & Thurber bar hammer, ring trigger pepperbox in excellent condition, a gun manufactured in Massachusetts before the turn of the 19th century. It is now offered for sale for $1,695 and your obvious interest may evoke a flood of papers from the seller.

You must look through this paperwork carefully before deciding that it amounts to a flood of provenance and that, as such, it will make your purchase both wise and secure. It is the author's experience that such paperwork is often meant to baffle the buyer, especially the novice buyer, rather than to shed light on a particular gun. In the midst of a buying and selling decision, copies of general articles about pepperboxes; Internet links to people who are researching Allen & Thurber; stories about the evolution of the firearm in America.... All of these will be interesting, but they will have nothing to do with your immediate purchasing option.

When you have a specific gun before you, it will have a specific history. Any documents relating to that specific serial numbered gun, to its specific owners, its use by the police or military and history of re-work are pertinent: bills of sale that allow you to trace its ownership history, contact information of former owners, certificates or letters from experts that verify the gun's authenticity (there are similar reproductions), receipts from restoration specialists who may have worked on the gun.... Everything else is irrelevant fog and could be thought of as either useless data or even a deliberate effort to mislead.

If the seller can provide true, specific provenance, you should proceed with the inspection and evaluation of the pepperbox. If the seller quietly overwhelms you with interesting but – at the moment of writing a check – irrelevant data, graphs, photocopies, book chapters and miscellaneous information, it is probably best to pass on his wares altogether.

Provenance, as we have noted, is the history of custody of the described material since its creation, including any changes successive custodians made to them. It can perhaps best be described with a hypothetical example:

A five-shot Kerr revolver made in England and dating from the Civil War era might bring $1,000; if it has documentation certifying that it belonged to a particular Confederate cavalryman, it might bring twice that; if it was the Kerr revolver belonging to Tom Custer, who was killed along with his brothers on the Little Big Horn battlefield in 1876, it might go at auction for a six-figure price.[17]

An actual entry that shows the importance of provenance is this from *Warman's Civil War Collectibles, 2nd Edition:*

"Import Kerr revolver, .44 caliber, serial number E5xx. The serial number is stamped inside the bottom of the frame and inside the trigger guard. It also has the initials "JS" surmounting an anchor stamped in the wood just below the lower tang (recognized as a Confederate inspection mark). Old letters with the revolver indicate that it was carried by Private Francis R. Frazer, Co. E, 56th Regiment of Virginia Infantry, boosting the value to $6,000-$7,500.[18] (James D. Julia Auctioneers)

But provenance is not only something that we in the gun trades are concerned about; it is a passion among antique collectors of all kinds. In fact, it is a virtual obsession among that ultimate of antique investigators, the archaeologist.

"Recording and mapping all findings during excavation," writes Michael Pante, a research team member at ArchaeologyInfo.com, "while time consuming, is the most important task an archaeologist has. Each level of a unit is described in various ways, including, start and stop depths, soil color and texture, and a list of what was bagged and removed from the hole, for example charcoal, soil samples, artifacts and bones. Every artifact and bone is placed in a bag designated to a unit and level, which intern receives a catalog number.

"When features or artifact and bone concentrations occur a plan map of the level is drawn to show there specific location and

At some point, conservation and preservation end and restoration begins. That point is reached when the alterations become irreversible.

when a unit is complete or not producing any further finds a profile map of the walls is drawn to show soil changes through the unit. Photographs of features and completed units are also taken to further document the excavation. Once a unit has been excavated there in no way to go back and check for overlooked information, which makes it imperative to continuously record all findings to maximize the knowledge we can obtain from any given excavation."[19]

Reversibility

Today, professional conservation and preservation efforts lean heavily toward the practice of reversibility. This means that all alterations should be clearly distinguishable from the original object or specimen, and that all of those alterations may be reversed or removed at some future time.

By "reversible," conservators speak of preventing permanent alterations, which is of course, precisely the opposite of what most restoration activities (the "life's too short to shoot an ugly gun" attitude) propose. Recall the cellophane tape we used when we were kids to put newspaper clippings in our scrapbooks. This tape causes heavy stains that eventually migrate through the paper or photograph and show on the front. With the passage of time, adhesive residues, tapes and stains become increasingly difficult to remove or reduce, and simply become worse. Using a touch of military or airline grade epoxy to hold a nagging frame screw in place when the threads are worn away – who will ever notice? – is another example of faux-reversibility, a permanent alteration when other options might be considered.

Even in the world of art, conservation is not considered the same as restoration. Restoration is generally a process that attempts to return the work of art to some previous state – presumably that of the day of its completion by the original master – at least, the state that the restorer imagines to be original. It was once a well-thought-of and common practice in museums around the world and it has been applied to many of the world's most magnificent paintings.

In the late 20th century, however, a different concept of conservation emphasizing preserving the work of art for the future took hold. This conservation was less about restoring, about making a painting or antique vase look pristine. Restoration, as we have said, is controversial, since it often involves irreversible changes to the original artwork or artifact with the goal of making it "look good." The attitude of art conservators in recent years is to make all the restoration they undertake after basic cleaning, reversible.

Reversibility preserves a piece "as is" for future generations rather than returning it to some presumed state of glory. It gives future conservators and historians, future collectors the option of applying their skills and – we hope – advanced techniques and materials to a painting or statue or firearm. Thus, it is hoped that they will not then have to first undo our work before proceeding with their own.

Footnotes

1   Nitrile examination gloves come in different sizes and can be purchased from most medical supply stores and some pharmacies. I recommend them because some people have serious allergic reactions to latex rubber; also, latex breaks down if it comes in contact with many paste waxes and cleaning materials.

2   Voltek produces sheets of Volara in a range of thicknesses, color and hardness, which have proven to be very stable, conservation-grade materials and are used in many museums for padding storage shelves and exhibit fixtures. For the nearest supplier contact VOLTEK, Division of Sekisui America Corporation, 100 Shepard Street, Lawrence, MA 01843 (800) 225-0668, or at www.sekisuivoltek.com.

3   Kodak Photo-Flo is a non-ionic detergent available at camera stores or from Internet suppliers.

4   KleenBore makes a stiff nylon bore brush that I like a lot. They also make black powder brushes with bristles that extend to the tip. Contact Kleen-Bore, 16 Industrial Parkway, Easthampton, MA 01027, (800) 445-0301, or at www.kleen-bore.com.

5   Liberon/Star Finish Supply offers a very good 0000 grade of steel wool, but it can be difficult to find. Another source is Conservation Support Systems in Santa Barbara, CA. They can be reached at (800) 482-6299 or on the web at www.silcom.com/~css.

6   Choice of oil for this purpose is not critical. I happen to use CRC 3-36, but WD-40 or any similar product will work fine as a scalpel lubricant.

7   The best discussion I've found on the importance of matching screwdriver tips to screw heads (and removing fasteners in general) is an excellent pair of articles by David R. Chicoine. See *American Gunsmith*, December 2003 and January 2004, entitled "Disassembling Fine Old Guns: The Right Way" (parts 1 & 2).

8   See Warren E. Roberts "Wood Screws as an Aid to Dating Wooden Artifacts" in *The Chronicle*, March, 1978 (An Early American Industries publication. Also, The Canadian Conservation Institute's excellent *Technical Bulletin #17*, "Threaded Fasteners in Metal Artifacts" by George Prytulak, 1977. The latter includes additional information on cleaning metals.

9 The National Rifle Association is a very good source for books on firearms assembly. Their address is: 11250 Waples Mill Road, Fairfax, VA 22030 www.nrastore.com. Search their technical references.

10 Take a look at: http://home.howstuffworks.com. Search on either Machineguns or Flintlocks.

11 Kiwi Bois can be ordered from www.kingdomrestorations.com. It comes in seven different wood tones. I frequently use "walnut." As far as I can tell, Mohawk and Behlen are the same product with different packaging. Mohawk's Blue Label brown wax can be ordered directly from Mohawk Finishing Products, 4715 State HWY 30, Amsterdam, NY 12010-9921, (800) 545-0047 or at www.mohawk-finishing.com. Behlen Blue Label brown wax can be ordered from Olde Mill Cabinet Shoppe, 1660 Camp Betty Washington Road, York, PA 17402, (717) 755-8884 or at www.oldemill.com. Black Bison waxes are available from12 Liberon/Star through www.kingdomrestorations.com.

12 Renaissance Wax can be ordered from Woodcraft (formerly Woodcraft Supply), 560 Airport Industrial Park, PO Box 1686, Parkersburg, WV 26102 (800) 225-1153 or at www.woodcraft.com.

13 David Arnold recommends "Preserving the Metal on Your Guns and Swords" in the October 2004 issue of *Man at Arms* (www.manatarmsbooks.com). It is a very thorough, balanced discussion of options for coating historic arms.

14 Incralac acrylic lacquer is offered in 12 oz. spray cans by Custom Aerosol Packaging, P.O. Box 1411, Piqua, OH 45356, (937) 773-1824 (www.custom-aerosol.com).

15 Hide glue is actually made up of tendons and other connective tissues. It is easy to use and should be prepared in small batches whenever needed. It is available from Woodcraft, Olde Mill, Liberon and many other fine woodworking suppliers. It is the only wood adhesive I use and recommend.

16 AIC, 1717 K Street N.W., Suite 301, Washington, D.C. 20005. (202) 452-9545. Best done initially on their web site at http://aic.stanford.edu/.

17 The Custer Kerr, by the way, was purchased from a private collection about 25 years ago and was verified with his initials – "TWC" for the two-time Medal of Honor winner Thomas Ward Custer – engraved in the negative on the gun's backstrap. It is now on display at the Custer Battlefield Museum, Town Hall, P.O. Box 200, Garryowen, MT 59031 (406) 638-1876 www.custermuseum.org. Featuring an extensive collection of Custer battlefield and period artifacts, as well as a Lewis and Clark exhibit, the museum is open from 8:00 am to 8:00 pm Memorial Day to Labor Day and from 9:00 am to 5:00 pm the balance of the year. Cost of admission is adults $4, seniors and children $3, and children under 12 Free. Closed major holidays; guided tours by special arrangement (406) 638-1876.

18 Graf, page 354.

19 For additional information on the Hominidae Project, the "new face of human evolution," visit www.archaeologyinfo.com/perspectives001.htm.

Chapter Six

What Is Restoration?

What seems obvious is, sometimes, not clear at all. Such is the case with the subject of restoring antique firearms. A rusted, heavily pitted century-old gun with a frozen hammer and missing grip or broken stock should surely be fixed-up...or surely not. Why not have such a junky old gun restored to its former beauty; what's the matter with having something people can look at and enjoy? Wouldn't people learn more – not to mention appreciate more – an antique gun that looks like it did a century ago, one they can actually operate by at least turning the cylinder and pulling the trigger if not firing for real? So kill the rust and re-blue the barrel, action,

Plenty can usually be done to antique guns to "improve" their appearance, because they are more than a century old, have perhaps been fired and sometimes maintenance is not to a museum curator's standards. After all, what's the point in "shooting (or owning) an ugly gun?" Recall that most experts believe that the difference between preservation and restoration is "reversibility." Thus, re-bluing, sanding and re-staining the stock, or attaching new barrels – with the old serial numbers and lettering re-stamped in place – would all be well beyond the point of accepted reversibility.

chamber and frame. Find cool new mother-of-pearl grips. Maybe have it handsomely engraved in the style of the day. Whatever you do to it, the gun will always be an 1860s Bacon Pocket Revolver or an 1865 Spencer Repeating Rifle. Having it re-blued or adding your initials somewhere unobtrusive will not change that.

Or will it?

Some would argue that the very best way to proceed would be to preserve it "as is," frozen hammer and all, after halting the active oxidation. They would claim that one should carefully photograph the gun and assemble all of the documentation that might be available, especially if it is a valuable antique. They would suggest that, now that you have the gun itself in your collection, the fun comes in the sleuthing. Where was this piece produced? What year was this serial number built? Who was the designer? Are there any variations that distinguish it from earlier or later versions? Who has owned

Is this a perfect restoration of an 1873 Blackpowder SAA or is it perhaps an Italian copy? After you pick it up, the first thing you will study are the stamps on metal. If you feel any slight "dishing" – and a person's skin is the most sensitive "organ" of the body – be very careful evaluating the gun.

"I'm totally opposed to firearms restoration," says firearms expert, author and auctioneer Jim Supica. "For my collection and my personal tastes…speaking as a collector and not as a dealer…any type of modern restoration other than minor mechanical repairs is something I am opposed to on a collectible firearm."

it and how have they used it? And so on to provide as complete a record as possible of the gun's provenance.

So what is the answer? Should these guns be restored to their as-manufactured condition or as close to that as reasonable given the cost and a gun's value...or should they be left forever as is?

The Firearms Expert, Collector, Dealer and Auction Owner

"I'm totally opposed to firearms restoration," says Jim Supica, author and firearms expert.

[Any kind of restoration?] "Yes. For my collection and my personal tastes...speaking as a collector and not as a dealer...any type of modern restoration other than minor mechanical repairs is something I am opposed to on a collectible firearm. If it is an older gun that is collectible, I dislike restoration on it."

[What do you mean by minor mechanical repair?] "Just to get a gun functioning, I'm not opposed...unless a gun has extraordinary historical provenance, and then I would be opposed to repairing or restoring it.

"For example, there was a big brouhaha a good number of years ago about the John Wilkes Booth-Lincoln assassination derringer and a question about whether the National Park Service had restored a broken screw in it. Any gun that has that type of important historical provenance, I'd be opposed to any change on it. If it's just a good collectible gun and somebody wants to get it functioning, I have no

"...any type of modern restoration other than minor mechanical repairs is something I am opposed to on a collectible firearm," says Jim Supica, firearms expert, author, auctioneer and collector.

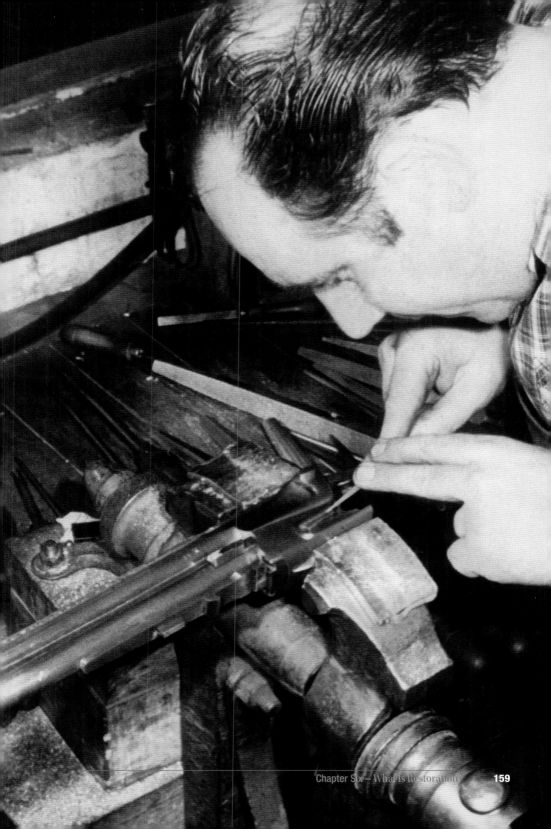

problem with that, with minor internal mechanical repairs. I'm less enthusiastic when you start changing large external components.[1]

[So for Tom Custer's English Kerr pistol now on display at the Custer Battlefield Museum?] "I would oppose any type of alteration from the way it was found other than something that was absolutely necessary to preserve the gun and prevent further deterioration."[2]

The Gunsmith and Restoration Specialist

"The last thing they [someone considering having a firearm undergo restoration] should do in my opinion is to go on a forum and ask other people's opinion," says Dean Dillabaugh of Dean's Gun Restorations in Jacksboro, Tennessee. "They'll get a thousand different opinions from a thousand different people.

"My belief, is that what they do when they refinish it is they limit their market if they ever go to resell it. A lot of people like to use the word 'destroy,' that you destroy the value of a gun when you have it refinished, and that is not true. I have proven it in the past with highly collectible M1s that I've refinished that have sold for a great deal more than they would have as just a collector item.

"But they [hard core collectors] like to think that they have the exclusive last word in the market, that their rules are the only ones that apply and it's not always true, but what is true is that when you do refinish you limit your resale market, because you have taken the hard core avid collectors out of the market, the ones that say that nothing should be done to a collectible firearm. They don't even want you to clean it.

"So it's all in how you approach your collecting. I have many, many customers all over the United States that absolutely love 100 percent correct firearms, but they want them refinished. Number one, they want to know that it is going to be preserved and that is what our Parkerizing does, it preserves the metal. Number two, they want the gun to look good. They want to be able to pull it out of the safe and show it to somebody and unless they are an avid collector themselves, most people don't appreciate [a gun that appears to be old and worn out].

"A good example – and I have a lot of them – was in California. I had a guy who was a [Mauser] K98 collector and we took one that

The venerable .30 M1 carbine had a high practical rate of fire. This, and the carbine's lightweight, compactness and low recoil made it a convenient self-defense weapon. A total of 6.25 million M1 Carbines of various models were manufactured, thus making it the most produced small arm in American military history. Despite being designed by Winchester, the great majority of these were made by other companies. The Auto-Ordnance division of Kahr Arms began production of an M1 Carbine replica in 2005. It is largely a faithful reproduction of the original, albeit with a different buttstock (birch vs. walnut) and lever-safety (instead of the more common button safety). Could this newly-made example be faked to resemble an original WWII- or Korean-era rifle? Yes; but values for the originals have not yet reached the point where this would be worthwhile. A far greater danger is "built-up" carbines assembled from spare or newly-made parts.

was not collectible and I refinished it for him. He had two or three K98s original, nothing done to them. And so he brought over his navy friends – he was a chief in the navy [chief petty officer] – and everybody wanted to see the one that was refinished. He got so mad he sold me the refinished one.

"'These stupid blah, blah guys. They don't know to appreciate...' Well, they appreciated the nice looking one. In time he says, 'I guess my idea of a collectible is different.' I called him a radical collector, but one who deserved his chance at it.

"Now what I do if I get a collectible rifle sent in is to call the customer and talk to him. Ninety percent of the time they don't realize it. 'What do you want to do with this firearm? Maybe you should just set this one aside and buy another one and let me refinish it, make it into a shooter.' I use this type of approach. Then again, usually, they say, 'I know, Dean. I know it's collectible, but I can't stand looking at it. Make it pretty.' And so I do." [3]

The Firearms Expert for Historical Arms and Militaria

"Refinishing antique guns is generally frowned upon," Norm Flayderman writes; "in quite a few instances, it actually detracts from value, resulting in a less desirable and less valuable item…. The practice of making a relatively worn gun, or one that has been heavily used, look like new is rather incongruous, and the effect on the gun is quite the same. Any antique item, especially a gun, used, and no longer new, should look its age and stand on its own merits. Refinishing is akin to taking an 80-year-old man and dressing him in the clothes of a teenager. Such a gun is, of course, simply detected and, for the most part, has the same value refinished as unrefinished However the restored status has changed the weapon's demand and desirability on the collector's market." [4]

Other Gunsmiths

"Restoration is the question that everyone will battle over till the end of time," say the fellows at Bose's Guns: Gunsmithing, Repair and Restoration Services in Emerson, Nebraska. "To the collector the answer will always be, they have to be originals, to be worth anything they have to be 'untouched.' [We] believe that a 98 to 100 percent gun that is 100 years old and has never been touched is truly

Has this gun been restored or is the patina on the brass authentic? Do the screws match and are they uniformly worn? If this rifle was restored 50 years ago…or 100 years ago…would that diminish its value? *(Photo courtesy Rock Island Auctions)*

a find and worth a premium. To find a firearm in this condition is like finding the Holy Grail. Outside of a collection, however, finding this is getting to be next to impossible.

"So why is firearm restoration looked down upon; reducing the firearm's worth to 60 percent of its value according to the so-called 'Grail hunters?' Because if you don't tell them they don't know, other than it looks too good to be original. This of course is the best compliment we can receive on our work.

"We pride ourselves at reproducing the original polishing lines and finish on all of our restoration jobs. If you were the type of customer who wanted to have the firearm restored to 95 to 98 percent quality, we have techniques that can age the finish to give it that 'used just a little bit' finish or we can leave it 100 percent museum or show quality. The choice is up to the customer because only they will know."[5]

The Firearms Appraiser and Collector

"Restoration of an old gun is a desecration," says Denver firearms appraiser Joe Cornell. "I can't think of a worse thing – well, of course I can – but I feel very strongly that it should only be done in very rare instances.

"There's a guy [out East] who is talented and does work on Winchesters and Colts, but when he does the work, he alters the serial number most of the time and puts his initials around that serial number to show that he has done the work. Let's say you had a 1 of 100 '76 and it was trashed…but still, a legitimate gun. Under some circumstances I could see someone doing work to bring that 1 of 100 back if it was identified.

"Way back in the '70s or '80s I had a Bulgarian Luger that was nickeled and the Luger book I had said there were only four known. Now, it was pitted, which was a tragedy because it was supposed to be extremely rare. I sold it to one of the biggest Luger dealers in the U.S. and then saw it a couple years later. It was in absolutely new condition! I recognized the serial number at a gun show and some dealer was selling it as new. The dealer's employee said the gun was discovered in some little old guy's stuff when the old man passed away. He had a story about where the gun came from.

"Right then I decided to study all the finishes of major manufacturers and to commit them to memory so that when I saw a Winchester, for instance, I could say that I recognized restoration work immediately."[6]

Whether you are for or against restoration in general, there are several issues upon which most points of view agree…or sometimes agree to disagree. Those points are:

- That restoration work almost always affects the value of a gun.
- That some guns should never be re-touched or only altered if it is absolutely necessary to preserve them.
- That interior, mechanical restoration is one thing – whereas exterior, surface restoration is something else entirely.
- That alterations to some guns will be immediately noticed and alterations to others will probably not matter a thousand years from now.
- And finally, that once an antique gun is worked on in any manner, the owner/collector is ethically obligated to disclose it – especially in any sales transaction.

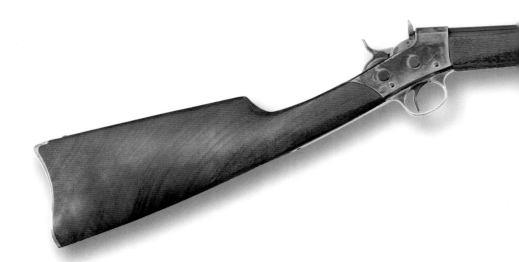

Pre-restoration vs. Post-restoration Value

On this single point, there is almost universal agreement. That there is an acknowledged and significant difference in the value that guns are given prior to and following an effort at restoration or repair. Once a gun is altered from its "original state" its value changes and, while values fluctuate for many reasons, the normal repairs or restorations can never be undone. Discarding old, cracked grips and replacing them with new grips or refinishing the stock, for example, are permanent, as is re-bluing or re-stamping the serial number to make it more legible. Assuming that items in a collection "turn over" with some regularity – from every couple years to the death of the owner – the new owners may not appreciate the changes recently made. Hence the emphasis by professional conservators on *reversibility*.

What's more, value depends on the buyer or the potential pool of buyers. A "serious collector" would almost surely devalue a restored gun unless it were used by a famous person or in some notorious manner, in which case – social responsibility be damned – all guns become increasingly valuable in proportion to the heinousness of the crime. A person buying with some other motive, though – a nice old Civil War era gun to hang on the wall of the office – might actually prefer the restoration and be willing to pay an additional premium for it!

If this rifle were used by Geronimo or Sitting Bull, or by Wyatt Earp or Billy the Kid, it should perhaps never be considered for restoration – only for conservation and preservation – so that future generations would have something original, genuinely representative of the frontier era to study. In fact…it is an Italian reproduction by Uberti.

Single action revolvers from U.S. FireArms: "USFA maintains the Douglas F. Donnelly collection, the largest Colt archive of original documents which contain the original Ledger Books of the founding of Sam Colt's company in 1855. The entire civil war history including shipments to the U.S. Government, detailed production history and a manufacturing and engineering archive allows us to look back into history of the Single Action Revolver."

"As the passion for golf shows no sign of abating," David Nicholls writes from Australia, "there is a market for most hickory shaft clubs in reasonable condition. There are many potential buyers of old clubs, who, while not collectors in the strict sense, may well be entranced by finding an old hickory shaft club attractively presented. This puts some pressure on the dealer to undertake some form of restoration, to achieve the potential value of the club."[7]

The "Untouchables."

Virtually everyone would agree that some guns, especially those linked to a major historical incident, should probably never be retouched for restoration or repair, only preserved "as is" for future generations. Examples of these guns might be the .44 caliber derringer with which Booth shot Abraham Lincoln or the Carcano M91/38 Fucile Corto (short rifle) that Lee Harvey Oswald used to kill John F. Kennedy.

Production of the 1849 Colt Pocket Revolver began in 1850 and continued through 1873. Hartford built about 325,000 and London chipped in 11,000. More Model 1849s in all its variations were produced than any other Colt percussion firearm. Flayderman reports discovering fake Pocket Revolvers, even with values for good condition hovering at the $500 level.

Such "untouchables," the special guns, regardless of their condition are typically worth far more to collectors (institutional or private) than other guns that are exactly the same only without the illuminated provenance. Here is an example that shows the power of a "name:"

• "Standard" Remington New Model Army revolvers used by the Union and described in Adams-Graf's *Warman's Civil War Collectibles, 2nd Edition* sold for about $1,000: $1,095 (legible cartouche, "PH," on the left grip), $975 (a repaired crack in the right grip only and no evidence of a cartouche), $1,495 (45 percent blue and clear government inspector's cartouche) and $895 (an early production piece).[8]

• In their December 8-10, 2007 auction, Rock Island Auction offered Lot #3287: "The Victor of The Battle of Gettysburg, General George Meade Presentation Nimschke Engraved Ivory Stocked Cased Remington New Model Army Revolver." Prior to the auction, Rock Island inspectors estimated a low auction price of $300,000 to an estimated high of as much as $400,000. The actual sales price was $287,500.[9]

One hidden issue here is that as our technologies improve and our theories become increasingly sophisticated, conservationists a century from now will almost certainly be able to use more precise tools and better formulations of chemicals to study antique firearms. And, barring some international disaster, the historical reference materials will probably be enhanced with additional years of study and investigation. This is one of the reasons, for instance, that ar-

The prescription for anyone interested in restoring (or faking) is a box of parts certified for Sharps and Springfield rifles. The For Sale sign noted that the box includes one engraved percussion hammer with extended nose, four plain percussion hammers, one conversion hammer, two 1873 and one 1970 trapdoor breechblocks, early trapdoor receiver, two Sharps lock plates, one Sharps percussion breechblock, three mainsprings, one Sharps lever, three trigger guards, four barrel bands, a forearm tip, sling swivel, partial sling bar, three pins, one barrel band retention spring, two screws, two tools and a few other parts. All items were estimated in fair or better condition and the seller asked $1,000-$1,500.

chaeologists excavating a site only sample it rather than complete a 100 percent excavation to bare soil, unless that site is threatened by development or some other catastrophe.

Inside-Outside

That acceptable repairs or restoration may depend upon whether such is performed inside the gun, where it is not visible, or on the surface seems illogical. The interior of the weapon is its heart and what makes one firearm model different, unique and collectible is surely its action and the mechanical design, more so than its raw appearance. It only stands to reason that a change in the primary mechanics would be more fundamental – and, from some points of view – more detrimental because they seem hidden, than in the veneer of appearance. Perhaps beauty is only skin deep, after all.

Maybe the ultimate irony is that antique guns that seem to look too good to be true are immediately mistrusted by collectors.

Of course, we as a human species have a long tradition of preferring what looks good on the outside to what is happening on the inside. My Oyster Perpetual Day-Date Rolex wristwatch, for example, was purchased for $10 from a street vendor in Paris. A similar model (#118208) on www.alanfurman.com sells for $17,150. (The difference perhaps is that mine keeps excellent time.) A knowledgeable friend realized that my watch was a fake the instant I showed it to her: "It's too light," she said. "That's not a real Rolex."

Many are Called, but Few are Chosen

There are quite literally millions of antique guns in the world. There are millions of American antique guns, for that matter – at least, millions were made in the antique (pre-1899) period, which is not a floating date: it does not change with the passing of time, such as curios and replicas, or with firearms innovation. How many total guns or total of any one manufacturer or model have survived to today is often anyone's guess. Informed sources note that perhaps six of the "Coffee Mill" Sharps, a minor Civil War variation on a Model 1859 or 1863 whose stock was rebuilt to incorporate a trial system for grinding corn or wheat in the stock, have been authenticated

This gun appears to be in the style of a Colt Dragoon. It has no special provenance – though its serial numbers are intact and legible. A good rule of thumb here is: If you don't know exactly what it is, don't buy it!

– out of the hundred that were authorized. Whether there are more of these valuable collector's items in basements or attic chests around the world is unknown and unknowable. On occasion, however, precious guns do unexpectedly surface.

At a recent trade show, Christopher Cranmer, president of International Military Antiques (IMA), was selling antique guns from the Royal Armory of Nepal, an incredible find of an enormous cache of weapons in a Nepalese palace. Evidence of this find appears occasionally in advertisements from various suppliers such as IMA and Atlanta Cutlery. These companies have been selling such recently discovered items as Snider cavalry carbines, Sharps slant breech rifles, Pattern 1862 muskets and Martini Henry infantry rifles among tons (quite literally) of other old military surplus items, from cutlasses to cannons. The discovery was potentially worth millions of dollars ... a good thing since the Nepalese charged them millions to rescue the cache.[10]

So the world of antique guns, like the universe, is expanding even though one would expect that every year a number of guns are lost or stolen and dismantled and perhaps even discarded. Thus it is almost certainly acceptable to restore some antique guns, even some very old guns, and no one will either be the wiser or care.

To take an old "Coffee-Mill" Sharps, however, and to have it engraved would certainly be a sin. Besides, Sharps is such a popular and collectible name in antique guns that any change in such a highly sought-after item (The "Coffee-Mill" Sharps is valued at $12,500 in only good condition.)[11] would be readily apparent, even to semi-experts. If you were to engrave – indeed,

A bit of ageing and some sleight-of-hand and this short, twin-hammer Coach Gun could be turned in to a valuable sale at a regional gun show.

completely restore – a six-shot James Warner Pocket Model Revolver which was manufactured during that same period (and is, by contrast, valued at $250 in good condition)[12] almost no one would ever look closely enough at it to care.

Nevertheless, whether anyone would ever know or care, an owner would have to give considerable thought to making any permanent change to such an old gun, inside or outside.

Don't Ask, Don't Tell

Once some significant restoration is made to an old gun, it is incumbent on the owner or a seller to so identify and document (provide provenance for) the re-work; in writing, if one is selling. In the case mentioned above of the "Coffee-Mill" Sharps, firearms expert Norm Flayderman warns, "Extreme caution should be exercised in purchasing any specimen of this rare variant; not a few spurious examples have been made over the past half century...and longer."[13] Thus, a refinishing mark such as the one used by Dean Dillabaugh of Dean's Gun Restorations (quoted earlier) becomes not only crucial to evaluating a firearm's authenticity and value, but becomes a mark of the owner's – and yes, sometimes the restorer's – integrity.

Thus it seemed interesting that Dillabaugh, in our interview noted above, said, "I just saw last week where a fellow found an M1 stamped 'USMC Rifle Team,' with the date also and, well, they [the USMC] never did that. One precaution for the seller is to know what was done and not done originally.

"There was a guy in Arizona who made a living faking things – and he was a friend...well, not a friend, but an acquaintance of mine. He got caught by the M1 Collector's Association stamping stocks and in his defense, he said, 'Hell, Dean, my dad was stamping them back in the '40s.'

"What that implies is that even if it looks original now it might not be. It takes an educated eye to know the difference and I'm not educated in [some of those fine points] well enough to know. There are guys out there who have studied cartouches and stamping though who can distinguish an original from a non-original probably 90 percent of the time but they even get faked out, too."

Footnotes

1   Read a fascinating case report titled "The Booth Deringer – Genuine Artifact or Replica?" written by Sally A. Schehl, Associate Editor, Forensic Science Communications-Forensic Science Research Unit and Carlo J. Rosati, Firearms Examiner, Firearms-Toolmarks Unit, Federal Bureau of Investigation, Washington, DC on line at www.fbi.gov/hq/lab/fsc/backissu/jan2001/schehl.htm.

2   Excerpted from the author's February 2008 interview with Jim Supica. Supica is partner – "I'm the gun end and he's the auction management end" – with Dan Kull in Kull & Supica Firearms Auctions http://armsbid.com.

3   Excerpted from the author's February 2008 interview with Dean Dillabaugh, Dean's Gun Restorations, 452 Jane Way Lane, Jacksboro, TN 37757 (423) 562-2010 www.dgrguns.com. Dean's specialty is U.S. M1s.

4   Flayderman, page 32

5   www.bosesofnebraska.com/

6   Excerpted from the author's March 2008 interview with Joe Cornell. His web site is located at www.weappraiseguns.com.

7   David C. Nicholls "Old Golf Clubs: Their Restoration and Cleaning" as reprinted on line at www.home.aone.net.au/~byzantium/golf/restore.html.

8   Graf, page 350

9   Rock Island Auction Co., 4507 49th Ave., Moline, IL 61265 (800) 238-8022 www.rockislandauction.com

10 Chris Pelzer made an interesting 60-minute documentary film about the discovery and excavation of the Nepalese armory. It is available from International Military Antiques, 1000 Valley Rd., Gillette, NJ 07933 (908) 903-1200 or through www.ima-usa.com. After a 30-year search, Cranmer found not only weapons that dated back through the Napoleonic wars but also more recent World War II firearms including Enfield No.1 and No. 4 rifles and U.S. M3 "grease guns." Ninety seven percent of the weapons retrieved dated before 1898, and in addition to firearms, Cranmer also found artillery pieces, swords, Kukris fighting knives, bayonets and huge numbers of spare barrels, locks, musket balls and flints.

11 Flayderman, page 171.

12 Flayderman, page 324.

13 Flayderman, page 171.

Chapter Seven

Antiques, Authentic Reproductions
& Their Market

*T*here is a great deal of interest today in black powder and reproduction firearms, although one could argue that the civilian interest in black powder never entirely disappeared. From the pleasure of collecting to the active enjoyment of participating in reenacting or hunting or cowboy shooting, the field is broad – and growing – in North America, Europe and around the world.

Applying finishing touches to a modern reproduction handgun in the U.S. FireArms facility in Hartford, Connecticut.

While some enthusiasts prefer to carry – and shoot – the original guns of the period, this group is small in comparison to those who use modern reproduction or replica firearms. Using an original 19th century Colt, for example, would certainly add excitement to any shooting venue. It would attract quite a bit of attention, thus stroking one's vanity (except for the scoffers and doubters), and the 150-year-old firearm might perform flawlessly. The same could be said for that 18th century Kentucky rifle, the family heirloom resting in brackets above the fireplace for a century, when carried to a rendezvous.

On the other hand, even a well-cared-for 150- or 200-year-old black powder gun, cleaned and with the correct powder and shot load, might not perform flawlessly...and all that attention might not be welcome. About 10,500 Third Model Dragoon blackpowder .44s were manufactured in Hartford from 1851 to 1861, and so they can occasionally be found at antique gun shows, and sometimes at a reasonable price. However, even a standard civilian model – not the more desirable military grade preferred by collectors – in good condition would be valued at more than $25,000 even in a depressed market.[1] Thus, substantial public attention might not be a good thing.

Besides, Sam Colt, Horace Smith and Dan Wesson are not manufacturing these guns any longer. To use one and risk damage, injury or theft is probably not a responsible option when plenty of reproductions – guns that, to the untrained eye, look precisely like the original (except perhaps that they are too shiny and new!) – are available. True antique firearms such as an old Kentucky muzzleloading rifle are part of our American heritage. Despite the fact that a particular model may not be in especially short supply or may not be greatly desired by collectors, it should nevertheless be respected as a priceless heirloom.

The Antique & Reproduction Market

How many ways can you think of to have fun with a firearm? A complete list would be extensive, and one person would be hard-pressed to participate in everything, from collecting to cowboy action to varmint shooting. All of these activities are served by specialty manufacturers in the U.S. and abroad, however, (especially in and around the city of Brescia, Italy) businesses that produce superior, absolutely realistic straight shootin' black powder replicas. Some of them even produce kits which allow the handyman to try building his own firearm.

What follows is a review of the most popular and most publicized activities, and a sampling of the original firearms upon which the new replicas are based. This contrast between the current weapons and the originals, the antiques themselves, which is, in a sense, the real story of this book – their apparent similarity yet enormous difference in date and value – highlights both the opportunity, the inducement and the fascination with altering or faking a firearm.

These activities or hobbies or movements are not just about people getting together and forming bonds around shared shooting interests. They are also about people using and enjoying firearms recreationally. After all, they bring thousands of endorsements into the community supporting our Second Amendment rights. And so they are doubly important.

Note that these firearms all require black powder (or Pyrodex pellets), not today's most advanced smokeless powders. The advent

The Gun Digest Book of® Firearms Fakes and Reproductions

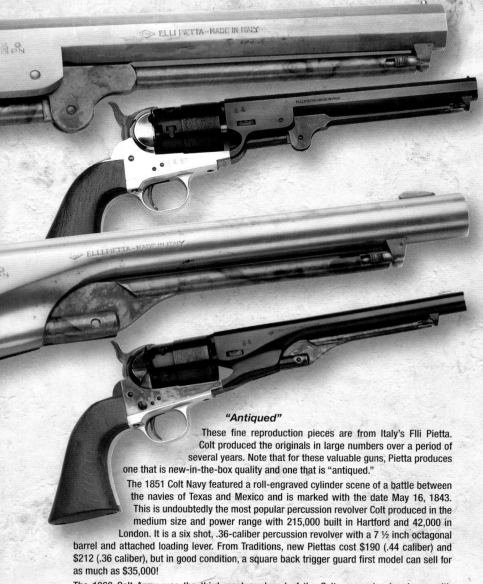

"Antiqued"

These fine reproduction pieces are from Italy's Flli Pietta. Colt produced the originals in large numbers over a period of several years. Note that for these valuable guns, Pietta produces one that is new-in-the-box quality and one that is "antiqued."

The 1851 Colt Navy featured a roll-engraved cylinder scene of a battle between the navies of Texas and Mexico and is marked with the date May 16, 1843. This is undoubtedly the most popular percussion revolver Colt produced in the medium size and power range with 215,000 built in Hartford and 42,000 in London. It is a six shot, .36-caliber percussion revolver with a 7 ½ inch octagonal barrel and attached loading lever. From Traditions, new Piettas cost $190 (.44 caliber) and $212 (.36 caliber), but in good condition, a square back trigger guard first model can sell for as much as $35,000!

The 1860 Colt Army was the third most produced of the Colt percussion handguns with 127,156 delivered. It was the primary revolver used by the Union Army during the Civil War. The Army is a six shot .44-caliber gun with either a 7 ½ or an 8 inch barrel. The frame, hammer and loading lever are case colored; the barrel and cylinder, either fluted, which is scarce, or round, which have the roll-engraved naval combat scene, are blued. In good condition, the full-fluted cylinder version is valued at $15,000; with the navy engraved scene on the cylinder, a martial-marked gun may go for $7,500 and a civilian for $6,000.

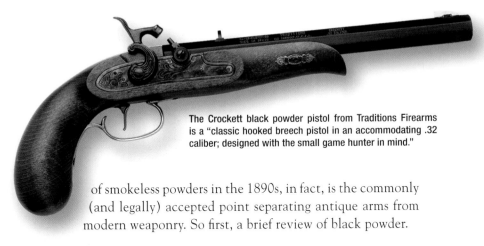

The Crockett black powder pistol from Traditions Firearms is a "classic hooked breech pistol in an accommodating .32 caliber; designed with the small game hunter in mind."

of smokeless powders in the 1890s, in fact, is the commonly (and legally) accepted point separating antique arms from modern weaponry. So first, a brief review of black powder.

Black Powder

No one is sure where gunpowder was invented. Traditionally, we have thought it was a Chinese development, but continuing study of ancient manuscripts and tracing the paths of old trade routes hints at the possibility of an Arabic or Middle Eastern origin.

Like so many inventions or discoveries, however, multiple minds were working independently along similar paths. The 21-year-old Sam Colt sailed to Europe in 1835 to patent his revolving cylinder concept, fearing that more advanced European gun makers were about to capitalize on that inspiration.

Black powder is a mixture of potassium nitrate (KNO_3 or saltpeter), sulfur (S) and charcoal (although not a basic element, charcoal is 85 to 98 percent carbon, and so, for convenience, most sources refer to it simply as C). The world standard

HS-7 pistol and shotgun powder for reloaders from Hodgdon. Smokeless and black powders are not interchangeable. People who reload shells and cartridges for more than one activity – cowboy action shooting and trap shooting, for instance – need to carefully separate their powders and components.

for mixing those ingredients eventually became 15/2/3 or 15/3/2 of $KNO^3/S/C$. This widely accepted standard allowed for shared consistency of arms chamber strength, and the opportunity to use powder from various sources.

A problem with black powder is that the ingredients, being granules of diverse sizes, tend to separate – inside a canister while riding in a bumpy wagon, the smaller granules sifted to the bottom – and this led to uneven burn rates, even to explosions. Consequently, in the late 1700s the mechanical mixture of ingredients was changed to a form in which the elements would not separate. This was accomplished by mixing the ingredients as uniformly as possible and then wetting the mixture so that it formed clumps. These clumps were then mechanically broken up (a dangerous task) into smaller kernels. Hence the term "corning."

John M. Marlin was born in Connecticut in 1836, and served his apprenticeship as a tool and die maker. During the Civil War, he worked at the Colt's plant in Hartford, and in 1870 began manufacturing his own line of revolvers and derringers in New Haven.

He produced the Models 1891 and 1893, which are today known as Models 39 and 336 respectively, the oldest shoulder arm designs in the world still being produced. The lever action .22 repeater (now Model 39) even became the favorite of many exhibition shooters, including the great Annie Oakley whom Sitting Bull called "Little Miss Sure Shot." (Annie Oakley photo by Richard K. Fox, 1899, courtesy Library of Congress Reproduction #LC-USZ62-7873)

In the early 1800s, testing confirmed that different granulations of corned powder were appropriate to different applications. This ultimately led to the grading system that is still in use today, in which the letters "F" (representing the size of screen mesh a granule must pass through) and "g" (a specific granulation). Thus the smallest granulation commonly available is FFFFg or "4F". It is used principally in the priming pans of flintlocks, but has some application in strong but small-chambered revolvers of .22 to .32 caliber. FFFg or "3F" is usually recommended for muzzleloading rifles of .50 caliber or less, and FFg in larger rifles. It also performs well in target loads in cartridge pistols when the modern cartridge case with a smaller internal dimension is used. The largest granulation is termed Fg and is used principally in cannons, though it is applicable to large bore (10 gauge and up) shotguns and double rifles of 8-, 6- and 4-bore.

Although delivery did not begin for several years, the U.S. Army adopted the .30-40 smokeless Krag-Jorgensen rifle in 1892. The military wanted to multiply the effectiveness of each fighting man by increasing both rate of fire and the range at which that fire could be delivered. The former required a newer rifle than the venerable Springfield "Trapdoor," while the latter required a higher velocity, and that called for a smaller diameter projectile. Since black powder residue fouls bores so thoroughly, and is more pronounced about doing so in smaller bores, few shots could be fired before it was necessary to swab a bore. The change to the lesser fouling, emerging smokeless powder was inevitable.

The recoil driven mechanisms of both the machine gun and the newly developed auto-loading pistols could not long tolerate the continual build-up of residue. The new technology of gas operated semi-automatic and fully automatic arms did not tolerate the residue in their more intricate mechanisms, either.

Black powder continued to be used in military revolver cartridges for quite some time, however, because there were great quantities of these guns in storage. U.S. issue black powder rifles and ammunition were eventually shunted down the military food chain to the National Guard and were last used in the Spanish-American War of 1898-1900.

Civilian demand caused the production of black powder to remain high for some time. The civilian life cycle for an individual firearm far exceeded that of the military. Long after the introduction of smokeless powder, many serviceable older arms remained in use for hunting and target shooting. Because of either their materials or design, these arms could not safely endure the increased chamber pressures associated with modern smokeless powders.

Black powder is classified as an explosive because its performace after ignition meets an admittedly arbitrary standard that takes it beyond the sense of "burning," even burning that, to our senses, appears to be instantaneous. Black powder will indeed explode with great force if ignited when contained. It has a long history in mining where it was poured down cracks or into drilled holes to blast apart rock, something that we have often seen on television and in movies.

Thus, references to the "burn rate" of black powder indicate the speed of passage of the flame front that brings ignition through the mass of powder. It does not refer to the speed of the reaction of the ignited powder itself.

The term "black powder," by the way, stems from the fact that the first smokeless powder was a light gray in color, in comparison to the commonly dark black of the propellant it largely supplanted. Before that, black powder was just called gunpowder.

Today, black powder is "corned," by forming the ingredients into cakes with water and alcohol. The cakes are dried to a specific water content, and crumbled. The kernels are then glazed with graphite, and graded by passage – or failure to pass – through successively smaller size screens.

The Mountain Man Movement

The mountain man movement might be thought of as reenacting or "buckskinning," although the first is more public and the second more lifestyle. The buckskin brigade offers a chance to relive an earlier period of history, says Ragnar of Elandris – known in this incarnation as Jim Schippnick of New York, who is himself a mountain man (as well as a Viking reenactor, a member of the Society of Creative Anachronism and, in the 21st century, owner of the informative web site www.ragweedforge.com).

"Reenacting at a mountain man rendezvous is done for the participants, not for an audience," says Schippnick. "In fact, the public is usually excluded. This makes it easier to feel that you are inside the period you are portraying. To some extent it is real, because one lives in conditions quite different than one's day-to-day life and more like those of the earlier period.

"Buckskinners relive the North American fur trade era. In the eastern part of the country that often means the colonial period of the so-called "longhunter" while in the west it means the Rocky Mountain fur trade era. Both groups are represented in most camps. Officially, it's usually pre-1840. That means that participants clothing, firearms, tents and anything else visible, must appear to be from the period.

"Muzzleloader shooters started buckskinning when they began dressing to match the period of their rifles. They went on recreate the entire lifestyle including the long river expeditions of the French voyageurs. Since the original interest was shooting, early participants were a bit light on historical accuracy. This has improved tremendously, but there's still a strong emphasis on shooting.

"Gatherings of mountain men are called 'rendezvous,' and are modeled after the Rocky Mountain gatherings where trappers met dealers to trade furs, buy supplies…and party. After all, these men had been in the bush for months and sometimes for years. The original sponsoring body for the rendezvous was the National Muzzleloading Rifle Association, and membership is required for attendance at sanctioned events.

"The best way to get started is to attend a rendezvous, talk to a lot of people and see what it's all about. As a rule, the major ten-day events are closed to the public, but they will have one or two visitor's days. Weekend events often allow visitors for a few hours on

Saturday. If you are on site any other time you must be registered and dressed for the period."

Schippnick says that because a variety of eras are represented at a rendezvous a wide variety of firearms will be carried. "An 18th century longhunter, an 18th century farmer, a 17th century trapper, an Indian or a voyageur will all have different outfits and at a large rendezvous or reenactment you can compare," he says, cautioning that one wants goods suitable for the French and Indian War period, or the Revolutionary War period, but NOT the popular (and later) Civil War period."

Several magazines are devoted to this smokepole era. *Muzzle Blasts* comes with a membership to the National Muzzle Loading Rifle Association (www.nmlra.org). Others are *Muzzleloader* (www.muzzleloadermag.com) and the newspaper printed by the *Smoke & Fire* folks (1-800-SMOKE-FI), which has excellent event listings, both large and small.

More information is available from the White Oak Society (www.whiteoak.org). The Coon 'n Crockett Club (www.coon-n-crockett.org) is strong on the shooting and hunting aspects, while the American Mountain Men (www.xmission.com/~drudy/amm/gateway.html) are more interested in outdoor skills from the later Rocky Mountain fur trade era. If your interest is in this later period you will want to become familiar with the Northwest Journal (www.northwestjournal.ca).

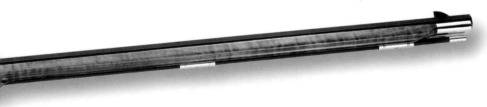

This Pedersoli replica, stocked in select American maple or European walnut, reproduces faithfully the original rifles built during the golden age of the American long rifle (1760- 1840). As with the squirrel rifles of this period, renowned for their accuracy at any range, this model has an octagonal rifled barrel that is rust browned. The rifle is provided with adjustable double set triggers. Trigger guard and butt plate are made of brass, lock and fittings are color case hardened. The maple models are available with a patch-box.

Firearms for the Mountain Man

For more than 50 years, Italy's Davide Pedersoli (www.davide-pedersoli.com) has produced "superior replica guns that faithfully duplicate models of the old American tradition and of the European gunsmith's history." The company manufactures military guns from the independence wars of the Old and New Worlds, and civilian models of those periods as well. These guns represent the culture and the history of Europe, as well as the expansion of the American Frontier toward the center and west of the American continent.

Replicas of Indian Trade Muskets, for example, are used at mountain man rendezvous. Pedersoli builds a faithful reproduction, a smooth bore based on a design that, since the late 1700s, was used by most well known trading companies (Northwest, Hudson's Bay, American Fur) for exchanges with American Indians…and white hunters, as well. The finish and fit of originals was often not carefully done in consideration of the rough use and infrequent cleanings those guns would receive. Still, they showed the classical lines of old country muskets produced both by European and American manufacturers (Leman, Henry, Tryon). A wooden ramrod and large trigger guard (to accommodate rough hands in mittens) were typical. The specifications were: 52 inches long, 7-¼ pounds, a rust brown color 36-inch barrel and a walnut stock. Trade muskets shot a 0.614-inch diameter round lead ball weighing 345 grains. Indian Trade Muskets are available stateside for $695 through Dixie Gun Works: www.dixiegunworks.com.

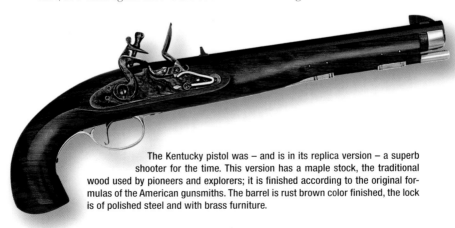

The Kentucky pistol was – and is in its replica version – a superb shooter for the time. This version has a maple stock, the traditional wood used by pioneers and explorers; it is finished according to the original formulas of the American gunsmiths. The barrel is rust brown color finished, the lock is of polished steel and with brass furniture.

For a pistol, a modern day buckskinner might carry a .50-caliber Queen Anne, just like one of the original beaver trappers. Pedersoli makes a true copy of this famous 2.2-pound, 13-inch English smoothbore pistol that came into use in Europe and the Americas between the end of 1600 and the beginning of 1700, during "Queen Anne's War." As with the originals, this reproduction is characterized by a metal mask under the buttstock. The single shot pistol is made with a European walnut half stock with a satin finish. Featuring a chromed 7-9/16-inch tapered round barrel, glazed outside, coin finished and polished brass furniture with a single trigger, it shoots a 177-grain round ball and costs $300 from Dixie Gun Works. (In kit form, should you have an interest in building the gun yourself, this pistol is only $260.)

According to Massachusetts' Al Hodgson, original Indian Trade Muskets are highly sought after collector's items with prices for guns in good condition or with apparent Indian provenance sometimes reaching tens of thousands of dollars. Guns were sometimes based on the famous "Northwest gun" style but were more often built out of cut down military muskets, and sometimes assembled from leftover military parts. These guns were often cut down in the barrel, and sometimes the butt as well. Almost always its native owner added a personal touch in the form of brass tacks, inlaid beads and paint. Repairs to the stock were usually done by wrapping with wet rawhide, which would shrink and then harden as it dried.

Ted Bell of Oregon's Antique Arms America (www.antiquearmsamericainc.com) recently sold a "Superb Hudson Bay Company Indian Trade Musket." He described it this way:

"You won't find better. This example appears to be unfired. The lock plate retains original faded case color and is marked 'Parker Field & Co. 1874 London.' It is unusual to find a flintlock dated this late, however, the trading posts and the government did not want the Indians to have the most sophisticated and up to-date weapons, which might be used against them. This full stocked weapon has a 36-inch barrel with virtually all of the original finish and a brass serpentine side plate as well as a brass butt plate. The stock bears a deep and near perfect impressed Hudson Bay Co. cartouche in a circle with the sitting fox. The sitting fox also appears on the side of the lock with the letters 'E.B.' under it. The best and completely original." [Bell says this gun sold for $4,000.]

Interpreting History – Civil War Reenacting

According to a recent 2008 survey by Ohio State University and published online (http://ehistory.osu.edu/osu/links/reenactors.cfm), there are approximately 40,000 Civil War reenactors in the U.S. Considering that more than that number showed up at Gettysburg a few years ago for the 135th anniversary of that great battle, there may very well be twice that many for all anyone truly knows. There are reenactor organizations around the world from Europe to several very active groups in Australia. Indeed, there are avid and knowledgeable living history participants for the colonial era, for farms before electricity, for Vikings, for the gunfight at the OK Corral and practically any striking incident in recorded history.

Anyone who doubts that Civil War reenacting has become a mainstream grown-up hobby only needs to attend one anniversary battle or a camp out. The participants, often entire families, dress in period woolens and silks, camp in canvas tents and carry weaponry

Re-enacting of the U.S. Civil War is based upon the terrifying reality that more than 600,000 men were killed and several million maimed in four years…in a nation with only 31 ½ million residents. On Wednesday, September 17, 1862, 5,500 men died in this "bloody lane." *(Alexander Gardner photo, Library of Congress Prints and Photographs Division Washington, D.C. 20540 Digital ID # ppmsca 07751)*

The Gun Digest Book of® Firearms Fakes and Reproductions

Civil War Reenacting

From cannons to cavalry with plenty of smoke, the fascination of reenacting the U.S. Civil War is not only limited to the major battles of the central states: Pennsylvania and Virginia. Even the very small engagement in Gainesville, Florida fought on August 17, 1864, which was more of a skirmish with casualties than a full-blown battle, is memorialized and draws a crowd of curious onlookers (as did actual battles early in that war). Each of the participants, except perhaps the surgeons, was armed.

The reenacting movement (along with cowboy action shooting) has opened the floodgates for new collectors – and perhaps new shooters as well – as men and women search for their own place in and perhaps their own piece of history. Beginning with replica firearms manufactured by Pedersoli, Uberti, Armi Sport or others, it is an easy and natural step to begin collecting authentic period weaponry.

Ralph Epifano, dressed as a Confederate infantryman, says that he scouts flea markets to find authentic clothing and accoutrements from the Civil War era. "I've seen plenty of fake stuff at flea markets, though," Ralph laughs. "The 'antique' powder horn with bright, shiny copper on the inside. The standard bullet-in-the-belt-buckle – seen plenty of those. I've seen reproductions that would fool experts and don't believe anything any more."

The brass frame of the .44-caliber 1866 Henry Sporting rifle has given the new company, Henry Repeating Arms, the "Golden Boy" name to hang on several rifles. This, however, was a Pietta replica. Early or late brass frame originals are valued at $10,000 and up.

used during the Civil War. Perhaps this is all dress-up and play, or perhaps George Patton was right when, on the eve of the Allied invasion of France in June 1944, he addressed his troops about the difficulties of the days immediately ahead of them and said, in part, "Americans love to fight, traditionally. All real Americans love the sting and clash of battle."[2]

Civil War reenacting draws people of all ages who work very hard to duplicate the events and the feel of the mid-19th century. Participants may even attend classes to learn how to dress, cook, eat and fight, just like real Civil War combatants and even the hovering wives, politicians and miscellaneous civilians (nurses, sutlers, journalists).

Honoring the 135th anniversary year since the battle of Gettysburg took place in Pennsylvania in July, 1863, more than 41,000 reenactors and nearly 50,000 spectators crowded onto the grounds of Gettysburg National Military Park (www.nps.gov/gett/).[3]

Why do so many people enjoy these reenactments or living history events? Is today's life generally so bleak in the affluent U.S. that people must turn to bitter and bloody events of the past to be fulfilled?

Historical reenactors have almost as many reasons for participating, as there are reenactors. Many are certainly interested by the historical perspective. Some trace their ancestry to participants, not only to the famous Gettysburg battle, of course, but also to thousands of other engagements around the country (and they are not limited to the eastern states). Others perhaps simply enjoy being out-of-doors and participating in a community of individuals without issues of family, politics or religion haunting a weekend. And even though one of the issues of the Civil War was bitter sectionalism, many reenactors have kits – uniforms and accoutrements – that allow them to participate as either a Federal or a Confederate, depending upon their whim or perhaps the need of the venue. All in all, however, most reenactors say they are "just having fun."

Enactments of U.S. Civil War events fall into two general categories:

- Living history is meant for public edification and may simply portray the life of the common soldier at a place and time during that long and terrible conflict. Commonly, the rifled muzzleloaders and muzzleloading cannons of the day are demonstrated with a light load of powder only, bands play tunes from the 1860s and sutlers (peddlers who followed the armies to sell food and supplies) offer sarsaparilla, hard candies and even antiques and replicas.

- Battles either loosely reenact particular events or are scripted tightly to follow the actions of units and individuals of the 1860s, often with narrators, as part of a wider recreation of period military tactics.

Firearms for the Civil War Reenactor

Incorporated 50 years ago, Armi Sport (www.armisport.com) is the foundation of the Chiappa Firearms group if Italy. Chiappa, better known as Armi Sport in the U.S., has established a reputation for precision craftsmanship with an eye for historical accuracy and detail. The company says it "has evolved with experience and a commitment to its customers to uniquely blend old world hand craftsmanship with the most modern of machining technology. This

blend of craftsmanship and technology has yielded treasures of the past which are truly antique art in the form of arms."

Armi Sport produces a replica of the model 1861 Springfield percussion rifled musket that was the principle firearm of Civil War infantry, and which is today carried by many reenactors. By the end of 1863 most infantrymen were armed with either this musket or an Enfield.

The Armi Sport reproduction features a one-piece forged barrel; steel butt plate, trigger guard and three barrel bands; a walnut stock with oil finish and a swelled ramrod...just like the original. The lock is marked "1861 Springfield" with an eagle, and features a one-piece American walnut, oil-finished stock. This musket measures 56 inches in length and is built with a 40-inch barrel in the authentic .58 caliber. The barrel has military style sights and the gun weighs nine pounds. The price is $600 from Cabela's and $615 from www.replicagunsswords.com.

Depending upon their condition, any known provenance, and the actual manufacturer, at auction, authentic period rifled muskets can bring anywhere from several hundred to several thousand dollars. Approximately a million Model 1861s were manufactured, a quarter of them by Springfield itself, and the balance by a number of subsidiary producers under contract with the U.S. Government. Antique, yes; especially rare, no.

While many Civil War soldiers, sailors and marines carried the newer American-made revolvers of the day, mostly Colts and Remingtons, the LeMat was well known in the Confederate States. It was quite a different and innovative design known popularly as the "Grape Shot Revolver."

Although significant advances were being made in hand-held firearms during the mid-19th century, beyond the arrival of the percussion gun, many of them did not make it into combat and a wide variety of weapons was used, especially among the Confederate troops.

The LeMat was developed in New Orleans in 1856 by Dr. Jean LeMat and backed by P.G.T. Beauregard, who was to become a general of the Confederacy. Approximately 2,900 were produced, many in Europe. The 2nd edition of *Warman's Civil War Collectibles*[4] notes that a French built .42-caliber LeMat percussion with an 18-gauge shotgun barrel sold for $6,900 with James D. Julia Auctioneers (http://juliaauctions.net/) – below the usual $7,000 to $9,000 value because the loading assembly was not original and *the serial numbers on the frame and barrel housing appeared to have been re-stamped.*

Cabela's sells an accurate Pietta reproduction of the First Model LeMat cavalry version with a nine shot, .44-caliber cylinder and rifled 6 ½-inch barrel. What set the LeMat apart from other revolver designs, Cabela's notes, is the 20-gauge, 5-inch smoothbore barrel, originally intended for firing buckshot. Both barrels are fired by a pivoting striker. In 19th century combat, the close range firepower from the pistol barrel plus a hefty dose of "blue whistlers" from the diminutive shotgun barrel made the LeMat a fearsome weapon. Accurate details such as the swivel lanyard ring and trigger guard spur duplicate those on original guns. The loading lever is mounted on the left side ($750 at www.cabelas.com).

The Colt 1836 patent was due to expire in 1849, but demonstrating that his company had not used it to its full capacity, Sam was able to renew it until February 25, 1857. The extension gave him a chance to squeeze the competition and thus, Remington waited and experimented until just prior to the outbreak of war.

When the Colt patent finally expired Remington quickly brought out a solid frame revolver design, which was both elegant and reliable. With more than 122,000 produced, the Remington New Model Army steel frame percussion blackpowder pistol was a favorite among cavalrymen because they could reload while riding simply by ejecting the spent cylinder and inserting a full cylinder. The reliability and accuracy of this gun made it so famous that, at the end of the Civil War when the Government gave Union officers an opportunity to take a gun home, the prevailing choice was this Remington revolver.

The specifications of the three-pound, .44-caliber Remington single action Pedersoli reproduction are: 18 3/5 inches length over-all, six shot, 8-inch blue octagonal barrel, fixed sights, twist/grooves 1:30 inches. The stock and grip are walnut and the frame is blued steel. The price of $285 was registered at www.replicagunsswords.com. Replaceable conversion cylinders are also available.

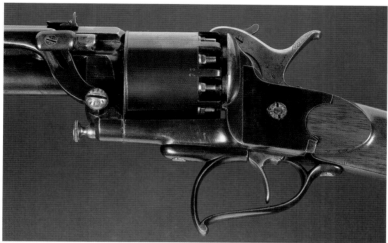

This is a truly extraordinary example of a Model 1863 LeMat Percussion Carbine (stock and barrel not shown). A very rare carbine with a .44 caliber rifled upper barrel and ten-shot cylinder, plus a rifled, single-shot .50 caliber barrel. The hammer has a selector spur to fire the lower barrel. The carbine has a loading lever attached to the left side of the barrel lug and is fitted with a two-leaf, folding, rear sight. The estimated value from Rock Island Auction is $100,000-$150,000. (Lot 3192)

James D. Julia Auctioneers (http://juliaauctions.net/) notes that these Remington revolvers in good condition usually sell for between $1,800 and $2,400. Flayderman's *Guide* suggests that $600 is appro-

The lower receiver tang of this factory-engraved .44 Henry Rifle manufactured in 1864 is stamped with a small "W" mark indicating personal inspection by Oliver Winchester. The receiver and buttplate heel are decorated with the factory scroll and floral pattern engraving attributed to Samuel J. Hoggson by George Maddis in *The Winchester Book*. The engraving features large floral designs on both sides of the forward portion of the receiver and large open scrollwork on a punch-dot background on the rest of the receiver and buttplate. Typical Hoggson factory engraving features an animal, in this case a dog on point, surrounded by scrollwork on the left side plate. Rock Island Auctions expected $30,000-$45,000 for this gun (Lot 1009).

priate for a pistol in good condition whereas a standard model with the government inspector's stamping on the left grip (initials within a cartouche) and sub-inspector initials on various other parts might fetch $2,000, if the gun were in fine condition.

Cowboy Action Shooting

In its own words, The Single Action Shooting Society (SASS: www.sassnet.com) is "an international organization created to preserve and promote the sport of Cowboy Action Shooting. SASS endorses regional matches conducted by affiliated clubs, stages END of TRAIL – The World Championship of Cowboy Action Shooting, promulgates rules and procedures to ensure safety and consistency in Cowboy Action Shooting matches, and seeks to protect its members' 2nd Amendment rights. SASS members share a common interest in preserving the history of the Old West and competitive shooting."

The Winchester New Model 94 with octagonal barrel hard at work shooting cowboy action. *(Photo courtesy Winchester)*

Due to the mystique or romance of the cowboys (or perhaps the Indians), SASS clubs have been formed in Europe (Austria, The Czech Republic, Denmark, England, Finland, Germany, Italy, The Netherlands, Norway and Switzerland) and "down under" in Australia and New Zealand.

So saith SASS, and furthermore, "One of the unique aspects of SASS approved Cowboy Action Shooting is the requirement placed

What could possibly be more fun than galloping around an arena and shooting at targets! The Western Shooting Horse Association offers competitive shooting as does the Single Action Shooting Society. The action combines elements of Wild West Show exhibition shooting along with the skills of barrel racing, pole bending and reining while using two .45 caliber single action revolvers (or a Winchester-style rifle) loaded with black powder blanks. The object is to shoot ten balloon targets while riding a mount through a variety of challenging courses. A timed sport, the competitor who rides the fastest with the least amount of missed targets wins. *(Photos courtesy WSHA)*

on costuming. Each participant is required to adopt a shooting alias appropriate to a character or profession of the late 19th century, a Hollywood western star, or an appropriate character from fiction. Their costume is then developed accordingly. Many event participants gain more enjoyment from the costuming aspect of our sport than from the shooting competition, itself. Regardless of a SASS member's individual area of interest, SASS events provide regular opportunities for fellowship and fun with like-minded folks and families."

And there is more. "Every SASS member is required to select a shooting alias representative of a character or profession from the Old West or the western film genre. Your alias may not in anyway duplicate or easily be confused with any other member's alias."

But what about the guns? "Cowboy Action Shooting is a multi-faceted shooting sport in which contestants compete with firearms typical of those used in the taming of the Old West: single action revolvers, pistol caliber lever action rifles and old time shotguns. The shooting competition is staged in a unique, characterized, Old West style. It is a timed sport in which shooters compete for prestige on a course of different shooting stages."

Wait! There are not only single action shooting clubs in every state and a dozen foreign nations, there is a horseback division as well.

Depending on your feelings about our equine neighbors, shooting horses may or may not be a good thing. The French eat horse-meat. A prime cut can be purchased in an open-air *chevalerie*. And without mentioning who, someone hunted the horse to extinction in North America about 10,000 years ago, along with the woolly rhinoceros and woolly mammoth…and this was before firearms!

Today, most Americans gag at the idea of eating horsemeat. We have, after all, a tradition of befriending the big equines, of making cartoon characters of them, pals. The stereotype is a cowboy kissing his horse and leaving the girl standing while he rides off into the sunset. Perhaps that is a wise choice, but it is also a good thing that we did not choose to ride cows or moose.

The rule book of the new, separate and independent Western Shooting Horse Association (www.westernshootinghorse.com) says that mounted shooting "...combines elements of Wild West Show exhibition shooting along with the skills of barrel racing, pole bending and reining while using two .45 caliber single action revolvers[5] loaded with black powder blanks." In the organization's rulebook, WSHA founder Ken Amorosano writes, "Only fixed sight single action revolvers of .45 Long Colt caliber, designed prior to 1898, or reproductions thereof are allowed." Most riders holster a couple of .45-caliber Colt reproductions from Cimarron or U.S. Firearms, or the new "old style" Ruger Vaquero.

Firearms for Cowboy Action Shooting

When someone begins to play a part in reenacting or cowboy action shooting (they must choose a stage name such as Ringo or Black Bart, although those names are already taken) they quickly choose an individual path. That is usually for the competition, be-

The China Camp Cowboy Action Gun from U.S. FireArms is designed and produced as an exact replica for the 80,000+ cowboy action shooters in the U.S. and abroad.

coming a state champion and eventually a Hall of Fame inductee, or it may be as a member of the SASS administrative structure, or a specialty cook or a vendor of unique belt buckles or cowboy knives.

Some shooters are natural organizers who, in their spare time enjoy developing the local club or helping refine the rules. Such was the case with Hall of Fame inductees Judge Roy Bean, SASS #1, and General U.S. Grant, SASS #2. These cowboys were prominent founders of Cowboy Action Shooting and the Single Action Shooting Society. They made essential contributions to the shooting sports by envisioning this family oriented game and creating innovative concepts that have endured for more than 25 years.

On the other hand, becoming famous in cowboy action circles may be for something as obvious as being a fancy dresser and role player. Alan Wah, also known as Wahoo, SASS #822, was a clothing visionary, a "snappy dresser," who designed and manufactured a line of Old West cowboy clothing with great attention to authenticity. Wah entered the Hall of Fame for his important contribution to this significant aspect of the sport. Not only did Wah provide important durable goods for the game, he also provided support as a long time major sponsor.

This old Civil War-era gun is heavily rusted and the stock is badly beaten-up. It may be good for a "decorator" gun or perhaps for a "parts gun" if collecting eventually leads you to become a gun trader.

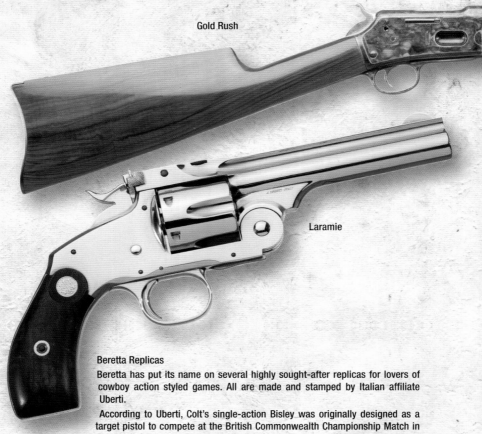

Gold Rush

Laramie

Beretta Replicas

Beretta has put its name on several highly sought-after replicas for lovers of cowboy action styled games. All are made and stamped by Italian affiliate Uberti.

According to Uberti, Colt's single-action Bisley was originally designed as a target pistol to compete at the British Commonwealth Championship Match in Bisley, England in 1894. The Bisley featured a longer grip-frame for its target grips and a lower profile, wide target hammer. Over 40,000 Colt Bisleys were made between 1894 and 1915. (Also available from Uberti with two-piece wood grips, case-hardened with 7 ½-inch barrel.)

The Laramie is a top-break six shot revolver. While keeping in mind the aesthetic and design of the late 1800's American western single action revolver, this model features a new safety system guaranteeing a lifetime of safety and performance. The new Laramie – blue or nickel – revolver is equipped with an automatic safety on the hammer consisting of a sliding bar.

Beretta's Gold Rush rifle and carbine combine the looks and feel of the Old West original with modern safety and reliability. Chambered for 45 LC and the 357 Mag/38 Special, the Gold Rush is a fast-handling pump-action longarm perfect for cowboy action, small-game hunting and target practice. Compared to the original, several modifications have been discretely incorporated that greatly enhance safety and reliability. A solid transfer-bar safety mechanism is housed in the hammer, making the gun absolutely safe to load and unload without having to lower the hammer. Feeding is improved considerably by ensuring that each cartridge is perfectly in line with the chamber. Lastly, a redesigned cycling mechanism makes it possible to obtain the desired speed without jams. All other aspects such as trigger-quality, accuracy

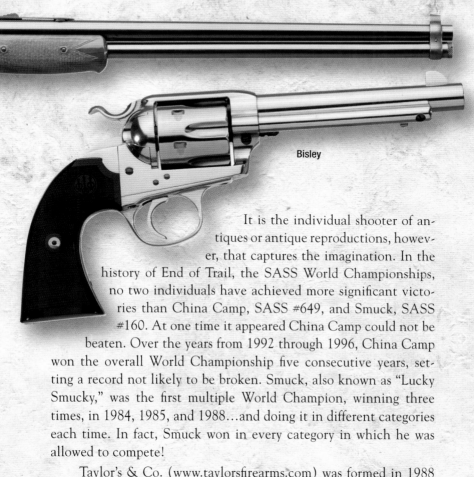

Bisley

It is the individual shooter of antiques or antique reproductions, however, that captures the imagination. In the history of End of Trail, the SASS World Championships, no two individuals have achieved more significant victories than China Camp, SASS #649, and Smuck, SASS #160. At one time it appeared China Camp could not be beaten. Over the years from 1992 through 1996, China Camp won the overall World Championship five consecutive years, setting a record not likely to be broken. Smuck, also known as "Lucky Smucky," was the first multiple World Champion, winning three times, in 1984, 1985, and 1988...and doing it in different categories each time. In fact, Smuck won in every category in which he was allowed to compete!

Taylor's & Co. (www.taylorsfirearms.com) was formed in 1988 by Sue Hawkins and Tammy Loy. Since then they have intensified their commitment to shooters who specialize in American firearms from the 1840s through 1892.

Taylor's notes it markets finely-crafted historical firearms that are "highly respected," and that its line of firearms and accessories is "historically correct." Manufactured using modern machinery and high quality modern materials, these firearms are faithful reproductions of firearms originally designed in the 19th century. It also carries an extensive inventory of parts "for our products as well as other models of firearms."[6]

These days a SASS shooter might carry a Smoke Wagon from Taylor's. This six-shooter is a second-generation, stagecoach style, single-action revolver. It boasts a low-profile hammer and wider-style sights that allow the user to acquire targets faster, without cocking the pistol. It also features a thin, richly detailed checkered grip. Taylor's says this is for comfort and improved aim, although all matters of fit are highly individual. Nevertheless, all of these features are available on both standard and deluxe models. The deluxe model also includes custom tuning; custom hammer and base pin springs; trigger-spring set at three pounds; jig-cut, positive angles on all triggers and sears for crisp, reliable action; a coil-loaded hand; and wire bolt and trigger springs. The suggested retail price for the standard model is $450 and for the deluxe, $575.

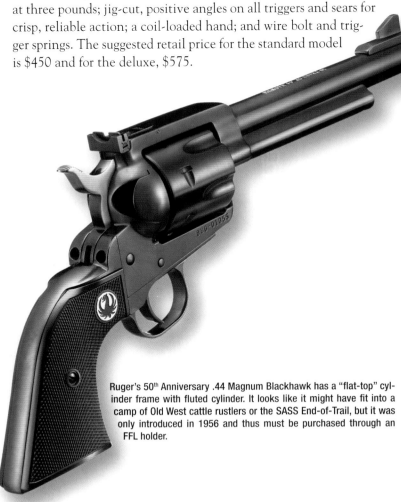

Ruger's 50th Anniversary .44 Magnum Blackhawk has a "flat-top" cylinder frame with fluted cylinder. It looks like it might have fit into a camp of Old West cattle rustlers or the SASS End-of-Trail, but it was only introduced in 1956 and thus must be purchased through an FFL holder.

Pietta calls it the New Sheriff, but Colt Sheriff models one through three were never chambered in the .357 magnum caliber. The .357 Magnum was created by Elmer Keith, Phillip Sharpe, Winchester and Smith & Wesson, based upon Smith & Wesson's earlier .38 Special. The .357 was only introduced in 1934. The Colt Sheriff or Storekeeper models had no ejector rods or housing and the frame was made without the hole in the right forward section to accommodate the ejector assembly.

At the higher end of the six-gun spectrum, a $1,170 nickel plated single-action .45 Colt reproduction from U.S. Firearms (www.usfirearms.com: bone case and blue for $975) might satisfy the most fastidious shooter. This gun also comes in .44 WCF, .44 special, .38 special, .38 WCF and .32 WCF. Barrel length options are 4 ¾, 5 ½ and 7 ½ inches. It is built with a modern cross-pin frame style for safety, hard rubber grips, a square notch rear sight and square front blade.

In the world of back-ups, a cowboy – especially one acquainted with city ways – might have stuck a derringer in his belt, down a pants pocket or even inside his boot. A 14-ounce, two-shot Big Bore Derringer from Cobra (www.cobrapistols.com) is available in calibers .22 Mag, .32 H&R Mag, .38 Special, .380 or 9mm. This derringer measures 4.65- x 3.31 inches and has a 2.75-inch barrel; grips are molded black synthetic and it is available finished in chrome, non-reflective black and satin nickel. During a recent auction at www.gunbroker.com this gun sold for $155.

When it comes to sighting down a longer barrel, the EMF Company (www.emf-company.com) is a leading source of historically accu-

With their unusual but collectible "bird's head" grip, the Model 1877 Thunderer was chambered for .41 Colt while the Model 1877 Lightning was chambered for .38 Colt. The names "Thunderer" and "Lightning" were apparently bestowed by Cincinnati distributor Ben Kittredge to give the new models an image boost. In good condition, both the Thunderer and Lightning are thousand-dollar guns. These are Pietta replicas — but unlike the originals, they're available in single-action only.

rate, collectible quality reproduction firearms of the Old West, cowboy and Civil War eras. Their offerings including black powder revolvers and rifles, single action revolvers, lever action rifles, shotguns, single shot rifles, derringers, accessories and more. "Our revolvers, pistols, shotguns, rifles and carbines match the originals in appearance, parts, construction and function, but are much lower in price."

The Model 1873 Winchester rifle, for example, was almost certainly the most popular civilian rifle used on the late frontier of the American West. By the turn of the century more than half a million had been produced. Late production of this extremely reliable rifle model was also a favorite south of the border to the very end of production in 1923, by which date more than 20,000 were produced.

EMF's authentic replicas of the 1873 Winchester and other guns of the era "match the originals in appearance, construction and function," EMF says. The '73 Winchester reproduction is available in two barrel lengths – 20 and 24 inches – and a choice of calibers (.32/20, .357, .45LC, .38/40, .44/40 and .45), each at $1,100. All parts are, of course, machined to exacting specifications.

At the end of the Civil War in April 1865, the U.S. War Department had to replace its millions of excellent muzzle loading muskets – such as the 1861 Springfield, already profiled – with metallic cartridge rifles although they were still loaded with black powder. Between 1865 and 1866 the first transformation of a muzzle loading Springfield musket was made by Allin and in 1868 the first "Trapdoor Rifle" was built, being further modified in 1870. Three years later a new rifle in the .45-70 caliber became available. Any of these might be seen at a cowboy action event.

During the following 20 years quite a large number of Springfield Trapdoor rifles were manufactured, among them also many versions with smooth barrels for cadets, for target shooting and even officers. "The Springfield Trapdoor rifle is a typical gun of the American soldiers," says reproduction manufacturer Pedersoli, "including General Custer. It equipped the troops also during the Spanish-American War (1898-1899). Davide Pedersoli Co. is pleased to be able to offer flawless reproductions of the three most significant models: the army rifle, the cavalry carbine and the officer's rifle, this last equipped with a

Collecting The Greatest Gunfight of All Time

George Armstrong Custer recklessly led his men of the 7th Cavalry into the perfect storm at the Little Big Horn and Sitting Bull, Crazy Horse, Gall and their Indian braves held nothing back. Custer's troop was annihilated to the last man.

For history buffs and collectors U.S. FireArms has recreated the pistol that Custer and many of his officers and men carried: each gun features correct style barrel address, patent markings and "US" stampings as well as single cartouche on the left grip. These guns are limited to the serial number range during which [Government Inspector Orville W.] Ainsworth inspected the

guns and use the exact old style hand numbering. All Government Inspector Series guns are available only in historically correct "US Government Cartridge" - 45 Colt."

Is this gun perhaps too authentic?

"It's all I had ever hoped for: the antique finish is dingy just like that original Colt SAA still on display at the battlefield's museum. Sights, firing pin, ejector rod head and grips are perfect renditions of those items found on original "Cavalry Colts." The "A" inspector's stampings are precisely where they are supposed to be, as is the cartouche on the left side of the walnut grip, and the U.S. stamp on the frame's left side. Furthermore, it has that fantastic quality in regards to fit and lock-up the U.S. Firearms Company has gained such a positive reputation for." – American Handgunner, January/ February 2006.

(George A. Custer photo, Library of Congress: Custer Digital ID #cwpb 05341)

single set trigger, rear sight and Creedmoor sight adjustable in elevation and windage. All of these follow the originals perfectly and blend traditional gunsmith handcraft arts to state of the art technology."

Pedersoli's Trapdoor Carbine DeLuxe is chambered for .45/70 with three 1:22 twists in the 22-inch barrel. The overall length is 41 ¼ and weight is 7 1/3 pounds. From Navy Arms (www.navyarms. com), the 1873 Officer's Model of this gun retails for $1,648.

And every now and then, of course, someone wanders onto a shooting venue with an authentic "Mare's Leg." According to big-bore six-gun specialist John Taffin[7], the Mare's Leg legend actually started with John Wayne's portrayal of Ringo in the 1939 movie *Stagecoach*. Actually an 1892 Winchester with a cut-off butt-stock and barrel, its otherwise most prominent feature was the large loop lever that Wayne and others following him – Chuck Connor's portrayal of Lucas McCain, for instance, in the television series *The Rifleman* – could twirl. (Taffin says Steve McQueen's Josh Randall in *Wanted Dead or Alive* actually twirled a lever action pistol related to an early Volcanic.) After reviewing ATF rulings, Taffin and builder Jim Buchanan have paperwork concluding that the Mare's Leg is a pistol...not a rifle. "Practical?" Taffin concludes in a May/June issue of the magazine *American Handgunner*. "Nope. But it sure is an attention-getter and fun-shootin' six-gun."

Buchanan's 1892 Mare's Leg custom lever action pistol can be viewed at (www.jbcustom.com). This six-shooter can be built in calibers

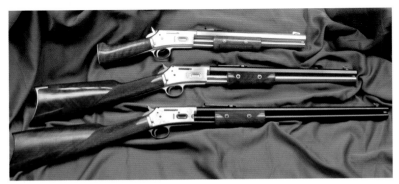

The American Western Arms Lightningbolt pistol (top) is a "Mare's Leg" version of the company's highly authentic Colt Lightning Magazine Rifle clones (bottom).

.45 Colt, .44-40, .44-magnum and .357-magnum. The overall length is 24 inches. The rear sight is adjustable while the dovetail front sight has a brass bead. The most notable feature, of course, is its big loop lever and it comes with a saddle ring and blue finish. The cost is $1,495. (And because a Mare's Leg revolver is going to be such a curiosity-piece, wearers will certainly want to spend $225 for one of Buchanan's special holster-and-belt set in black or brown to properly wear this unique gun.)

The Vintagers

Here is a relatively small group of shooters that has fun out of proportion to its numbers. They are the Vintagers (www.vintagers.org) and the mission of this not-for-profit corporation is to provide an opportunity for the use, appreciation and collection of side-by-side shotguns and rifles. Shotguns with hammers! The corporation was organized in 1994 when four friends who loved both side-by-side shotguns and the game of sporting clays recognized that the emphasis on score discouraged the use of fine game guns at sporting clay events. In response, they set up shoots for classic guns with emphasis on fun targets, Vintage attire, fine dining and good fellowship.

"We had too much fun shooting these old hammer guns to score targets," says Ray Poudrier, president of the Order of Edwardian Gunners, "and the group known as The Vintagers quickly became a success. Today, membership is open to anyone who shares our enthusiasm for the Double Gun."

The Vintagers, Order of Edwardian Gunners, like many other recreational groups has an interest that centers in old hammer guns and drillings.

Members are invited to all shooting and social events promoted by the Order of Edwardian Gunners or "Vintagers" and chartered affiliates. Members in good standing receive a periodic newsletter, which may contain historic double gun information, news from headquarters, a calendar of events and members' classified advertisements as well as other information of interest. They also receive free admission to regional and international Vintager Expositions.

"It's a shooting experience for gentlemen and gentlewomen who appreciate the guns, attire and habits of the Vintage Years, 1880 to 1914," Poudrier says. "A safe side-by-side cartridge gun of good quality that reflects the Vintage period in its nature is required as is clothing and accessories appropriate to the English Sportsman of the period and their guests." And before a reader jumps to the conclusion that these are just rich snobs in period clothing, note that the web site recommends rummaging through a local Salvation Army thrift store for antique clothing!

Shooting a drilling and dressed in the Edwardian style of the early 20th century, members of the Vintagers believe that these days, far too much emphasis is given to a person's score and far too little to the social environment of shooting.

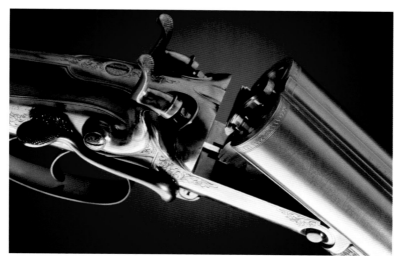

In practically new condition, this double-hammer shotgun would be a showpiece at any gathering, Vintagers or not.

Firearms of The Vintagers

It is the guns – and of course the old clothes, though there is no Hall of Fame for "sharp dressers" – that set the Vintagers apart and here were four of the antiques offered for sale in classified ads on their web site:

• LeFever 10 gauge side-by-side: Grade G, lots of case color, line engraving, heavy gun with 2 ¾ inch chambers, Prince of Wales grip, uncut but thick 31-inch Damascus barrels, mod/full chokes, extractors, no buggered screws, virtually untouched. A classic American waterfowler! $1,200.

• Westley Richards 10 gauge side-by-side: 30-inch Damascus barrels, lighter gun, Prince of Wales grip, 2 5/8-inch chambers, extractors, light mod/light mod chokes, worn checkering, 90 percent engraving, put back "on the face" by J.J. Perodeau with Champlin Arms. Best gun maker that needs a bit of tidying! $1,500.

• W.C. Scott 10 gauge side-by-side: "la creme de la creme" of the lot, with crystal cocking indicators, extractors, spectacular marbled French walnut, Prince of Wales grip, light case colors, line engraving with single flying duck, 30 inch Damascus barrels, full/full chokes, 2 ¾-inch chambers. A classic British ten in phenomenal condition! $2,500.

• L.C. Smith Specialty Grade 16 gauge two barrel set, manufactured 1914. Only one made with Damascus and steel barrels. All numbers match, all bores are pristine, 30 inch steel barrels are f/f, 26-inch Damascus barrels are im/f, splinter fore-end with ebony insert on both. $5995.

Cimarron Firearms (www.cimarron-firearms.com) offers a number of imported firearm replicas, dead ringers for the ones used taming the frontier and for shooting such as the Vintagers enjoy. "We believe we are a recognized leader in both quality and authenticity in replica shooting firearms," says owner Mike Harvey. (Harvey is known in SASS-speak as Texas Jack Omohundro. "We're SASS lifers," he says, "and have supported Cowboy Action Shooters since 1987. In 1988, in fact, we brought cowboy action shooting from End of Trail to Texas.")

"We offer the highest quality reproductions of Colt and Winchester replicas: the single action army, U.S. cavalry and artillery model, the 1872 open top, the Model 'P' (with old model, pre-war, or early pinched frame), the Model 'P' Jr., the Thunderer, Lightning, the Richards-Mason conversion. In long guns we have replicas of the Henry rifle, the 1866 Winchester Yellowboy, the 1873 Winchester lever action rifle, Carbine and Trapper, the Model 92 rifle, the Lightning Magazine Rifle, the Model 1876 Centennial, the 1885 Winchester high wall, the Spencer repeating rifle and the 1874 Sharps rifle, plus Buffalo Guns."

Cimarron sells a reproduction of an 1878 Coach Gun side-by-side with real working hammers. The 20-inch, blued steel barrels take 12-gauge shells and are bored for cylinder patterns. The wood is American walnut and the gun has a suggested retail price of $488.

Spain is well represented in the classic and collectible gun tradition, though not nearly so heavy perhaps in historic American pieces as Italy. This line-up of hand-built shotguns is from AYA (Aguirre y Aranzabal) in Eibar, Spain.

The Hunters

How many people hunt or shoot competitively with muzzleloaders? No one knows for sure, of course, but Winston Roland, the current president of the National Muzzle Loading Rifle Association (www.nmlra.org), believes that the number is 3-½ to 4 million in the U.S.

Competition shooting appears to be declining or perhaps only holding steady. And even though he believes the numbers of the North-South Skirmish Association (www.n-ssa.org) are probably no more than 5,000 active members, those members are avid about shooting and their skirmish (competition and Civil War campout) weekends.[8]

Interestingly, Roland feels that the advent of the in-line muzzleloader has been a significant boon to the shooting sports. People look at an older percussion or flintlock – the "real McCoy antique" or a replica – and feel intimidated, he says.

And although the NMLRA does not take any position relating to state seasons or the determination of weapon appropriateness, the organization has a basic policy stating that if a gun loads through the muzzle, it is a muzzleloader.

Black powder seasons require hunting with vintage weapons or replicas...right? Such hunting should put one in a special elite league, with fly fishermen, and with archers who prefer longbows and recurves rather than today's mechanically superior 300 fps cam bows. Black powder hunting is not for everyone, because it carries special disadvantages: shots will be closer, the gun will need to be cleaned more often and when the

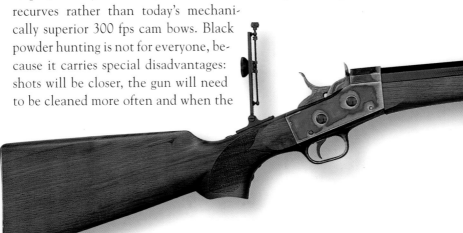

powder explodes and the smoke clears you will either have hit what you are shooting at or it will be long gone. In muzzleloader or black powder hunting, a second chance is rare...or is it?

Well, not all black powder hunting these days is with antiques or replicas of older style flintlocks or percussion guns. There has been considerable development of new styles of "in-line" muzzleloaders. At $430 suggested retail price, the Pursuit Pro Break-Open muzzle-loader, for example, is the newest and most advanced blackpowder rifle offered by Traditions (www.traditionsfirearms.com). This gun also gives owners the ability to change from a .50 caliber barrel to a .45 caliber or even a 12-gauge muzzleloading shotgun barrel quickly "so they can hunt virtually any game in the woods."

With its 28-inch fluted, tapered barrel, Traditions explains, "shooters have been getting exceptional accuracy out to 200 yards. The break open action gives the shooter fast and easy access to the 209 [a shotgun primer] ignition system. It also allows for quick and effortless cleanup. The solid aluminum ramrod features a reversible loading and cleaning jag giving you the extended length you need for the 28-inch barrel. The Pursuit Pro also incorporates two safety systems, a transfer bar safety on the inside of the frame and a cross-block safety in the trigger guard. Additional features include: Monte Carlo style synthetic stock, ambidextrous hammer spur for right and left handed shooters, drilled and tapped for scope mounting and projectile alignment system in the muzzle."

" Dear Sirs,

"Last year I ordered from your firm a sporting rifle, caliber .50. I received the rifle a short time prior to the departure of the Yellowstone Expedition.

"The Expedition left Fort Rice the 20th of June, 1873 and returned to Fort Abraham Lincoln, September 21, 1873. During the period of three months I carried the rifle referred to on every occasion and the following exhibits but a portion of the game killed by me: Antelope 41; buffalo 4; elk 4; blacktail deer 4; American deer 3; white wolf 2; geese, prairie chicken and other feathered game in large numbers.

"The number of animals killed is not so remarkable as the distance at which the shots were executed. The average distance at which the forty-one antelopes were killed was 250 yards by actual measurement. I rarely obtained a shot at an antelope under 150 yards, while the range extended from that distance up to 630 yards....."

Signed George Armstrong Custer.

Couple this fine in-line muzzleloader or one like the Fire Storm from Thompson/Center with the new Pyrodex palletized powders and modern jacketed, self-lubricating sabots and – not to make or hinder waves – one wonders if these guns belong in the black powder season or the general rifle season. Current muzzleloader seasons were designed to give those who limited their range and accuracy some extra time in the field and those hunters were shooting replica firearms from the 18th and 19th centuries.

Firearms for Hunters

In 1965, K. W. Thompson Tool was looking for a product to build and a gun designer named Warren Center was looking for someone to build his Contender pistol. It was a perfect match. Thompson expanded its facilities and Thompson/Center Arms (T/C) was formed. Two years later, the first Contender was shipped, starting a trend in high performance large caliber hunting handguns, which continues to grow. To date, more than 400,000 Contender pistols have been shipped and the pistol's reputation is difficult to dispute.

In the 1970s, antique rifles were selling for high prices, but most collectors opted not to fire them. Thus T/C saw that the market needed a quality replica rifle at a reasonable price and introduced its Hawken.

Here is a puzzle. The 1858 Bison is manufactured in Italy by F. Pietta. Traditions sells it for $283 claiming that it is "…modeled after the renowned Buntline Special reportedly given to Wyatt Earp by gun designer Ned Buntline." As a dime novelist, Buntline, of course, barely knew which end of the gun the bullet flew out of and the Buntline Special is a myth. This gun sells for $200 from Cabelas as the 1858 Buffalo brass frame black powder revolver. Cabelas says, "With its rugged frame construction and increased accuracy this gun gained great favor with shooters, hunters and soldiers." Baloney. This is essentially a new gun, which may be modeled after a mid-19th century Colt or Remington, but it is not a replica of an antique gun!

Currently, T/C produces an extensive line of single shot pistols and rifles, plus a full line of muzzleloading rifles and black powder accessories.

During the last 15 years, black powder hunting has broadened dramatically, as have hunters' demands. T/C believes that modern hunters are less interested in the nostalgia, which accompanies the guns of the 1800's, than performance: modern designs, greater accuracy at extended ranges and easier cleaning. Although T/C still offers the Hawken, most of today's T/C muzzleloaders are modern in-line styles capable of accepting magnum charges of 150 grains of FFG Black Powder, or Pyrodex equivalent (i.e., three each of 50 grain [50 caliber] Pyrodex pellets).

Today's in-line muzzleloaders are ideal for hunting from the ground or from trees. Still, whether or not they are more effective – more accurate and more powerful – than antique muzzleloaders in the hands of skilled shooters is open to question. *(Photos courtesy Mossy Oak)*

The Gun Digest Book of® Firearms Fakes and Reproductions

Thompson/Center guns are built by New Englanders, who take pride, the company says, in building a "sturdy product and selling it at a fair price." In addition, each new gun comes with a Lifetime Warranty. In 2007 T/C became part of Smith & Wesson Holdings and is recognized as Smith & Wesson Hunting.

T/C's .50 caliber Hawken with hooked breech system was designed for the American shooter. This is a top quality firearm, T/C says, as fine as the one your great, great granddaddy carried across his saddle pommel or packed along on the wagon train. It captures the romance of the original but is manufactured to standards of quality control that were unheard of in the early 1800's. "The proper use of the investment casting, improved methods of hardening parts and deep-hole drilling, continuously guarding against imperfections in the steel coupled to our constant attention to tolerances is what allows us to offer a Lifetime Warranty."

The 8-½-pound, 45-¼-inch long Hawken has a 28-inch polished and blued octagonal barrel that is 1-5/16 inches across the flats. It is drilled and tapped for scope mounts (using rear sight holes and breech plug hole) before leaving the factory, but otherwise has fully adjustable open hunting style rear sights with bead front sight. Triggers are

Throwing an atl-atl is fun, but not compared to firing a .50-caliber black powder Hawken Rifle reproduction from Thompson-Center. This old-timer – who goes by the name "Leggs" – would certainly not have carried a spear-thrower; would probably have disdained it, in fact. He would have been armed with the latest and most affordable technology, which may have been a powerful Hawken and he would have traded rough-and-ready muskets to the Indians with whom he did business for animal skins – beaver and felt hats being all the rage in Europe and America for nearly 300 years, from 1550 to 1850. The Indians tended to decorate the muskets with leather, paint, etching and even tacks of the era.

fully adjustable for a light, crisp pull and will function either as double set or single stage. The gun is complemented by solid brass hardware. The butt plate, trigger guard and contoured patch box are inletted and fitted to the American walnut stock. (With a suggested retail price of $787, the T/C Hawken was offered for sale through www.cheaper-thandirt.com for $630 or to CTD club members for $567.)

Originally, Hawken rifles were made in the anticipation of rugged use on the plains and thus, delicate touches were avoided. Built in St. Louis by Jacob (later joined by brother Samuel) Hawken, they were shorter rifles for big game than the customary Kentucky rifles of the time. The Hawkens expected that many of their guns would be used on horseback, so barrels were shortened and bores enlarged. Average barrel lengths were 36 to 38 inches; bores were 50 or 60 caliber; stocks were walnut or maple; and weights were between 9 and 14 pounds. Indications of Indian use, perhaps with decorations of brass tacks or any evidence that the stock may have been wrapped with rawhide, bring a premium in evaluation value.

"Without doubt the markings of the Hawken brothers and their St. Louis address are magic on any plains rifle," writes Norm Flayderman in the 8th edition of *Flayderman's Guide to Antique American Firearms...and their values*.[9] "Not only were they the originators of the type but their rifle was so widely accepted, used and respected that in some instances the Hawken name, like that of Henry Deringer, became the generic term for the entire style of rifle.... Examples of their work are now quite rare and any genuine specimen brings far in excess of what other plains rifles of contemporary makers fetch."

According to Flayderman, values for an original Hawken range from $10,000 for a gun in only fair condition to as much as $40,000 for one in very good condition. Still, the following Hawken sale at auction illustrates the volatility of the collectibles market, which is subject to – and professional economists spend lifetimes studying these things – everything from the price of a barrel of oil from Saudi Arabia to an indigestible lunch eaten quickly just prior to the auction. This is the listing that appeared on the Kull & Supica Firearms Auction site (www.armsbid.com/7antique-guns.htm) for April 2007:

Lot 196 - S. Hawken - plains rifle - .62 cal.; 32-5/8" octagon barrel, measures 1" across flats. - Well used condition. - Appears heavily used & unaltered since period of use. Dark metal with roughness & scaling. Legible barrel marking "S. HAWKEN ST. LOUIS". Lock plate marked "JAS. GOLCHER / PHILADA" with engraved game bird faint on rear of lock & faint light scroll engraving on lockplate & hammer. Buckhorn rear sight dovetailed in front of empty dovetail; 1-1/8" long German silver front sight blade on dovetailed base. Simple brass furniture; pewter nosecap. Iron underbarrel rib & ramrod thimbles. Half stock w/cheekpiece has crack at front of lock (with old woodscrew repair), bottom rear of buttstock, and on bottom from nearly front of the triggerguard tang running forward to the nosecap, with significant old losses around the front of the ramrod channel. - Double set trigger is not quite functioning. Front of lockplate is pulling away from stock. Iron tipped ramrod. Knowledgeable owner describes this as "non-typical large bore brass trim Hawken's Plain Rifle. Has been well used and has probably been reworked from a full stock at some point but lock & barrel markings are clear & correct". - {7sgar-1} – antique.

Kull and Supica[10] have an excellent reputation in the firearms auction market. Supica, who is a firearms expert in his own right, examined the Hawken and estimated its value at between $6,000 and $10,000. The gun sold for $5,390.

Footnotes

1   See the author's *Standard Catalog of Colt Firearms* (Krause Publications, Iola, WI; 2007) for an extended review of Colt firearms from Sam Colt's original Paterson, NJ models to the newest 9mm submachine gun.

2   For the full text of General George Patton's speech to the U.S. Third Army in England on June 5, 1944, the eve of "Operation Overlord" and the invasion of France go to www.pattonhq.com/speech.html.

3   For up-to-date information on the latest reenactment and camp-out at Gettysburg, the most famous and popular reenactment in the world, visit www.gettysburggreenactment.com. This annual event is coordinated through The Gettysburg Anniversary Committee, P.O. Box 3482, Gettysburg, PA 17325-3482 (717) 338-1525 gac3@comcast.net. The Gettysburg Anniversary Committee handles only the Annual Battle of Gettysburg Reenactment and due to limited staff, can only answer emails related to the reenactment. For information about planning a trip to Gettysburg, visit Gettysburg Convention & Visitors Bureau – www.gettysburg.travel and Gettysburg National Military Park – www.nps.gov/gett.

4   Adams-Graf's, page 355.

5   The Cowboy Mounted Shooting Association (www.cowboymountedshooting.com) also has a rifle shooting division. Its rules state, "The rifle used shall be one manufactured prior to 1900 or a reproduction thereof. It shall be a production weapon, not a one of a kind or a homemade weapon. It shall be a pump action, lever action, or revolving rifle. The pump action and lever action shall be 45 LC, 44/40 or 44 magnum calibers. The revolving rifle shall be 45 LC. Rifle barrel minimum length shall be 16 inches and overall rifle minimum length shall be 30 inches."

6   In choosing to own or use historical firearms, the user must recognize that there have been significant advances in firearms blueprints, materials and safety in the years since these firearms were originally designed. It is vital that users be familiar with their firearm and the possible safety risks that may be inherent in the design.

    Most significantly, the user should realize that the designs of safeties – or even the presence of adequate safeties – vary significantly on historical designs and do not offer the protection against accidental discharge that modern firearms safeties achieve.

    Similarly, any firearm that is fired using black powder (or Pyrodex) has basic risks not found in modern cartridge firearms. Black powder is a dangerous explosive and has to be used and handled with extreme caution. The slightest miscalculation or carelessness with black powder and black powder firearms can result in serious injuries to the user.

7   John Taffin, *Big Bore Sixguns* (Krause Publications, Iola, WI 1997)

8   The North-South Skirmish Association or N-SSA (www.n-ssa.org) "promotes the competitive shooting of Civil War firearms and artillery and encourages the preservation of battlefields, artifacts and education of the period."

9   Flayderman, page 565.

10   Jim Supica and Richard Nahas, *Standard Catalog of Smith & Wesson* (Gun Digest Books, Krause Publications, Iola, WI 2007)

Chapter Eight

Being A Collector

ny time that antique gun values, restoration and reproductions are mentioned in the same breath, the subject eventually turns to collecting. We are a generation of collectors, earnestly plowing the fields of nostalgia for re-runs of "The Lone Ranger" or "Star Trek" or "I Love Lucy." As kids we collected S&H Green Stamps with our moms; we pasted them into booklets and traded those for "valuable prizes." We collected coins and postage stamps; we had insect collections and baseball cards. We had the space and time, the parental encouragement to "get out of the house – go outside and play" as well as their suffrage when, in those days of only two or three channels of black and white television, we lay on the bed and sorted our Boy Scout Merit Badges.

With time off for school, work and families, we eventually resumed collecting as adults, many of us turning to the larger pursuit of big game trophies, sports cars and…valuable antique firearms.

Why We Hunt And Gather

In this book's Introduction, I suggested that collecting in general, and gun collecting in particular, was a rather meaningless activity. One could argue that, like stamp or coin collecting, it keeps we middle-age men off the streets at night, out of the pick-up bars and tattoo parlors. Nevertheless, I need just a few paragraphs to explain…and to promote an idea that is more sophisticated than those youthful passions.

Antiquing, in a very great degree, may be a quite useless activity and a pointless way to spend our time, our energies and our resources. Is it nostalgia run wild with the checkbook? Or is it something deep-

As part of becoming a complete collector with a special area of interest, it is worthwhile keeping one's eyes open for items that will one day be collectibles. Paulo Shanalingigua, for instance, was Tanzania's first Chief of Wildlife and first black professional hunter. Will his rifles, his trophies or autographs be valuable one day to Africanists, historians or members of SCI, the Safari Club International?

er, some need to surround ourselves with the "stuff" of our youth and thus to stay young ourselves? The things we remember our parents and grandparents talking about?

Today's old gun markets have almost everything a collector could possibly be interested in and most fields are deep enough that the idea of fakes is irrelevant. Many old Russian military guns, for example, are in good enough condition to shoot and retail for $150...no one would fake such a gun for so little financial reward.

A variety of collectibles and shooters (all are in operating condition), guns from all wars of the 20th century, fill a local retailer's wall. Your local gun store, followed by a gun show, are good places to identify your collecting interest.

We collect because it is fun to learn about and possess these old firearms, whether they are the Guns that Won the West or the sidearm grandpa carried at Belleau Wood. Good collecting, the most satisfying kind of hunting and gathering or "accumulating," becomes more than simple acquisition, more than decoration; it becomes a life-long passion that involves more than hiding artifacts in a safe. The deeper we get into antique firearms, for instance, the more questions we ask: Did Remington manufacture .38 rimfire Vest Pocket Pistols, its "Saw-Handle Deringer," or were these simply mis-gauged .41s? And how many .30- and .32- caliber models were made? Are these versions quite rare or simply odd? And always, "What were they thinking…?"

"Collecting, as opposed to gathering, can be an intellectual pursuit as well as a way to be with other people of a similar interest. In my experience, [fishing] lure collectors, in particular are the some of more fun loving bunch of people I've encountered.

"I don't know if this will translate to the Internet or not. How much fun is it to collect in front of your video screen?

"On the other hand, where else can you legally have this much fun and maybe make some money on your indulgences in the long run?

Firearms are not the only types of guns that are collectible and have interesting histories. More than nine million Daisy Red Ryder BB guns have been sold since its introduction in 1939. On their epic 19th century expedition, Lewis and Clark carried a very powerful air rifle for hunting and to impress the Indians … but not a Daisy.

"Bottom line: collect what you really like and wait on those boomers to show up about the time you want to buy a house in Montana, but don't quit the hobby just because it's hard to find a five dollar Heddon."

– Michael Echols, originally written in 1998 and since updated for Gabby Talkington's www.antiquelures.com. Used with permission.)

It is a challenge to dig into the unknown. There are so many peculiar and unanswered questions in every facet of firearms as to boggle the mind, and trying to decipher these puzzles keeps us on a learning curve when our human brains, by some medical and sociological accounts, have long since fossilized. Does it matter to the human race whether Remington manufactured .38 rimfire Deringers? Probably not, but it may matter to us, personally.

The mental stimulation of learning about any technology such as guns – the arguing, debating and researching – is sufficient reason, quite apart from actually owning them, to collect. It is really no different than a medieval monk laboriously transcribing an ancient parchment scroll. It is brain health.

But actually owning the old guns, turning them over in one's gloved hands, poring over them with a magnifying glass is also important. There is a story about an old duck hunter who has taken his grandson into the marsh. The old man calls and the cold wind blows and the boy shivers. Finally, the ducks swoop in and the old man points out the mallards and the blue wing teal and shows the

After World War II, there was an awakening to the quality of Japanese arms when returning soldiers brought thousands of them home as souvenirs. Today, they are highly collectible. This Type-14 Nambu was manufactured at the Nagoya Army Arsenal in February 1927. Rock Island Auction valued it between $950 and $1,100 (Lot 169) and said that "while the magazine is nickel and mismatched, the gun is in excellent condition. It retains approximately 90 percent original blue finish and 75 percent straw colors. The grips are very good with small chip out of left grip on bottom, the usual gouge from the safety lever and minor handling marks….the right side grip screw is locked up and the head is slightly marred."

boy how to tell them apart from the wood ducks, the drakes from the hens, and coaches him about lead, but the old man does not shoot.

As the next flight swings around the decoys, the boy does not raise his gun to shoot, either. "Why didn't you shoot?" the old man asks and the boy says, "I just want to be like you, grandpa." And the old man pats him on the back and says, "I've shot plenty of ducks in my time. Now it's your turn. You have to shoot 'em."

It is the same way with antique firearms. Beyond the biofeedback, the hand-to-brain hypothesis suggests that it is the stimulation of our restless hands and fingers that encourages our brain to learn: "You have to own them." Learning about old guns is wonderful and some might say a sufficient reason to be interested. That coin has another side, however, and that is actually making a purchase; taking home your first gun. And that thrill – and it is a thrill – is absolutely necessary to fully participate in and enjoy this antique field, whether or not it is ultimately a meaningless activity and whether our kids follow in our collecting footsteps.

Investing vs. the True Collector

According to Gabby Talkington of AntiqueLures.com, "The person who gets into collecting because he or she enjoys it is going to come out ahead, no matter what happens to the market. If they have fun studying old lures or whatever, then when a barrel of oil reaches $200 and the bottom drops out of the stock and collectible markets, they won't be hitting their head against the wall like they would if collecting was just some investment. If they're collecting because its fun to find and have this old stuff around and the prices go up...then that's kind of a double bonus."

"There is the risk that the bottom [of the collector market] will fall out tomorrow. The collectible decoy prices fell. Gold coins fell. Baseball cards fell.

"Think about it again. You didn't sell that lure for $1,000 last week...and the very next week the market crashes and we are back to the $5 lure! Don't laugh, it could happen. It has happened before.

BEST WISHES
DICK
Fred Bear 1983

No celebrity – movie star or politician – signs their own name to the thousands of photographs they give to their fans (unless they are retired athletes who are paid to appear and sign their name). In public, world famous archer and bowhunter Fred Bear would sign almost anything: bows, shirts, photos and, with enormous glee, the breasts of gullible ladies. In private, however, it was understood at Bear Archery that Fred had his secretary sign thousands of photos for him. Is this signature then a fake?

"In 1988-89 the prices went through the ceiling and crashed the next year as the rolling recession of the 1990-93 period started. With the Asian and Russian economies crashing in 1998 [and ultimately rebounding] we may see the same results sooner than later.

"Collecting is a mind game. Without the perception, in your mind, that something has value then there is none. What is the intrinsic value of a wood fishing lure? Well, we're back to the $5 lure."

– Michael Echols, writing for Gabby Talkington's www.antiquelures.com With permission.)

Perhaps it is the same in every collecting field. A group gets together for a beer and talk turns to "what Dad did in the war." The next time they have a neighborhood Bar-B-Q someone brings an old Nazi battle pennant and soon, someone else brings the Luger that his father smuggled home from Germany. Then someone buys a book such as the annual *Standard Catalog of Firearms*[1] or does an Internet search for "gun collecting" and a whole new pod of collectors springs to life.

The men and women in this hypothetical neighborhood group illustrate an excellent way to get started in collecting – start or become part of a group. One person's interest feeds that of another and enthusiasm, stories, good purchases and even screw-ups become a commonly shared experience. A quiet competitiveness is naturally awakened within the group.

While joining a club or hanging out with other collectors is a great way to get started, there is really no "wrong" way to begin (unless it is to rush out and buy something impulsively). Nevertheless, most collectors, writers and gun experts suggest that to get involved in collecting with the objective to make money buying and selling guns as investments is close to the wrong way. Becoming a "gun trader" involves an entirely different motivation and methodology, one that is strictly mercantile, commodity oriented.

While collecting values tend to be stable to gradually increasing – after all, as Mark Twain is supposed to have quipped about land, they are not making any more Model 1, First Type Smith & Wes-

It was a myth, perhaps one that fans of Old West stories want to believe, but dime novelist Ned Buntline never had these guns built for the Earps…or what was left of the Earps after the fallout from the OK Corral incident. Legend has it that Buntline presented special order Colt revolvers with 12-inch barrels and detachable shoulder stocks to Wyatt Earp, Bat Masterson and other noted Old West celebrities. Based on this story, the long-barreled Peacemakers came to be called "Buntline Specials." Uberti makes them now, with incredible 18-inch barrels, but are they really "reproductions?" Buntline wrote the sort of turn-of-the-century Dime Novel that popularized the gun as a method for settling arguments and made heroes – famous and infamous – out of many of the cutthroats, neer-do-wells and rascals who flooded west toward America's frontier. *(Courtesy Autry National Center)*

son .22s, for example (Or are they? Does one count a reproduction?) – those same values can be volatile and swings in the marketplace are as notorious as swings in the stock market. (Former Hoyt-USA president Joe Johnston recalls that the archery company got a terrific, although temporary boost when Sylvester Stallone used their product in his first Rambo movie in 1882.)

On the one hand, Nevada Colt collector Ed Cox warns, nothing is assured in the world of collecting. The generation of kids who grew up playing cowboys and Indians, the ones who are especially in love with cowboy action shooting and collecting antique Colt SAAs, are getting "along in years" now and whether the next generation wants these old guns is anyone's guess. (When members of the next generation arrive at their 50s, they may collect vintage iPods!)

But on the other hand Cox notes that, "If I had put my dollar in a savings account in the bank, it would never be worth $1,300. By buying the antique gun, though, it would surely go up in value. If I'd bought an antique gun when I was a kid the value would be $1,800-$2,500 now."

Florida's Norm Flayderman believes that gun collecting has so far been isolated from dramatic market swings because it has not attracted hordes of "investors," people hoping literally to get rich quick, the

Warren Buffets trying to corner the market on silver, for instance. What has given the antique or collectible gun market its continuing viability is that collectors know the guns and have an interest in them other than strictly their monetary value. Thus, as the economy swings, the gun market tends to remain steady to increasing – again, because the field is saturated with true collectors rather than investors who, Flayderman notes, "purchase only for the sake of financial gain with no appreciation for the arms themselves."

The Six Rules Of Smart Collecting

1) Read and Learn. The rules of satisfying collecting are perhaps everywhere the same. They begin with identifying your interest and – before collecting any firearms – collecting information, building a storehouse of knowledge. If you are enticed into the field by the romance of the American Frontier era and enjoy looking at old Colt firearms, your first purchase might be Doc O'Meara's book on the Colt SAA.[2] O'Meara's book will both inspire you to collect and alert you to some of the nuances of the field, Bisleys to Buntlines.

There are many steps to building a fine gun collection, but the first and perhaps most important is to find your specific interest, perhaps in a specific gun or era or even a particular style of shooting.

Developing a fine gun collection can bring problems greater than worrying about undisclosed alterations to a purchase. Insurance and passive security systems plus a cautious approach to talking about your treasures is well advised.

The more you read and learn, the easier it will be to narrow your interest and objective when you get that itch to write out a check. And the more secure you will feel when you return home without that sulkingly familiar "buyer's remorse." Every bookstore has an outdoor section that contains a sample of gun books, but the best references for these invaluable collector's aids can be found online with a minimum of searching.

2) Find People with Similar Interests. A second rule of good collecting is to affiliate with others and learn from them...or allow them to learn from you. While any group can exhibit a "flock mentality" and carry you over the edge to a disastrous purchase (the lemming mentality of group-think), there is strength in numbers. Within a group, the new collector can find a mentor and can, in turn, become a mentor. There are quite a few gun-collecting associations and we provide a brief listing of national groups in an Appendix at the end of this book.

Probably less than 1,000 of the Remington Revolving Percussion Rifle were made from about 1866-79 in .36- and .44 caliber. Larger cylinder and extra-long loading lever help identify authentic specimens. Although few were made, slight demand causes sales below $2,000 if in good condition. *(This is a recreation from Traditions/Pietta.)*

3) Attend Gun Shows. At an early stage, it is a wonderful use of your time to visit local gun shows. Unless they are so designated, local shows will not have many antique firearms, although many curio and relic (C&R) guns and a ton of reproductions will be on view and on sale. Gun shows are a great place to make contacts, to pick up business cards of men and women who may take time with a newcomer, to learn about organizations that provide contacts and information. They are not necessarily good places to make a purchase for a collection, however, because there is simply not time – and there are rarely facilities – to study and to thoroughly examine a gun. For that, one needs reference books, a good magnifying glass, good light and some peace and quiet, time without interruption to look and think; time to just sit and stare at the gun....

4) Avoid Impulse Buys. The fourth rule of good collecting is to avoid the rush to make a purchase. Everyone is, on occasion, struck with the craving to buy now, as in "right now." It is a strain of impatience that runs deep in the male species, men generally possessing the pro-buying, anti-shopping gene. Generally speaking, if something looks too good to be true, it probably is. Today, the field of American firearms holds many questions, but few surprises.

Still, every serious gun collector has a story about making an impulse decision to buy a firearm without thoroughly examining it or questioning its owner. It happens when one is distracted and can happen to an expert as well as a newbie. The field is littered – some say heavily – with altered and even downright faked firearms, and so when the impulse rises to make a snap decision that will cost hun-

An advertisement from 1878 offers Colt .45 New Model Army revolvers for $20. In good condition today, this black powder cartridge revolver might bring $10,000-$12,000. *(Library of Congress Digital File cph 3c10403)*

CARTRIDGE REVOLVING PISTOL.

The Drawing is one-half the size of the Pistol.

cal. .45 inch.   PRICE $20,00.

Sophisticated modern manufacturing techniques make this modern United States Fire Arms Custer .45 almost indistinguishable from the real thing of 130+ years ago.

dreds or perhaps thousands of dollars, your best course of action is to walk away. Ninety-nine percent of the time this will be the correct long-term decision.

The 16th Pennsylvania Volunteers kneeling, with rifles raised, in the Spanish-American War. This stereopticon photograph may have been taken strictly for public relations purposes, but as late as 1898 units of the U.S. Army were still using single-shot Springfields. Establishing a military provenance will automatically raise the value of a collectible firearm. *(J. F. Jarvis photo c. 1898, Library of Congress Digital File cph 3c19308)*

5) Make a Test Purchase. While avoiding the impulse buy, it ultimately becomes important to buy...something. As a youngster I wanted a telescope to look at the moon and stars. My father insisted that I read about telescopes first, learn the principles by which the mirrors worked and then once I knew what I was talking about, he said, we would buy a great telescope. Learning somewhat in a vacuum with only pictures and nothing to actually handle, manipulate, enjoy, I found words about objectives lenses and diopters and image stabilization to be terribly frustrating. I never got a telescope and eventually lost interest. I did not want an expensive motor-driven refracting telescope anyway...just something to play around with.

The recollection of that experience, and others since then, have led me to believe that nothing quite beats handling the real thing to stimulate interest. You must have something to "play around with." Only by investing in more than moving our eyes and perhaps our brain, only by making a real purchase can we extend the learning and enjoying experience.

An "exact re-creation." U.S. Fire Arms' Henry Nettleton Cavalry Revolver is "the first in the Government Inspector Series. It is an exact re-creation of the model inspected by Henry Nettleton, U.S. Government inspector of small arms in 1878. *The Nettleton features the exact cartouche branding and hand-stamped markings as the original.* Available only in historically correct 'US Government Cartridge' - 45 Colt, with one-piece walnut grips *[it] ... is an exact number for number re-creation of the original, using exact old style hand numbering.*

"These revolvers feature our Old Armory Bone Case Hardened Frame, Gate & Hammer. Artillery Model has 5 ½" barrel. A special *historically correct* Armory Blue {Military Polish} will be used on all other parts. This is not our standard Salt Bath Finish - Dome Blue. Armory Blue is a *Genuine pre-1900 finish* and is accomplished through the use of sterile parts heated in a forge. Although more costly, Armory Blue provides that *absolutely correct and durable blue.* Also available in Full Nickel Plate with U.S. Government Markings."

Nettleton {H.N.} was a U.S. Government Inspector of small arms produced for the Springfield Armory. He received his commission as Inspector in Springfield, Massachusetts on June 6, 1878. "The Nettletons comprise the most sought after examples of U.S. marked guns today. *We are proud to offer a replica of these exact serial number guns {47056 - 51083} for the experienced shooter and collector. These specific arms have exact Cartouche branding and all correct Inspector Handstamp markings, beveled cylinders & finishes."*

Perhaps it is a version of the "build it and they will come" philosophy. Your first purchase does not have to be expensive; it probably should not be expensive, in fact, but it has to excite you. Stimulate you to want to learn more, see more and, yes, possess more. (Hint: For your first purchase, buy down in desirability, but up in quality or grade.)

6) Build Relationships. Finally, when one has read and looked at pictures as much as one can stand, when one has narrowed one's interest and visited gun shows and even made an initial "test purchase," it is time to establish a relationship with a seller. One of the best ways to avoid being stuck with a turkey is to know the person who is selling to you; know where they will be two weeks after your

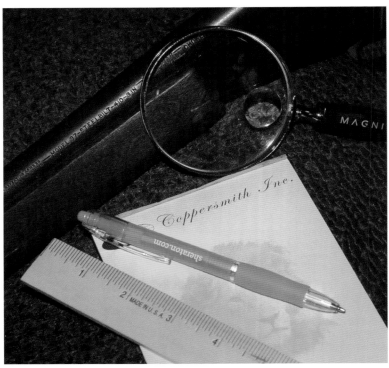

The best tools for the initial study of a collectible gun are a magnifying glass, ruler and good lighting, plus perhaps a ruler to measure the barrel and pen and paper to make notes including markinings, serial number, etc. You will not be able to take a camera into most gun shows, but if the seller is totally legitimate, you might be able to photograph the gun later and then use your reference books before making an offer.

check has cleared. By developing a long term relationship with a seller – whether it is an auction house or a private gun trader,[3] one begins to develop trust.

Replica powder horns and flasks to accent your collection are readily available. Produced to the same standards as the 18th century, they have become a cottage industry in the U.S. and Europe. Having the collectible firearm is a big step in entertaining your friends, but having a similar replica with accoutrements that allow you to fire it adds a whole new world of value to the collecting enterprise.

A serious caution is in order here, however. Even though you may be collecting for fun, money is changing hands and that makes some aspect of collecting a business. If it isn't a business for you, it almost certainly will be for the person who is selling to you and in a business relationship you must, in the words of Ronald Regan, "Trust, but verify." The first time your new best friend approaches with a Confederate Colt, show your interest and ask for the paperwork, the provenance, and for any independent evaluations that might be reasonable. If the seller is legitimate and the product is legitimate as well, your questions and requests for independent authentication will not be offensive.[4] You might also ask for a written, 90-day money-back guarantee. If you are afraid to speak up, you lose.

The Collector vs. the Accumulator

Decide now whether you are a collector or an accumulator, because in the antique field you will hear both terms used as if they are interchangeable; they are not.

Whereas both may be focused on an objective, the collector is specifically interested in a style of gun or a particular manufacturer or an era when a certain type of gun was used, perhaps that moment in time when percussion revolvers were being converted into cartridge guns.

The accumulator, on the other hand, is interested in gathering: a Civil War sword for the fireplace, a replica cannon for the hobby

For the collector who has it all, a replica "Old Ironsides" cannon from the U.S.S. Constitution, now from Traditions (Davide Pedersoli). Authentically styled although scaled down naval carriage and barrel in either .50 or .69/.70 caliber – $230.

farm, and a musket for the office wall. Accumulating is gathering for some other purpose than a focus on an object, and decorating a home can be sufficiently purposeful and fulfilling...it just isn't collecting.

Fakes and the Internet

As a collector, there are many sources for both information, documentation and collec-

Collecting Derringers (or Deringers) would be a fascinating specialty. This vest-pocket .31-caliber replica percussion Derringer from Traditions Firearms is brass with simulated ivory bird's head grips and an authentic spur trigger. "Those snug-fitting vests favored by the infamous riverboat gamblers concealed many a close-range pistol." $158 from Traditions or $2,500 for a first model Colt Deringer.

tor guns. The local firearms dealer often takes collectible guns on consignment, displaying them under the glass counters beside his new H&Ks, Rugers and S&Ws. Another source, of course, and an important one, is within the gun family, other collectors and collector clubs and associations. A minor and, to this collector and writer, sometimes troubling[5] source is the gun show and if an estate sale takes place in your area, they are often filled with curiosities – though rarely with collectible weaponry. There are publications such as *Gun Digest the Magazine*, *Shotgun News* (www.shotgunnews.com), gaveled auctions at companies such as Rock Island Auction Company (www.rockislandauction.com) and James D. Julia Auctioneers and Appraisers (http://juliaauctions.net) and Internet auction sites such as Auction Arms (www.auctionarms.com).

The elephant in the room, of course, is the Internet and much of our retail world has changed within the past dozen years to cope with this worldwide technological phenomenon. Just a few years ago, conventional wisdom said that only low-to-middle quality collectibles were found on the Internet, and for higher end guns one had to work through a gaveled auction. Judging by collectible offerings at multiple Internet auction sites, this may still be true in essence, but it also appears to be changing.

Internet sites provide everything these days except the feel of the gun in your hand. They are flush with photos of guns for sale; descriptions and details. If they are also a gaveled auction with the ability to take telephone or Internet bids, someone on their staff has probably looked over the guns to personally verify the basics of a seller's claims, to give the gun at least a perfunctory authentication. The purpose of the auction is to provide a competitive forum for the seller to maximize his return and, in a sense, for the buyer to confirm that he is getting good value for his money. Once the details are

Close-up of engraved receivers on replica pump-action Colt Lightning rifles from U.S. Fire-Arms. Note that the engraving extends to the first few inches of the octagonal barrels.

At some point, this firearm, built in the spirit of the Colt Hartford English Dragoon, will appear on the market. How would you value it for authenticity, scarcity, condition and demand? A gun produced in commemoration of an event such as the losing Republican ticket for 1996 – Bob Dole, president, and Jack Kemp, vice president – might not hold its value. *(Photo courtesy U.S. FireArms)*

wrapped and the gun is sent to the buyer, an inspection period begins – often three days – during which time the gun can be returned and the buyer's money – less shipping and handling fees – will be returned. Now that is cheap insurance.[6]

(The growth of the Internet, even for sales of firearms through neighborhood FFL holders, is both astonishing and alarming. We speak more to this topic with specific examples in the chapter, "Spotting Fakes.")

Another Viewpoint On Auctions

"Why is an auction the hottest spot for a person to be taken advantage of?" asks Denver firearms expert Joe Cornell.

"They state in unambiguous terms that everything is bought 'as-is' with no warranty expressed or implied – this is every auction house in U.S. – and they even go so far as to say that what the auctioneer says [during his spiel] doesn't matter.

"The auctioneer says before every session, 'Now you are the expert. You buy it – you know what it is and buy as-is, where-is – we don't even pretend to know what it is. When I drop my gavel, you own it.' So everybody at an auction is on their own.

"At least when you talk to a firearms dealer you can ask, 'Is this a straight gun?' And if he's wrong, you can take it back – or sue him."

"USFA's Gunslinger features a genuine 'browning' or patina process that gets better with use. This is not a wipe on/off finish or temporary acid treatment (gray appearance) such as the Italian imports. The Gunslinger antique finish is a process that involves the development of multiple patina layers, each building on the next, aging the surface without pitting the metal. Age and use will only enhance the character of this gun…. This is your great-great-grandfather's gun…fitted with our trademark aged hard rubber grip you'll swear Gunslinger has been around a long time and will become an instant heirloom." Aging techniques like this were unheard-of only a decade ago.

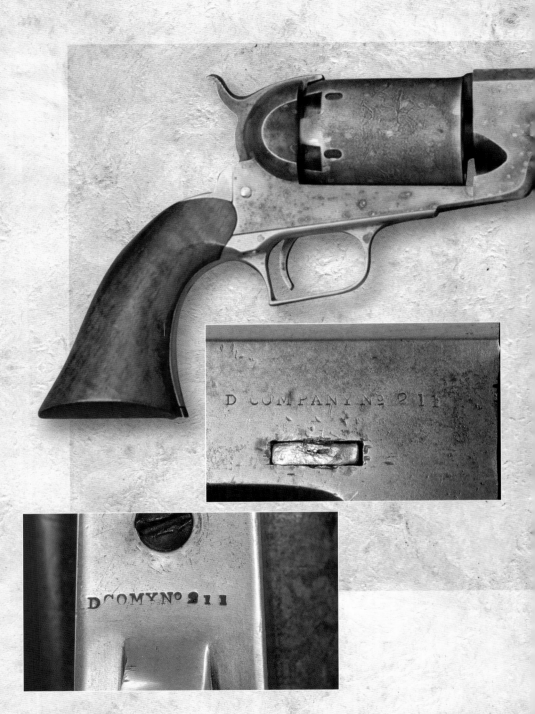

Close-ups from a "rare and desirable" U.S. Colt Walker Model 1847 percussion revolver marked for "D COMPANY" and numbered No. 211. The asking price for this gem of an antique is between $280,000 and $330,000 (Lot 1196) from Rock Island Auction (800-238-8022). With prices such as this for old guns, is it any wonder that fakes and frauds abound in antique Colt firearms? "This outstanding Colt Walker Revolver appears to be completely original except for the period replacement loading lever spring and plunger."

Footnotes

1   Dan Shideler, 2007 *Standard Catalog of Firearms: The Collector's Price & Reference Guide*, 17th Edition A Gun Digest Book for F&W Publications, Iola, WI 2007.

2   "Doc" O'Meara, *Colt's Single Action Army Revolver*, A Gun Digest Book for F&W Publications, Iola, WI 2005.

3   "A gun trader is not a collector, retailer or investor. He will buy any affordable firearm within his area of expertise so long as it meets his criteria for potential short-term profit. He will sell every firearm as soon as his profit objective can be reached, or as soon as it becomes apparent that his objective will not be reached.... The gun trader treats the gun as a marketable commodity...a marvelously interesting, beautiful and enjoyable commodity, but a commodity nonetheless." George Knight, *Successful Gun Trading*, Stoeger Books, Accokeek, MD 2006 (page 2).

4   The prospective collector of guns from the U.S. Civil War needs to take extreme care. "Rare models [of revolvers and pistols] are often faked or pieced together from parts," warns John Graf in Warman's Civil War Collectibles. "High-end purchases should be left to advanced, knowledgeable collectors. Though there are plenty of representative pieces available to collectors, handguns that have a historic provenance proving actual use in the Civil War are rather scarce, and, therefore, much more expensive. Provenance can add hundreds or thousands of dollars to the price of the most mediocre weapon." (page 340).

5   Why is the local gun show a "minor and troubling" source? Why does it have both attractive and repulsive qualities? In the author's experience, for every one genuine antique or collectible firearm displayed at a gun show, the prospective buyer must look over thousands of current and replica firearms often presented in a seemingly haphazard and mind-numbing manner. Guns will be tied to display boards, sometimes with extension chains, and while you may usually pick up a gun to look at it, the clerks behind the tables will hover, often not allowing it to be removed from the wire or chain. There are no facilities for close examination either, no special tables with lights, no reference books, and the aisles will be crowded. Chances are that the placeholder will not have any informative paper – or else he will inundate you with a ton of miscellaneous photocopies – being far too wrapped up in selling new guns and completing the required ATF paperwork. Unless a show is specifically labeled as an antique show or has a special wing or section for antiques, time spent in such an environment may not prove to be of significant value.

The other consideration is that gun shows forbid cameras. While they may have good organizational reasons for such a rule, anytime an organization or activity forbids cameras the author has come to believe that they have something to hide.

Appendix 1

DATA ON COMMONLY-FAKED FIREARMS

WINCHESTER SERIAL NUMBERS

MODEL	SERIAL NUMBER
1866	124995 to 170101
1873	1 to 720496 (N/A 497-610 and 199551-199598)
1876	1 to 63871
Hotchkiss	1 to 84555
1885*	1 to 109999 (N/A 74459-75556)
1886	1 to 156599 (N/A 146000-150799)
1887 & 1901	1 to 72999
1890	1 to 329999 (N/A 20000-29999)
1906	1 to 79999
1892	1 to 379999
1893	1 to 34050
1897	1 to 377999
1894	1 to 353999
1895	1 to 59999
Lee	1 to 19999
1903	1 to 39999
1905	1 to 29078
1906	1 to 79999
1907	1 to 9999
21	1 to 35000

* Single-Shot

COLT'S PATENT FIRE ARMS MANUFACTURING MODEL DATA

COLT PATERSON MODELS

Pocket or Baby Paterson Model No. 1

The Paterson was the first production revolver manufactured by Colt. It was first made in 1837. The Model 1 or Pocket Model is the most diminutive of the Paterson line. The revolver is serial numbered in its own range, #1 through #500. The numbers are not visible without dismantling the revolver. The barrel lengths run from 1.75" to 4.75". The standard model has no attached loading lever. The chambering is .28 caliber percussion and it holds five shots. The finish is all blued, and the grips are varnished walnut. It has a roll-engraved cylinder scene, and the barrel is stamped "Patent Arms Mfg. Co. Paterson N.J. Colt's Pt."

Belt Model Paterson No. 2

The Belt Model Paterson is a larger revolver with a straight-grip and an octagonal barrel that is 2.5" to 5.5" in length. It is chambered for .31 caliber percussion and holds five shots. The finish is all blued, with varnished walnut grips and no attached loading lever. It has a roll-engraved cylinder scene, and the barrel is stamped "Patent Arms Mfg. Co. Paterson N.J. Colt's Pt." The serial number range is #1-#850 and is shared with the #3 Belt Model. It was made from 1837-1840.

Belt Model Paterson No. 3

This revolver is quite similar to the Model #2 except that the grips are curved outward at the bottom to form a more handfilling configuration. They are serial numbered in the same #1-#850 range. Some attached loading levers have been noted on this model, but they are extremely rare and would add approximately 35 percent to the value.

Ehlers Model Pocket Paterson

John Ehlers was a major stockholder and treasurer of the Patent Arms Mfg. Co. when it went bankrupt. He seized the assets and inventory. These revolvers were Pocket Model Patersons that were not finished at the time. Ehlers had them finished and marketed them. They had an attached loading lever, and the abbreviation "Mfg Co." was deleted from the barrel stamping. There were 500 revolvers involved in the Ehlers variation totally, and they were produced from 1840-1843.

Ehlers Belt Model Paterson

The same specifications apply to this larger revolver as they do to the Ehlers Pocket Model. It falls within the same 500 revolver involvement and is rare.

Texas Paterson Model No. 5

This is the largest and most sought after of the Paterson models. It is also known as the Holster Model. It has been verified as actually seeing use by both the military and civilians on the American frontier. It is chambered for .36 caliber percussion, holds five shots, and has an octagonal barrel that ranges from 4" to 12" in length. It has been observed with and without the attached loading lever, but those with it are rare. The finish is blued, with a case-colored hammer. The grips are varnished walnut. The cylinder is roll-engraved; and the barrel is stamped "Patent Arms Mfg. Co. Paterson, N.J. Colts Pt." Most Texas Patersons are well used and have a worn appearance. One in excellent or V.G. condition would be highly prized. A verified military model would be worth a great deal more than standard, so qualified appraisal would be essential. The serial number range is #1-#1000, and they were manufactured from 1838-1840. The attached loading lever brings approximately a 25 percent premium.

COLT REVOLVING LONG GUNS 1837-1847

First Model Ring Lever Rifle

This was actually the first firearm manufactured by Colt; the first revolver appeared a short time later. There were 200 of the First Models made in 1837 and 1838. The octagonal barrel of the First Model is 32" long and browned, while the rest of the finish is blued. The stock is varnished walnut with a cheekpiece inlaid with Colt's trademark. The ring lever located in front of the frame is pulled to rotate the 8-shot cylinder and cock the hammer. The rifle is chambered for .34, .36, .38, .40, and .44 caliber percussion. The cylinder is roll-engraved, and the barrel is stamped "Colt's Patent/Patent Arms Mfg. Co., Paterson, N. Jersey." This model has a top strap over the cylinder. They were made both with and without an attached loading lever. The latter is worth approximately 10 percent more.

Second Model Ring Lever Rifle

This model is quite similar in appearance to the First Model. Its function is identical. The major difference is the absence of the top strap over the cylinder. It had no trademark stamped on the cheekpiece. The Second Model is offered with a 28" and a 32" octagonal barrel and is chambered for .44 caliber percussion, holding 8 shots. There were approximately 500 produced from 1838-1841. The presence of an attached cheekpiece would add approximately 10 percent to the value.

Model 1839 Shotgun

This model is quite similar in appearance to the 1839 Carbine. It is chambered for 16 gauge and holds six shots. It has a Damascus pattern barrel, and the most notable difference is a 3.5" (instead of a 2.5") long cylinder. There were only 225 of these made from 1839-1841. The markings are the same as on the Carbine.

Model 1839 Carbine

This model has no ring but features an exposed hammer for cocking and rotating the 6-shot cylinder. It is chambered for .525 smoothbore and comes standard with a 24" round barrel. Other barrel lengths have been noted. The finish is blued, with a browned barrel and a varnished walnut stock. The cylinder is roll-engraved, and the barrel is stamped "Patent Arms Mfg. Co. Paterson, N.J.-Colt's Pt." There were 950 manufactured from 1838-1841. Later variations of this model are found with the attached loading lever standard, and earlier models without one would bring approximately 25 percent additional. There were 360 purchased by the military and stamped "WAT" on the stock. These would be worth twice what a standard model would bring.

Model 1839/1850 Carbine

In 1848 Colt acquired a number of Model 1839 Carbines (approximately 40) from the state of Rhode Island. In an effort to make them marketable they were refinished and the majority fitted with plain cylinders (brightly polished) having integral ratchets around the arbor hole.

Barrel length 24"; caliber .525; barrel browned; cylinder polished; frame blued; furniture case hardened; walnut stock varnished.

Model 1854 Russian Contract Musket

In 1854 Colt purchased a large number of U.S. Model 1822 flintlock muskets that the company altered to percussion cap ignition and rifled. The reworked muskets are dated 1854 on the barrel tang and at the rear of the lockplate. In most instances the original manufactory marks, such as Springfield or Harpers Ferry at the rear of the lockplate, have been removed, while the U.S. and eagle between the hammer and bolster remain. The percussion nipple bolster is marked COLT'S PATENT. Some examples have been noted with the date 1858.

Barrel length 42"; caliber .69; lock and furniture burnished bright; walnut stock oil finished. Breech-loading examples made in two styles are also known. Production of this variation is believed to have only taken place on an experimental basis.

COLT WALKER-DRAGOON MODELS

Walker Model Revolver

The Walker is a massive revolver. It weighs 4 lbs., 9 oz. and has a 9" part-round/part-octagonal barrel. The cylinder holds six shots and is chambered for .44 caliber percussion. There were 1,000 Walker Colts manufactured in 1847, and nearly all of them saw extremely hard use. Originally this model had a roll-engraved cylinder, military inspection marks, and barrel stamping that read "Address Saml. Colt-New York City." Practically all examples noted have had these markings worn or rusted beyond recognition. Because the Walker is perhaps the most desirable and sought-after Colt from a collector's standpoint and because of the extremely high value of a Walker in any condition, qualified appraisal is definitely recommended. These revolvers were serial numbered A, B, C, and D Company 1-220, and E Company 1-120.

Civilian Walker Revolver

This model is identical to the military model but has no martial markings. They are found serial numbered 1001 through 1100.

Whitneyville Hartford Dragoon

This is a large, 6-shot, .44 caliber percussion revolver. It has a 7.5" part-round/part-octagonal barrel. The frame, hammer, and loading lever are case colored. The remainder is blued, with a brass trigger guard and varnished walnut grips. There were only 240 made in late 1847. The serial numbers run from 1100-1340. This model is often referred to as a Transitional Walker. Some of the parts used in its manufacture were left over from the Walker production run. This model has a roll-engraved cylinder scene, and the barrel is stamped "Address Saml. Colt New York-City." This is an extremely rare model.

Walker Replacement Dragoon

This extremely rare Colt (300 produced) is sometimes referred to as the "Fluck" in memory of the gentleman who first identified it as a distinct and separate model. They were produced by Colt as replacements to the military for Walkers that were no longer fit for service due to mechanical failures. They were large, 6-shot, .44 caliber percussion revolvers with 7.5" part-round/part-octagonal barrels. Serial numbers ran from 2216 to 2515. The frame, hammer, and loading lever are case-colored; the remainder, blued, The grips, which are longer than other Dragoons and similar to the Walkers, are of varnished walnut and bear the inspectors mark "WAT" inside an oval cartouche on one side and the letters "JH" on the other. The frame is stamped "Colt's/ Patent/U.S." The letter "P" appears on various parts of the gun.

First Model Dragoon

Another large, 6-shot, .44 caliber percussion revolver. It has a 7.5" part-round/part-octagonal barrel. The frame, hammer, and loading lever are case colored; the remainder, blued with a brass grip frame and square backed trigger guard. The trigger guard is silver-plated on the Civilian Model only. Another distinguishing feature on the First Model is the oval cylinder stop notches. The serial number range is 1341-8000. There were approximately 5,000 made. The cylinder is roll-engraved; and the barrel stampings read "Address Saml. Colt, New York City." "Colt's Patent" appears on the frame. On Military Models the letters "U.S." also appear on the frame.

Second Model Dragoon

Most of the improvements that distinguish this model from the First Model are internal and not readily apparent. The most obvious external change is the rectangular cylinder-stop notches. This model is serial numbered from 8000-10700, for a total production of approximately 2,700 revolvers manufactured in 1850 and 1851. There is a Civilian Model, a Military Model, and an extremely rare variation that was issued to the militias of New Hampshire and Massachusetts (marked "MS.").

Third Model Dragoon

This is the most common of all the large Colt percussion revolvers. Approximately 10,500 were manufactured from 1851 through 1861. It is quite similar in appearance to the Second Model, and the most obvious external difference is the round trigger guard. The Third Model Dragoon was the first Colt revolver available with a detachable shoulder stock. There are three basic types of stocks, and all are quite rare as only 1,250 were produced. There are two other major variations we will note—the "C.L." Dragoon, which was a militia-issued model and is rare, and the late-issue model with an 8" barrel. These are found over serial number 18000, and only 50 were produced.

Hartford English Dragoon

This is a variation of the Third Model Dragoon. The only notable differences are the British proofmarks and the distinct #1-#700 serial number range. Other than these two features, the description given for the

Third Model would apply. These revolvers were manufactured in Hartford but were finished at Colt's London factory from 1853-1857. Some bear the hand-engraved barrel marking "Col. Colt London." Many of the English Dragoons were elaborately engraved, and individual appraisal would be a must. Two hundred revolvers came back to America in 1861 to be used in the Civil War.

Model 1848 Baby Dragoon

This is a small, 5-shot, .31 caliber percussion revolver. It has an octagonal barrel in lengths of 3", 4", 5", and 6". Most were made without an attached loading lever, although some with loading levers have been noted. The frame, hammer, and loading lever (when present) are case colored; the barrel and cylinder, blued. The grip frame and trigger guard are silver-plated brass. There were approximately 15,500 manufactured between 1847 and 1850. The serial range is between 1-5500. The barrels are stamped "Address Saml. Colt/New York City." Some have been noted with the barrel address inside brackets. The frame is marked "Colt's/Patent." The first 10,000 revolvers have the Texas Ranger/Indian roll-engraved cylinder scene; the later guns the stagecoach holdup scene. This is a popular model, and many fakes have been noted.

Model 1849 Pocket Revolver

This is a small, either 5- or 6-shot, .31 caliber percussion revolver. It has an octagonal barrel 3", 4", 5", or 6" in length. Most had loading gates, but some did not. The frame, hammer, and loading lever are case colored; the cylinder and barrel are blued. The grip frame and round trigger guard are made of brass and are silver plated. There are both large and small trigger guard variations noted. This is the most plentiful of all the Colt percussion revolvers, with approximately 325,000 manufactured over a 23-year period, 1850-1873. There are over 200 variations of this model, and one should consult an expert for individual appraisals. There are many fine publications specializing in the field of Colt percussion revolvers that would be helpful in the identification of the variations. The values represented here are for the standard model.

London Model 1849 Pocket Revolver

Identical in configuration to the standard 1849 Pocket Revolver, the London-made models have a higher quality finish and their own serial number range, 1-11000. They were manufactured from 1853 through 1857. They feature a roll-engraved cylinder scene, and the barrels are stamped "Address Col. Colt/London." The first 265 revolvers, known as early models, have brass grip frames and small round trigger guards. They are quite rare and worth approximately 50 percent more than the standard model that has a steel grip frame and large oval trigger guard.

Model 1851 Navy Revolver

This is undoubtedly the most popular revolver Colt produced in the medium size and power range. It is a 6-shot, .36-caliber percussion revolver with a 7.5" octagonal barrel. It has an attached loading lever. The basic model has a case colored frame hammer, and loading lever, with silver-plated brass grip frame and trigger guard. The grips are varnished walnut. Colt manufactured approximately 215,000 of these fine revolvers between 1850 and 1873. The basic Navy features a roll-engraved cylinder scene of a battle between the navies of Texas and Mexico. There are three distinct barrel stampings—serial number 1-74000, "Address Saml. Colt New York City"; serial number 74001-101000 "Address Saml. Colt. Hartford, Ct."; and serial number 101001-215000 "Address Saml. Colt New York U.S. America." The left side of the frame is stamped "Colt's/ Patent" on all variations. This model is also available with a detached shoulder stock, and values for the stocks today are nearly as high as for the revolver itself. Careful appraisal should be secured before purchase. The number of variations within the 1851 Navy model designation makes it necessary to read specialized text available on the subject.

London Model 1851 Navy Revolver

These revolvers are physically similar to the U.S.-made model with the exception of the barrel address, which reads "Address Col. Colt. London." There are also British proofmarks stamped on the barrel and cylinder. There were 42,000 made between 1853 and 1857. They have their own serial number range, #1-#42,000. There are two major variations of the London Navy, and again a serious purchaser would be well advised to seek qualified appraisal as fakes have been noted.

COLT-ROOT SIDE HAMMER GUNS

Model 1855 Side Hammer "Root" Pocket Revolver

The "Root," as it is popularly known, was the only solid-frame revolver Colt ever made. It has a spur trigger and walnut grips, and the hammer is mounted on the right side of the frame. The standard finish is a case colored frame, hammer, and loading lever, with the barrel and cylinder blued. It is chambered for both .28 caliber and .31 caliber percussion. Each caliber has its own serial number range—1-30000 for the .28 caliber and 1-14000 for the .31 caliber. The model consists of seven basic variations, and the serious student should avail himself of the fine publications dealing with this model in depth. Colt produced the Side Hammer Root from 1855-1870.

1855 Sporting Rifle, 1st Model

This is a 6-shot revolving rifle chambered for .36 caliber percussion. It comes with a 21", 24", 27", or 30" round barrel that is part octagonal where it joins the frame. The stock is walnut with either an oil or a varnish finish. The frame, hammer, and loading lever are case colored; the rest of the metal, blued. The hammer is on the right side of the frame. The 1st Model has no forend, and an oiling device is attached to the barrel underlug. The trigger guard has two spur-like projections in front and in back of the bow. The roll-engraved cylinder scene depicts a hunter shooting at five deer and is found only on this model. The standard stampings are " Colt's Pt./1856" and "Address S. Colt Hartford, Ct. U.S.A."

1855 Half Stock Sporting Rifle

Although this rifle is quite similar in appearance and finish to the 1st Model, there are some notable differences. It features a walnut forend that protrudes halfway down the barrel. There are two types of trigger guards—a short projectionless one or a long model with a graceful scroll. There is a 6-shot model chambered for .36 or .44 caliber or a 5-shot model chambered for .56 caliber. The cylinder is fully fluted. The markings are "Colt's Pt/1856" and "Address Col. Colt/Hartford Ct. U.S.A." There were approximately 1,500 manufactured between 1857 and 1864.

1855 Full Stock Military Rifle

This model holds 6 shots in its .44 caliber chambering and 5 shots when chambered for .56 caliber. It is another side hammer revolving rifle that resembles the Half Stock model. The barrels are round and part-octagonal where they join the frame. They come in lengths of 21", 24", 27", 31", and 37". The hammer and loading lever are case colored; the rest of the metal parts, blued. The walnut buttstock and full length forend are oil finished, and this model has sling swivels. The cylinder is fully fluted. Military models have provisions for affixing a bayonet and military-style sights and bear the "U.S." martial mark on examples that were actually issued to the military. The standard stampings found on this model are "Colt's Pt/1856" and "Address Col. Colt Hartford, Ct. U.S.A." There were an estimated 9,300 manufactured between 1856 and 1864.

1855 Full Stock Sporting Rifle

This model is similar in appearance to the Military model, with these notable exceptions. There is no provision for attaching a bayonet, there are no sling swivels, and it has sporting-style sights. The buttplate is crescent shaped. This model has been noted chambered for .56 caliber in a 5-shot version and chambered for .36, .40, .44, and .50 caliber in the 6-shot variation. They are quite scarce in .40 and .50 caliber and will bring a 10 percent premium. The standard markings are "Colt's Pt/1856" and "Address Col. Colt/Hartford Ct. U.S.A." Production on this model was quite limited (several hundred at most) between the years 1856 and 1864.

Model 1855 Revolving Carbine

This model is similar in appearance to the 1855 Military Rifle. The barrel lengths of 15", 18", and 21" plus the absence of a forend make the standard Carbine Model readily identifiable. The markings are the same. Approximately 4,400 were manufactured between 1856 and 1864.

Model 1855 Artillery Carbine

Identical to the standard carbine but chambered for .56 caliber only, it has a 24" barrel, full-length walnut forend, and a bayonet lug.

Model 1855 British Carbine

This is a British-proofed version with barrel lengths of up to 30". It has a brass trigger guard and buttplate and is chambered for .56 caliber only. This variation is usually found in the 10000-12000 serial number range.

Model 1855 Revolving Shotgun

This model very much resembles the Half Stock Sporting Rifle but was made with a 27", 30", 33", and 36" smoothbore barrel. It has a 5-shot cylinder chambered for .60 or .75 caliber (20 or 10 gauge). This model has a case-colored hammer and loading lever; the rest of the metal is blued, with an occasional browned barrel noted. The buttstock and forend are of walnut, either oil or varnish-finished. This model has no rear sight and a small trigger guard with the caliber stamped on it. Some have been noted with the large scroll trigger guard; these would add 10 percent to the value. The rarest shotgun variation would be a full stocked version in either gauge, and qualified appraisal would be highly recommended. This model is serial numbered in its own range, #1-#1100. They were manufactured from 1860-1863.

Model 1861 Single-Shot Rifled Musket

With the advent of the Civil War, the army of the Union seriously needed military arms. Colt was given a contract to supply 112,500 1861-pattern percussion single-shot muskets. Between 1861 and 1865, 75,000 were delivered. They have 40" rifled barrels chambered for .58 caliber. The musket is equipped with military sights, sling swivels, and a bayonet lug. The metal finish is bright steel, and the stock is oil-finished walnut. Military inspector's marks are found on all major parts. "VP" over an eagle is stamped on the breech along with a date. The Colt address and a date are stamped on the lockplate. A large number of these rifles were altered to the Snyder breech loading system for the Bey of Egypt.

COLT PERCUSSION REVOLVERS

Model 1860 Army Revolver

This model was the third most produced of the Colt percussion handguns. It was the primary revolver used by the Union Army during the Civil War. Colt delivered 127,156 of these revolvers to be used during those hostilities. This is a 6-shot .44 caliber percussion revolver. It has either a 7.5" or 8" round barrel with an attached loading lever. The frame, hammer, and loading lever are case colored; the barrel and cylinder are blued. The trigger guard and front strap are brass, and the backstrap is blued steel. The grips are one-piece walnut. The early models have the barrels stamped "Address Saml. Colt Hartford Ct." Later models are stamped "Address Col. Saml. Colt New-York U.S. America." "Colt's/Patent" is stamped on the left side of the frame; ".44 Cal.," on the trigger guard. The cylinder is roll engraved with the naval battle scene. There were a total of 200,500 1860 Army Revolvers manufactured between 1860 and 1873. The civilian model is found in either 3- or-4 screw variations and it may or may not be cut for a shoulder stock. Civilian models are usually better finished.

Model 1861 Navy Revolver

This model is a 6-shot, 7.5" round-barreled, .36 caliber percussion revolver. The frame, hammer, and attached loading lever are case colored. The barrel and cylinder are blued. The grip frame and trigger guard are silver-plated brass. The grips are of one-piece walnut. The cylinder has the roll-engraved naval battle scene, and the barrel stamping is "Address Col. Saml. Colt New-York U.S. America." The frame is stamped "Colts/Patent" with "36 Cal." on the trigger guard. There are not many variations within the 1861 Navy model designation, as less than 39,000 were made between 1861 and 1873.

Military Model

Marked "U.S." on frame, inspector's cartouche on grip. 650 were marked "U.S.N." on the butt.

Shoulder Stock Model

Only 100 3rd-type stocks were made. They appear between serial #11000-#14000. These are very rare revolvers.

Fluted Cylinder Model

Approximately the first 100 were made with full fluted cylinders.

Model 1862 Pocket Navy Revolver

This is a smaller, 5-shot, .36 caliber percussion revolver that resembles the configuration of the 1851 Navy. It has a 4.5", 5.5", or 6.5" octagonal barrel with an attached loading lever. The frame, hammer, and loading lever are case colored; the barrel and cylinder, blued. The grip frame and trigger guard are silver-plated brass; and the one-piece grips, of varnished walnut. The stagecoach holdup scene is roll-engraved on the cylinder. The frame is stamped "Colt's/Patent"; and the barrel, "Address Col. Saml. Colt New-York U.S. America." There were approximately 19,000 manufactured between 1861 and 1873. They are serial numbered in the same range as the Model 1862 Police. Because a great many were used for metallic cartridge conversions, they are quite scarce today. The London Address Model with blued steel grip frame would be worth more than the standard model.

Model 1862 Police Revolver

This is a slim, attractively designed revolver that some consider to be the most aesthetically pleasing of all the Colt percussion designs. It has a 5-shot, half-fluted cylinder chambered for .36 caliber. It is offered with a 3.5", 4.5", 5.5", or 6.5" round barrel. The frame, hammer, and loading lever are case colored; the barrel and cylinder, blued. The grip frame is silver-plated brass; and the one-piece grips, varnished walnut. The barrel is stamped "Address Col. Saml Colt New-York U.S. America"; the frame has "Colt's/Patent" on the left side. One of the cylinder flutes is marked "Pat Sept. 10th 1850." There were approximately 28,000 of these manufactured between 1861 and 1873. Many were converted to metallic cartridge use, so they are quite scarce on today's market.

The London Address Model would be worth approximately twice the value of the standard model.

COLT METALLIC CARTRIDGE CONVERSIONS

Thuer Conversion Revolver

Although quite simplistic and not commercially successful, the Thuer Conversion was the first attempt by Colt to convert the percussion revolvers to the new metallic cartridge system. This conversion was designed around the tapered Thuer cartridge and consists of a ring that replaced the back part of the cylinder, which had been milled off. This ring is stamped "Pat. Sep. / 15. 1868." The ejection position is marked with the letter "E." These conversions have rebounding firing pins and are milled to allow loading from the front of the revolver. This conversion was undertaken on the six different models listed; and all other specifications, finishes, markings, etc., not directly affected by the conversion would be the same as previously described. From a collectible and investment standpoint, the Thuer Conversion is very desirable. Competent appraisal should be secured if acquisition is contemplated. Found on Models 1849, 1851, 1860, 1861 and 1862.

Richards Conversion, 1860 Army Revolver

This was Colt's second attempt at metallic cartridge conversion, and it met with quite a bit more success than the first. The Richards Conversion was designed for the .44 Colt cartridge and has a 6-shot cylinder and an integral ejector rod to replace the loading lever that had been removed. The other specifications pertaining to the 1860 Army Revolver remain as previously described if they are not directly altered by the conversion. The Richards Conversion adds a breechplate with a firing pin and its own rear sight. There were approximately 9,000 of these Conversions manufactured between 1873 and 1878.

Transition Richards Model

This variation is marked by the presence of a firing pin hammer.

Richards-Mason Conversion, 1860 Army Revolver

This conversion is different from the Richards Conversion in a number of readily apparent aspects. The barrel was manufactured with a small lug much different in appearance than seen on the standard 1860 Army. The breechplate does not have its own rear sight, and there is a milled area to allow the hammer to contact the base of the cartridge. These Conversions were also chambered for the .44 Colt cartridge, and the cylinder holds 6 shots. There is an integral ejector rod in place of the loading lever. The barrels on some are stamped either "Address Col. Saml. Colt New-York U.S. America" or "Colt's Pt. F.A. Mfg. Co. Hartford, Ct." The patent dates 1871 and 1872 are stamped on the left side of the frame. The finish of these revolvers, as well as the grips, were for the most part the same as on the unconverted Armies; but for the first time, nickel-plated guns are found. There were approximately 2,100 of these Conversions produced in 1877 and 1878.

Richards-Mason Conversions 1851 Navy Revolver

These revolvers were converted in the same way as the 1860 Army previously described, the major difference being the caliber .38, either rimfire or centerfire. Finishes are mostly the same as on unconverted revolvers, but nickel-plated guns are not rare.

Richards-Mason Conversion 1861 Navy Revolver

The specifications for this model are the same as for the 1851 Navy Conversion described above, with the base revolver being different. There were 2,200 manufactured in the 1870s.

Model 1862 Police and Pocket Navy Conversions

The conversion of these two revolver models is the most difficult to catalogue of all the Colt variations. There were approximately 24,000 of these produced between 1873 and 1880. There are five basic variations with a number of sub-variations. The confusion is usually caused by the different ways in which these were marked. Depending upon what parts were utilized, caliber markings could be particularly confusing. One must also consider the fact that many of these conversion revolvers found their way into secondary markets, such as Mexico and Central and South America, where they were either destroyed or received sufficient abuse to obliterate most identifying markings. The five basic variations are all chambered for either the .38 rimfire or the .38 centerfire cartridge. All held 5 shots, and most were found with the round roll-engraved stagecoach holdup scene. The half-fluted cylinder from the 1862 Police is quite rare on the conversion revolver and not found at all on some of the variations. The finishes on these guns were pretty much the same as they were before conversion, but it is not unusual to find nickel-plated specimens. Blued models will bring a premium over nickel in the same condition. The basic variations are listed.

Model 1871-1872 Open Top Revolver

This model was the first revolver Colt manufactured especially for a metallic cartridge. It was not a conversion. The frame, 7.5" or 8" round barrel, and the 6-shot cylinder were produced for the .44 rimfire metallic cartridge. The grip frame and some internal parts were taken from the 1860 Army and the 1851 Navy. Although this model was not commercially successful and was not accepted by the U.S. Ordnance Department, it did pave the way for the Single-Action Army that came out shortly thereafter and was an immediate success. This model is all blued, with a case colored hammer. There are some with silver-plated brass grip frames, but most are blued steel. The one-piece grips are of varnished walnut. The cylinder is roll-engraved with the naval battle scene. The barrel is stamped "Address Col. Saml. Colt New-York U.S. America." The later production revolvers are barrel stamped "Colt's Pt. F.A. Mfg. Co. Hartford, Ct. U.S.A." The first 1,000 revolvers were stamped "Colt's/Patent." After that, 1871 and 1872 patent dates appeared on the frame. There were 7,000 of these revolvers manufactured in 1872 and 1873.

COLT DERRINGERS AND POCKET REVOLVERS

First Model Derringer

This is a small all-metal single-shot. It is chambered for the .41 rimfire cartridge. The 2.5" barrel pivots to the left and downward for loading. This model is engraved with a scroll pattern and has been noted blued, silver, or nickel-plated. The barrel is stamped "Colt's Pt. F.A. Mfg. Co./ Hartford Ct. U.S.A/ No.1." ".41 Cal." is stamped on the frame under the release catch. There were approximately 6,500 of this model manufactured from 1870-1890. It was the first single-shot pistol Colt produced.

Second Model Derringer

Although this model has the same odd shape as the First Model, it is readily identifiable by the checkered varnished walnut grips and the "No 2" on the barrel after the address. It is also .41 rimfire and has a 2.5" barrel that pivots in the same manner as the First Model. There were approximately 9,000 of these manufactured between 1870 and 1890.

Third Model Derringer

This model was designed by Alexander Thuer who was also responsible for Colt's first metallic cartridge conversion. It is often referred to as the "Thuer Model" for this reason. It is also chambered for the .41 rimfire cartridge and has a 2.5" barrel that pivots to the right (but not down) for loading. The Third Model has a more balanced appearance than its predecessors, and its commercial success (45,000 produced between 1875 and 1910) reflects this. The barrel on this model is stamped "Colt" in small block letters on the first 2,000 guns. The remainder of the production features the "COLT" in large italicized print. The ".41 Cal." is stamped on the left side of the frame. This model will be found with the barrel blued or plated in either silver or nickel and the bronze frame plated. The grips are varnished walnut.

House Model Revolver

There are two basic versions of this model. They are both chambered for the .41 rimfire cartridge. The 4-shot version is known as the "Cloverleaf" due to the shape of the cylinder when viewed from the front. Approximately 7,500 of the nearly 10,000 House revolvers were of this 4-shot configuration. They are offered with a 1.5" or 3" barrel. The 1.5" length is quite rare, and some octagonal barrels in this length have been noted. The 5-shot round-cylinder version accounts for the rest of the production. It is found with serial numbers over 6100 and is offered with a 2-7/8" length barrel only. This model is stamped on the top strap "Pat. Sept. 19, 1871." This model has brass frames that were sometimes nickel-plated. The barrels are found either blued or plated. The grips are varnished walnut or rosewood. There were slightly fewer than 10,000 of both variations manufactured from 1871-1876.

Open Top Pocket Revolver

This is a .22-caliber rimfire, 7-shot revolver that was offered with either a 2-3/8" or a 2-7/8" barrel. The model was a commercial success, with over 114,000 manufactured between 1871 and 1877. There would undoubtedly have been a great deal more sold had not the cheap copies begun to flood the market at that time, forcing Colt to drop this model from the line. This revolver has a silver or nickel-plated brass frame and a nickel-plated or blued barrel and cylinder. The grips are varnished walnut. The cylinder bolt slots are found toward the front on this model. "Colt's Pt. F.A. Mfg. Co./Hartford, Ct. U.S.A." is stamped on the barrel and ".22 Cal." on the left side of the frame.

New Line Revolver .22

This was the smallest framed version of the five distinct New Line Revolvers. It has a 7-shot cylinder and a 2.25" octagonal barrel. The frame is nickel-plated, and the balance of the revolver is either nickel-plated or blued. The grips are of rosewood. There were approximately 55,000 of these made from 1873-1877. Colt also stopped production of the New Lines rather than try to compete with the "Suicide Specials." "Colt New .22" is found on the barrel; and ".22 Cal.," on the frame. The barrel is also stamped "Colt's Pt. F.A. Mfg.Co./Hartford, Ct. U.S.A."

New Line Revolver .30

This is a larger version of the .22 New Line. The basic difference is the size, caliber, caliber markings, and the offering of a blued version with case colored frame. There were approximately 11,000 manufactured from 1874-1876.

New Line Revolver .32

This is the same basic revolver as the .30 caliber except that it is chambered for the .32-caliber rimfire and .32-caliber centerfire and is so marked. There were 22,000 of this model manufactured from 1873-1884. This model was offered with the rare 4" barrel, and this variation would be worth nearly twice the value of a standard model.

New Line Revolver .38

There were approximately 5,500 of this model manufactured between 1874 and 1880. It is chambered for either the .38 rimfire or .38 centerfire caliber and is so marked. This model in a 4" barrel would also bring twice the value.

New Line Revolver .41

This is the "Big Colt," as it was sometimes known in advertising of its era. It is chambered for the .41 rimfire and the .41 centerfire and is so marked. The large caliber of this variation makes this the most desirable of the New Lines to collectors. There were approximately 7,000 of this model manufactured from 1874-1879. A 4"-barreled version would again be worth a 100 percent premium.

New House Model Revolver

This revolver is similar to the other New Lines except that it features a square-butt instead of the bird's-head configuration, a 2.25" round barrel without ejector rod, and a thin loading gate. It is chambered for the .32 (rare), .38, and the .41 centerfire cartridges. The finish was either full nickel-plated or blued, with a case colored frame. The grips are walnut, rosewood or (for the first time on a Colt revolver) checkered hard rubber, with an oval around the word "Colt." The barrel address is the same as on the other New Lines. The frame is marked "New House," with the caliber. There were approximately 4,000 manufactured between 1880-1886. .32 caliber model would bring a 10 percent premium.

New Police Revolver

This was the final revolver in the New Line series. It is chambered for .32, .38, and .41 centerfire caliber. The .32 and .41 are quite rare. It is offered in barrel lengths of 2.25", 4.5", 5.5", and 6.5". An ejector rod is found on all but the 2.5" barrel. The finish is either nickel or blued and case colored. The grips are hard rubber with a scene of a policeman arresting a criminal embossed on them; thusly the model became known to collectors as the "Cop and Thug" model. The barrel stamping is as the other New Lines, and the frame is stamped "New Police .38." There were approximately 4,000 of these manufactured between 1882-1886.

COLT'S SINGLE-ACTION ARMY REVOLVER

The Colt Single-Action Army, or Peacemaker as it is sometimes referred to, is one of the most widely collected and recognized firearms in the world. With few interruptions or changes in design, it has been manufactured from 1873 until the present. It is still available on a limited production basis from the Colt Custom Shop. The variations in this model are myriad. It has been produced in 30 different calibers and barrel lengths from 2.5" to 16", with 4.75", 5.5", and 7.5" standard. The standard finish is blued, with a case colored frame. Many are nickel-plated. Examples have been found silver- and gold-plated, with combinations thereof. The finest engravers in the world have used the SAA as a canvas to display their artistry. The standard grips from 1873-1883 were walnut, either oil-stained or varnished. From 1883 to approximately 1897, the standard grips were hard rubber with eagle and shield. After this date, at serial number 165000, the hard rubber grips featured the Rampant Colt. Many special-order grips were available, notably pearl and ivory, which were often checkered or carved in ornate fashion. The variables involved in establishing values on this model are extreme. Added to this, one must also consider historical significance, since the SAA played a big part in the formative years of the American West. Fortunately for those among us interested in the SAA, there are a number of fine publications available dealing exclusively with this model. It is our strongest recommendation that they be acquired and studied thoroughly to prevent extremely expensive mistakes. The Colt factory records are nearly complete for this model, and research should be done before acquisition of rare or valuable specimens.

For our purposes we will break down the Single-Action Army production as follows:

Antique or Black Powder, 1873-1898, serial number 1-175000: The cylinder axis pin is retained by a screw in the front of the frame.

Pre-war, 1899-1940, serial number 175001-357859: The cylinder axis pin is retained by a spring-loaded button through the side of the frame. This method is utilized on the following models, as well.

Post-war 2nd Generation, 1956-1978: Serial number 0001SA-99999SA

3rd Generation, 1978-Present: Serial #SA1001 – .

COLT ANTIQUE SINGLE-ACTION ARMY REVOLVERS

1st Year Production "Pinched Frame" 1873 Only

It is necessary to categorize this variation on its own. This is one of the rarest and most interesting of all the SAAs—not to mention that it is the first. On this model the top strap is pinched or constricted approximately one-half inch up from the hammer to form the rear sight. The highest surviving serial number having this feature is #156, the lowest #1. From these numbers, it is safe to assume that the first run of SAAs were all pinched-frame models; but there is no way to tell how many there were, since Colt did not serial number the frames in the order that they were manufactured. An educated guess would be that there were between 50 and 150 pinched frame guns in all and that they were all made before mid-July 1873. The reason for the change came about on the recommendation of Capt. J.R. Edie, a government inspector who thought that the full fluted top strap would be a big improvement in the sighting capabilities of the weapon. The barrel length of the first model is 7.5"; the standard caliber, .45 Colt; and the proper grips were of walnut. The front sight blade is German silver. Needless to say, this model will rarely be encountered; and if it is, it should never be purchased without competent appraisal.

Early Military Model 1873-1877

The serial number range on this first run of military contract revolvers extends to #24000. The barrel address is in the early script style with the # symbol preceding and following. The frame bears the martial marking "US," and the walnut grips have the inspector's cartouche stamped on them. The front sight is steel as on all military models; the barrel length, 7.5". The caliber is .45 Colt, and the ejector rod head is the bull's-eye or donut style with a hole in the center of it. The finish features the military polish and case colored frame, with the remainder blued. Authenticate any potential purchase; many spurious examples have been noted.

Early Civilian Model 1873-1877

This model is identical to the Early Military Model but has no military acceptance markings or cartouches. Some could have the German silver front sight blade. The early bull's-eye ejector rod head is used on this model. The Civilian Model has a higher degree of polish than is found on the military models, and the finish on these early models could be plated or blued with a case colored frame. This model also has a script barrel address. The grips are standard one-piece walnut. Ivory-grip models are worth a premium.

.44 Rimfire Model 1875-1880

This model was made to fire the .44 Henry Rimfire cartridge. It was to be used as a compatible companion sidearm to the Henry and Winchester 1866 rifles that were used extensively during this era. However, this was not the case; and the .44 Rimfire was doomed to economic failure as soon as it appeared on the market. By that time, it had already been established that large-caliber centerfire cartridges were a good deal more efficient than their rimfire counterparts. The large-caliber rimfires were deemed obsolete before this Colt ever hit the market. The result of this was that Colt's sales representatives sold most of the production to obscure banana republics in South and Central America, where this model received much abuse. Most had the original 7.5" barrels cut down; and nearly all were denied even the most basic maintenance, making the survival rate of this model quite low. All this adds to its desirability as a collector's item and makes the risk of acquiring a fake that much greater. This model is unique in that it was the only SAA variation to have its own serial number range, starting with #1 and continuing to #1892, the latest known surviving specimen. The block style barrel markings were introduced during this production run. At least 90 of these revolvers were converted by the factory to .22 rimfire, and one was shipped chambered for .32 rimfire.

Late Military Model 1878-1891

The later Military Models are serial numbered to approximately #136000. They bear the block-style barrel address without the # prefix and suffix. The frames are marked "US," and the grips have the inspector's cartouche. The finish is the military-style polish, case colored frame; and the remainder, blued. Grips are oil-stained walnut. On the military marked Colts, it is imperative that potential purchases be authenticated as many fakes have been noted.

Artillery Model 1895-1903

A number of "US" marked SAAs were returned either to the Colt factory or to the Springfield Armory, where they were altered and refinished. These revolvers have 5.5" barrels and any combination of mixed serial numbers. They were remarked by the inspectors of the era and have a case colored frame and a blued cylinder and barrel. Some have been noted all blued within this variation. This model, as with the other military marked Colts, should definitely be authenticated before purchase. Some of these revolvers fall outside the 1898 antique cutoff date that has been established by the government and, in our experience, are not quite as desirable to investors. They are generally worth approximately 20 percent less.

London Model

These SAAs were manufactured to be sold through Colt's London Agency. The barrel is stamped "Colt's Pt. F.A. Mfg. Co. Hartford, Ct. U.S.A. Depot 14 Pall Mall London." This model is available in various barrel lengths. They are generally chambered for .45 Colt, .450 Boxer, .450 Eley, .455 Eley, and rarely .476 Eley, the largest of the SAA chamberings. A good many of these London Models were cased and embellished, and they should be individually appraised. This model should be authenticated as many spurious examples have been noted.

Frontier Six-Shooter 1878-1882

Several thousand SAAs were made with the legend "Colt's Frontier Six Shooter" acid-etched into the left side of the barrel instead of being stamped. This etching is not deep, and today collectors will become ecstatic if they discover a specimen with mere vestiges of the etched panel remaining. These acid-etched SAAs are serial numbered #45000-#65000. They have various barrel lengths and finishes, but all are chambered for the .44-40 caliber.

Sheriff's or Storekeeper's Model 1882-1898

This model was manufactured with a short barrel (2.5"-4.75"). Most have 4" barrels. It features no ejector rod or housing, and the frame is made without the hole in the right forward section to accommodate the ejector assembly. The Sheriff's or Storekeeper's Model is numbered above serial #73000. It was manufactured with various finishes and chambered for numerous calibers. This model continued after 1898 into the smokeless or modern era. Examples manufactured in the prewar years are worth approximately 20 percent less. Although faking this model is quite difficult, it has been successfully attempted.

Flattop Target Model 1888-1896

This model is highly regarded and sought after by collectors. It is not only rare (only 925 manufactured) but is an extremely attractive and well-finished variation. It is chambered for 22 different calibers from .22 rimfire to .476 Eley. The .22 rimfire, .38 Colt, .41, and .45 Colt are the most predominant chamberings. The 7.5" barrel length is the most commonly encountered. The serial number range is between #127000-#162000. Some have been noted in higher ranges. The finish is all blued, with a case colored hammer. The checkered grips are either hard rubber or walnut. The most readily identifying feature of the flattop is the lack of a groove in the top strap and the sight blade dovetailed into the flattop. The front sight has a removable blade insert. The values given are for a standard production model chambered for the calibers previously mentioned as being the most common. It is important to have other calibers individually appraised as variance in values can be quite extreme.

Bisley Model 1894-1915

This model was named for the target range in Great Britain, where their National Target Matches were held since the nineteenth century. The model was designed as a target revolver with an odd humped-back grip that was supposed to better fill the hand while target shooting. It is also easily identified by the wide low profile hammer spur, wide trigger, and the name "Bisley" stamped on the barrel. The Bisley production fell within the serial number range #165000-#331916. There were 44,350 made. It was offered in 16 different chamberings from .32 Colt to .455 Eley. The most common calibers were .32-20, .38-40, .41, .44-40, and .45 Colt. The barrel lengths are 4.75", 5.5", and 7.5". The frame and hammer are case-colored; the remainder, blued. Smokeless powder models produced after 1899 utilized the push-button cylinder pin retainer. The grips are checkered hard rubber. This model was actually designed with English sales in mind; and though it did sell well over there, American sales accounted for most of the Bisley production.

Bisley Model Flattop Target 1894-1913

This model is quite similar to the Standard Bisley Model, with the flattop frame and dovetailed rear sight feature. It also has the removable front sight insert. It has an all-blued finish with case-colored hammer only and is available with a 7.5" barrel. Smokeless powder models produced after 1899 utilized the push-button cylinder pin retainer. The calibers are the same as the standard Bisley. Colt manufactured 976 of these revolvers. The advice regarding appraisal would also apply.

Standard Civilian Production Models 1876-1898

This final designated category for the black powder or antique

SAAs includes all the revolvers not previously categorized. They have barrel lengths from 4.75", 5.5", and 7.5" and are chambered for any one of 30 different calibers. The finishes could be blued, blued and case colored, or plated in nickel, silver, gold, or combinations thereof. Grips could be walnut, hard rubber, ivory, pearl, stag, or bone. The possibilities are endless. The values given here are for the basic model, and we again strongly advise securing qualified appraisal when not completely sure of any model variation.

COLT PRE-WAR SINGLE-ACTION ARMY REVOLVER 1899-1940

Standard Production Pre-war Models

The 1899 cutoff has been thoroughly discussed, but it is interesting to note that the actual beginning production date for smokeless models was 1900. The pre-war Colts are, all in all, quite similar to the antiques — the finishes, barrel lengths, grips, etc. Calibers are also similar, with the exception of the obsolete ones being dropped and new discoveries added. The most apparent physical difference between the smokeless powder and black powder models is the previously discussed method of retaining the cylinder axis pin. The pre-war Colts utilized the spring-loaded button through the side of the frame. The black powder models utilized a screw in the front of the frame. The values we furnish for this model designation are for these standard models only. The serial number range on the pre-war SAAs is 175001-357859. Note that any variation can have marked effects on value fluctuations, and qualified appraisal should be secured. Note: Scarce chamberings command 30 percent to 100 percent premium.

Long Fluted Cylinder Model 1913-1915

Strange as it may seem, the Colt Company has an apparent credo they followed to never throw anything away. That credo was never more evident than with this model. These Long Flute Cylinders were actually left over from the model 1878 Double-Action Army Revolvers. Someone in the hierarchy at Colt had an inspiration that drove the gunsmiths on the payroll slightly mad: to make these cylinders fit the SAA frames. There were 1,478 of these Long Flutes manufactured. They are chambered for the .45 Colt, .38-40, .32-20, .41 Colt, and the .44 Smith & Wesson Special. They were offered in the three standard barrel lengths and were especially well-polished, having what has been described as Colt's "Fire Blue" on the barrel and cylinder. The frame and hammer are case colored. They are fitted with checkered hard rubber grips and are particularly fine examples of Colt's craft. Rare.

WINCHESTER REPEATING ARMS

Henry Rifle

With the development of B. Tyler Henry's improvements in the metallic rimfire cartridge and his additional improvements in the Volcanic frame, the direct predecessor to the Winchester lever-action repeater was born. The new cartridge was the .44 caliber rimfire, and the Henry rifle featured a 24" octagon barrel with a tubular magazine holding 15 shells. The rifle had no forearm, but was furnished with a walnut butt-stock with two styles of buttplates: an early rounded heel crescent shape seen on guns produced from 1860 to 1862 and the later sharper heel crescent butt found on guns built from 1863 to 1866. The early models, produced from 1860 to 1861, were fitted with an iron frame, and the later models, built from 1861 to 1866, were fitted with brass frames. About 14,000 Henry rifles were made during the entire production period; only about 300 were iron frame rifles.

Martially Inspected Henry Rifles

Beginning in 1863 the Federal Government ordered 1,730 Henry Rifles for use in the Civil War. Most of these government-inspected rifles fall into serial number range 3000 to 4000 while the balance are close to this serial-number range. They are marked "C.G.C." for Charles G. Chapman, the government inspector. These Henry rifles were used under actual combat conditions and for that reason it is doubtful that there are any rifles that would fall into the excellent condition category.

NOTE: There are many counterfeit examples of these rifles. It is strongly advised that an expert in this field be consulted prior to a sale.

Winchester's Improvement Carbine

Overall length 43-1/2"; barrel length 24"; caliber .44 rimfire. Walnut stock with a brass buttplate; the receiver and magazine cover/forend of brass; the barrel and magazine tube blued. The magazine loading port is exposed by sliding the forend forward. This design was protected by O.F. Winchester's British Patent Number 3285 issued December 19, 1865. Unmarked except for internally located serial numbers. Approximately 700 manufactured in December of 1865 and early 1866, the majority of which were sold to Maximilian of Mexico. Prospective purchasers are strongly advised to secure an expert appraisal prior to acquisition.

Model 1866

In 1866 the New Haven Arms Company changed its name to the Winchester Repeating Arms Company. The first firearm to be built under the Winchester name was the Model 1866. This first Winchester was a much-improved version of the Henry. A new magazine tube developed by Nelson King, Winchester's plant superintendent, was a vast improvement over the slotted magazine tube used on the Henry and its predecessor. The old tube allowed dirt to enter through the slots and was weakened because of it. King's patent, assigned to Winchester, featured a solid tube that was much stronger and reliable. His patent also dealt with an improved loading system for the rifle. The rifle now featured a loading port on the right side of the receiver with a spring-loaded cover. The frame continued to be made from brass. The Model 1866 was chambered for the .44 caliber Flat Rimfire or the .44 caliber Pointed Rimfire. Both cartridges could be used interchangeably.

The barrel on the Model 1866 was marked with two different markings. The first, which is seen on early guns up to serial number 23000, reads "HENRY'S PATENT-OCT. 16, 1860 KING'S PATENT-MARCH 29, 1866." The second marking reads, "WINCHESTER'S-REPEATING-ARMS.NEW HAVEN, CT. KING'S-IMPROVEMENT-PATENTED MARCH 29, 1866 OCTOBER 16, 1860."

There are three basic variations of the Model 1866:

1) Sporting Rifle round or octagon barrel. Approximately 28,000 were produced.

2) Carbine round barrel. Approximately 127,000 were produced.

3) Musket round barrel. Approximately 14,000 were produced.

The rifle and musket held 17 cartridges, and the carbine had a capacity of 13 cartridges. Unlike the Henry, Model 1866s were fitted with a walnut forearm. The Model 1866 was discontinued in 1898 with approximately 170,000 guns produced. The Model 1866 was sold in various special order configurations, such as barrels longer or shorter than standard, including engraved guns. The prices listed represent only standard-model 1866s. For guns with special-order features, an independent appraisal from an expert is highly recommended.

First Model

This first style has both the Henry and King patent dates stamped on the barrel, a flat-loading port cover, and a two-screw upper tang. Perhaps the most distinctive feature of the First Model is the rapid drop at the top rear of the receiver near the hammer. This is often referred to as the "Henry Drop," a reference to the same receiver drop found on the Henry rifle. First Models will be seen up through the 15000 serial number range.

Second Model

The second style differs from the first most noticeably in its single screw upper tang and a flare at the front of the receiver to meet the forearm. The Second Model also has a more gradual drop at the rear of the receiver than the First Model. The Second Style Model 1866 appears through serial number 25000.

Third Model

The third style's most noticeable characteristic is the more moderately curved receiver shape at the rear of the frame. The serial number is now stamped in block numerals behind the trigger, thus allowing the numbers to be seen for the first time without removing the stock. The barrel marking is stamped with the Winchester address. The Third Model is found between serial numbers 25000 and 149000. For the first time, a musket version was produced in this serial-number range.

Fourth Model

The fourth style has an even less pronounced drop at the top rear of the frame, and the serial number is stamped in script on the lower tang under the lever. The Fourth Model is seen between serial number 149000 and 170100 with the late guns having an iron buttplate instead of brass.

Model 1866 Iron Frame Rifle Musket

Overall length 54-1/2"; barrel length 33-1/4"; caliber .45 centerfire. Walnut stock with case hardened furniture, barrel burnished bright, the receiver case hardened. The finger lever catch mounted within a large bolster at the rear of the lever. Unmarked except for serial numbers that appear externally on the receiver and often the buttplate tang. Approximately 25 made during the early autumn of 1866. Prospective purchasers are strongly advised to secure an expert appraisal prior to acquisition.

Model 1866 Iron Frame Swiss Sharpshooters Rifle

As above, but in .41 Swiss caliber and fitted with a Scheutzen style stock supplied by the firm of Weber Ruesch in Zurich. Marked Weber Ruesch, Zurich on the barrel and serial numbered externally. Approximately 400 to 450 manufactured in 1866 and 1867. Prospective purchasers are strongly advised to secure an expert appraisal prior to acquisition. Model 1867 Iron Frame Carbine

Overall length 39-1/4"; barrel length 20"; caliber .44 rimfire. Walnut stock with case hardened furniture; the barrel and magazine tube blued; the receiver case hardened. The finger lever catch mounted within the rear curl of the lever. Unmarked except for serial numbers that appear externally on the receiver and often the buttplate tang. Approximately 20 manufactured. Prospective purchasers are strongly advised to secure an expert appraisal prior to acquisition.

Model 1868 Iron Frame Rifle Musket

Overall length 49-1/2" (.455 cal.), 50-1/2" or 53" (.45 and .47 cal.); barrel length 29-1/2" (.455 cal.) and 30-1/4" or 33" (.45 and .47 cal.); calibers .45, .455, and .47 centerfire. Walnut stock with case hardened or burnished bright (.45 and .47 cal.) furniture; the barrel burnished bright; the receiver case hardened or burnished bright (.45 and .47 cal.). The finger lever catch mounted on the lower receiver tang. The rear of the finger lever machined with a long flat extension on its upper surface. Unmarked except for serial number. Approximately 30 examples made in .45 and .455 caliber and 250 in .47 caliber. Prospective purchasers are strongly advised to secure an expert appraisal prior to acquisition.

Model 1868 Iron Frame Carbine

Overall length 40"; barrel length 20"; caliber .44 centerfire. Walnut stock with case hardened furniture; barrel and magazine tube blued; the receiver case hardened. The finger lever catch as above. Unmarked except for serial numbers (receiver and buttplate tang). Approximately 25 manufactured. Prospective purchasers are strongly advised to secure an expert appraisal prior to acquisition.

Model 1873

This Winchester rifle was one of the most popular lever-actions the company ever produced. This is the "gun that won the West" and with good reason. It was chambered for the more powerful centerfire cartridge, the .44-40. Compared to the .44 Henry, this cartridge was twice as good. With the introduction of the single-action Colt pistol in 1878, chambered for the same cartridge, the individual had the convenience of a pistol for protection and the accuracy of the Winchester for food and protection. The .44-40 was the standard cartridge for the Model 1873. Three additional cartridges were offered but were not as popular as the .44. The .38-40 was first offered in 1879 and the .32-20 was introduced in 1882. In 1884 the Model 1873 was offered in .22 caliber rimfire, with a few special order guns built in .22 extra long rimfire. Approximately 19,552 .22 caliber Model 1873s were produced.

Early Model 1873s were fitted with an iron receiver until 1884, when a steel receiver was introduced. The Model 1873 was offered in three styles:

1) Sporting Rifle, 24" round, octagon, or half-octagon barrel. Equipped standard with a crescent iron buttplate, straight-grip stock and capped forearm.

2) Carbine, 20" round barrel. Furnished standard with a rounded iron buttplate, straight-grip stock, and carbine style forend fastened to the barrel with a single barrel band.

3) Musket, 30" round barrel. Standard musket is furnished with a nearly full-length forearm fastened to the barrel with three barrel bands. The buttstock has a rounded buttplate.

The upper tang was marked with the model designation and the serial number was stamped on the lower tang. Caliber stampings on the Model 1873 are found on the bottom of the frame and on the breech end of the barrel. Winchester discontinued the Model 1873 in 1919, after producing about 720,000 guns.

The Winchester Model 1873 was offered with a large number of extra-cost options that greatly affect the value of the gun. For example, Winchester built two sets of special Model 1873s: the 1-of-100 and the 1-of-1000. Winchester sold only eight 1-of-100 Model 1873s, and 136 of the 1-of-1000 guns that were built. In 1991 a few of these special guns were sold at auction and brought prices exceeding $75,000. The prices listed here are for standard guns only. For Model 1873 with special features, it is best to secure an expert appraisal. Model 1873s with case colored receivers will bring a premium.

First Model

The primary difference between the various styles of the Model 1873 is found in the appearance and construction of the dust cover. The First Model has a dust cover held in place with grooved guides on either side. A checkered oval finger grip is found on top of the dust cover. The latch that holds the lever firmly in place is anchored into the lower tang with visible threads. On later First Models, these threads are not visible. First Models appear from serial number 1 to about 31000.

Second Model

The dust cover on the Second Model operates on one central guide secured to the receiver with two screws. The checkered oval finger grip is still used, but on later Second Models this is changed to a serrated finger grip on the rear of the dust cover. Second Models are found in the 31000 to 90000 serial number range.

Third Model

The central guide rail is still present on the Third Model, but it is now integrally machined as part of the receiver. The serrated rear edges of the dust cover are still present on the Third Model.

Model 1873 .22 Rimfire Rifle

Winchester's first .22 caliber rifle and the first .22 caliber repeating rifle made in America was introduced in 1884 and discontinued in 1904. Its drawback was the small caliber. The general preference during this period of time was for the larger-caliber rifles. Winchester sold a little more than 19,000 .22 caliber Model 1873s.

Model 1876

Winchester's Model 1876, sometimes referred to as the Centennial Model, was the company's response to the public's demand for a repeater rifle capable of handling larger and more potent calibers. Many single-shot rifles were available at this time to shoot more powerful cartridges, and Winchester redesigned the earlier Model 1873 to answer this need. The principal changes made to the Model 1873 were a larger and stronger receiver to handle more powerful cartridges. Both the carbine and the musket had their forearms extended to cover the full length of the magazine tube. The carbine barrel was increased in length from 20" to 22", and the musket barrel length was increased from 30 to 32". The Model 1876 was the first Winchester to be offered with a pistol-grip stock on its special Sporting Rifle. The Model 1876 was available in these calibers: .45-77 W.C.F., .50-95 Express, .45-60 W.C.F., .40-60 W.C.F. The Model 1876 was offered in four different styles:

1) Sporting Rifle, 28" round, octagon, or half-octagon barrel. This rifle was fitted with a straight-grip stock with crescent iron buttplate. A special sporting rifle was offered with a pistol-grip stock.

2) Express Rifle, 26" round, octagon, or half-octagon barrel. The same sporting rifle stock was used.

3) Carbine, 22" round barrel with full length forearm secured by one barrel band and straight-grip stock.

4) Musket, 32" round barrel with full-length forearm secured by one barrel band and straight-grip stock. Stamped on the barrel is the Winchester address with King's patent date. The caliber marking is stamped on the bottom of the receiver near the magazine tube and the breech end of the barrel. Winchester also furnished the Model 1876 in 1-of-100 and 1-of-1000 special guns. Only 8 1-of-100 Model 1876s were built and 54 1-of-1000 76s were built. As with their Model 1873 counterparts, these rare guns often sell in the $75,000 range or more. Approximately 64,000 Model 1876s were built by Winchester between 1876 and 1897.

First Model

As with the Model 1873, the primary difference in model types lies in the dust cover. The First Model has no dust cover and is seen between serial number 1 and 3000.

Second Model

The Second Model has a dust cover with guide rail attached to the receiver with two screws. On the early Second Model an oval finger guide is stamped on top of the dust cover while later models have a serrated finger guide along the rear edge of the dust cover. Second Models range from serial numbers 3000 to 30000.

Northwest Mounted Police Carbine

The folding rear sight is graduated in meters instead of yards. Beware of fakes! NOTE: Be very cautious if factory records do not confirm NPW use. A Model 1876 NWP in excellent condition is very rare. Proceed with caution.

Third Model

The dust cover guide rail on Third Model 76s is integrally machined as part of the receiver with a serrated rear edge on the dust cover. Third Model will be seen from serial numbers 30000 to 64000.

Winchester Hotchkiss Bolt-Action Rifle

This model is also known as the Hotchkiss Magazine Gun or the Model 1883. This rifle was designed by Benjamin Hotchkiss in 1876, and Winchester acquired the manufacturing rights to the rifle in 1877. In 1879 the first guns were delivered for sale. The Hotchkiss rifle was a bolt-action firearm designed for military and sporting use. It was the first bolt-action rifle made by Winchester. The rifle was furnished in .45-70 Government, and although the 1884 Winchester catalog lists a .40-65 Hotchkiss as being available, no evidence exists that such a chamber was ever actually furnished. The Model 1883 was available in three different styles:

1) Sporting Rifle, 26" round, octagon, or half-octagon barrel fitted with a rifle-type stock that included a modified pistol grip or straight-grip stock.

2) Carbine, 24" round or 22-1/2" round barrel with military-style straight-grip stock.

3) Musket, 32" or 28" round barrel with almost full-length military-style straight-grip stock. Winchester produced the Model 1883 until 1899, having built about 85,000 guns. NOTE: Beware of military guns "converted" into sporting rifles.

First Model

This model has the safety and a turn button magazine cut-off located above the trigger guard on the right side. The Sporting Rifle is furnished with a 26" round or octagon barrel while the carbine has a 24" round barrel with a saddle ring on the left side of the stock. The musket has a 32" round barrel with two barrel bands, a steel forearm tip, and bayonet attachment under the barrel. The serial number range for the First Model is between 1 and about 6419.

Second Model

On this model the safety is located on the top left side of the receiver, and the magazine cutoff is located on the top right side of the receiver to the rear of the bolt handle. The sporting rifle remains unchanged from the First Model with the above exceptions. The carbine has a 22-1/2" round barrel with a nickeled forearm cap. The musket now has a 28" barrel. Serial number range for the Second Model runs from 6420 to 22521.

Third Model

The Third Model is easily identified by the two-piece stock separated by the receiver. The specifications for the sporting rifle remain the same as before, while the carbine is now fitted with a 20" barrel with saddle ring and bar on the left side of the frame. The musket remains unchanged from the Second Model with the exception of the two-piece stock. Serial numbers of the Third Model range from 22552 to 84555.

Model 1885 (Single-Shot)

The Model 1885 marks an important development between Winchester and John M. Browning. The Single-Shot rifle was the first of many Browning patents that Winchester would purchase and provided the company with the opportunity to diversify its firearms line. The Model 1885 was the first single-shot rifle built by Winchester. The company offered more calibers in this model than any other. A total of 45 centerfire calibers were offered from the .22 extra long to the 50-110 Express, as well as 14 rimfire caliber from .22 B.B. cap to the .44 Flat Henry. Numerous barrel lengths, shapes, and weights were available as were stock configurations, sights, and finishes. These rifles were also available in solid frame and takedown styles. One could almost argue that each of the 139,725 Model 1885s built are unique. Many collectors of the Winchester Single-Shot specialize in nothing else. Beware of rechamberings!

The Model 1885 was offered in two basic frame types:

1) The High Wall was the first frame type produced and is so called because the frame covers the breech and hammer except for the hammer spur.

2) The breech and hammer are visible on the Low Wall frame with its low sides. This frame type was first introduced around the 5000 serial number range.

Both the High Wall and the Low Wall were available in two type frame profiles; the Thickside and the Thinside. The Thickside frame has flat sides that do not widen out to meet the stock. The Thickside is more common on the low wall rifle and rare on the High Walls.

The Thinside frame has shallow milled sides that widen out to meet the stock. Thinside frames are common on High Wall guns and rare on Low Wall rifles.

1) The standard High Wall rifle was available with octagon or round barrel with length determined by caliber. The butt stock and forearm were plain walnut with crescent buttplate and blued frame.

2) The standard Low Wall featured a round or octagon barrel with length determined by caliber and a plain walnut stock and forearm with crescent buttplate.

3) The High Wall musket most often had a 26" round barrel chambered for the .22 caliber cartridge. Larger calibers were available as were different barrel lengths. The High Wall Musket featured an almost full length forearm fastened to the barrel with a single barrel band and rounded buttplate.

4) The Low Wall musket is most often referred to as the Winder Musket named after the distinguished marksman, Colonel C.B. Winder. This model features a Lyman receiver sight and was made in .22 caliber.

5) The High Wall Schuetzen rifle was designed for serious target shooting and was available with numerous extras including a 30" octagon barrel medium weight without rear sight seat; fancy walnut checkered pistol grip Schuetzen-style cheekpiece; Schuetzen-style buttplate; checkered forearm; double set triggers; spur finger lever, and adjustable palm rest.

6) The Low Wall carbine was available in 15", 16", 18", and 20" round barrels. The carbine featured a saddle ring on the left side of the frame and a rounded buttplate.

7) The Model 1885 was also available in a High Wall shotgun in 20 gauge with 26" round barrel and straight-grip stock with shotgun style rubber buttplate. The Model 1885 was manufactured between 1885 and 1920 with a total production of about 140,000 guns.

CALIBER NOTE: As stated above it is difficult to provide pricing on specific rifles, especially calibers, because of the wide range of variables. However, the collector may find it useful to know that the most common rimfire calibers were the .22 Short, .22 WCF, and .22 Long, in that order, with the .22 Long Rifle a distant fourth. The most common centerfire chambers were the .32 WCF and the .32-40. Other popular centerfire calibers were the .38-55, .25-20, .44 WCF, .32 Long WCF, and the .45-70. There were a number of chamberings that are extremely rare (one of each built). It is strongly recommended that research is done prior to a purchase.

Model 1886

Based on a John Browning patent, the Model 1886 was one of the finest and strongest lever-actions ever utilized in a Winchester rifle. Winchester introduced the Model 1886 in order to take advantage of the more powerful centerfire cartridges of the time.

Model 1886 rifles and carbines were furnished with walnut stocks, case hardened frames, and blued barrels and magazine tubes. In 1901 Winchester discontinued the use of case hardened frames on all its rifles and used blued frames instead. For this reason, case hardened Model 1886 rifles will bring a premium. Winchester provided a large selection of extra cost options on the Model 1886, and for rifles with these options, a separate valuation should be made by a reliable source. The Model 1886 was produced from 1886 to 1935 with about 160,000 in production.

The rifle was available in 10 different chambers:

.45-70 U.S. Government............................. .50-110 Express
.45-90 W.C.F. .... .40-70 W.C. F.
.40-82 W.C.F. .... .38-70 W.C. F.
.40-65 W.C.F. 50-100-450
.38-56 W.C.F. .... .33 W.C. F.

The most popular caliber was the .45-70 Government. Prices of the Model 1886 are influenced by caliber, with the larger calibers bringing a premium. The 1886 was available in several different configurations.

1) Sporting Rifle, 26", round, octagon, or half-octagon barrel, full or half magazine and straight-grip stock with plain forearm.

2) Fancy Sporting Rifle, 26", round or octagon barrel, full or half magazine and fancy checkered walnut pistol-grip stock with checkered forearm.

3) Takedown Rifle, 24" round barrel, full or half magazine with straight-grip stock fitted with shotgun rubber buttplate and plain forearm.

4) Extra Lightweight Takedown Rifle, 22" round barrel, full or half magazine with straight-grip stock fitted with shotgun rubber buttplate and plain forearm.

5) Extra Lightweight Rifle, 22" round barrel, full or half magazine with straight-grip stock fitted with a shotgun rubber butt-plate and plain forearm.

6) Carbine, 22" round barrel, full or half magazine, with straight-grip stock and plain forearm.

7) Musket, 30" round barrel, musket-style forearm with one barrel band. Military-style sights. About 350 Model 1886 Muskets were produced.

Model 1892

The Model 1892 was an updated successor to the Model 1873 using a scaled down version of the Model 1886 action. The rifle was chambered for the popular smaller cartridges of the day, namely the .25-20, .32-20, .38-40, .44-40, and the rare .218 Bee. The rifle was available in several different configurations:

1) Sporting Rifle, solid frame or takedown (worth an extra premium of about 20 percent), 24" round, octagon, or half-octagon barrel with 1/2, 2/3, or full magazines. Plain straight-grip walnut stock with capped forearm.

2) Fancy Sporting Rifle, solid frame or takedown (worth 20 percent premium), 24" round, octagon, or half-octagon barrel with 1/2, 2/3, or full magazine. Checkered walnut pistol-grip stock with checkered capped forearm.

3) Carbine, 20" round barrel, full or half magazine, plain walnut straight-grip stock with one barrel band forearm. Carbines were offered only with solid frames.

4) Trapper's Carbine, 18", 16", 15", or 14" round barrel with the same dimensions of standard carbine. Federal law prohibits the possession of rifles with barrel lengths shorter than 16". The Model 1892 Trapper's Carbine can be exempted from this law as a curio and relic with a federal permit providing the trapper is an original trapper and left the factory with the short trapper barrel. Beware of fakes!

5) Musket, 30" round barrel with full magazine. Almost full-length forearm held by two barrel bands. Buttstock is plain walnut with straight grip.

The Model 1892 was built between 1892 and 1932 with slightly more than 1 million sold. The Model 1892 carbine continued to be offered for sale until 1941.

Model 1894

Based on a John M. Browning patent, the Model 1894 was the most successful centerfire rifle Winchester ever produced. This model is still in production, and the values given here reflect those rifles produced before 1964, or around serial number 2550000. The Model 1894 was the first Winchester developed especially for smokeless powder and was chambered for these cartridges: .32-40, .38-55, .25-35 Winchester, .30-30 Winchester, and the .32 Winchester Special. The rifle was available in several different configurations:

1) Sporting Rifle, 26" round, octagon, or half-octagon barrel, in solid frame or takedown. Full, 2/3 or 1/2 magazines were available. Plain walnut straight or pistol-grip stock with crescent buttplate and plain capped forearm.

2) Fancy Sporting Rifle, 26" round, octagon, or half-octagon barrel, in solid frame or takedown. Full, 2/3, or 1/2 magazines were available. Fancy walnut checkered straight or pistol-grip stock with crescent buttplate and checkered fancy capped forearm.

3) Extra Lightweight Rifle, 22" or 26" round barrel with half magazine. Plain walnut straight-grip stock with shotgun buttplate and plain capped forearm.

4) Carbine, 20" round barrel, plain walnut straight-grip stock with carbine style buttplate. Forearm was plain walnut uncapped with one barrel band. Carbines were available with solid frame only. Carbines made prior to 1925 were fitted with a saddle ring on the left side of receiver and worth a premium over carbines without saddle ring.

5) Trapper's Carbine, 18", 16", 15", or 14". Buttstock, forearm, and saddle ring specifications same as standard carbine. Beware of fakes!

All Model 1894s were furnished with blued frames and barrels, although case hardened frames were available as an extra-cost option. Case colored Model 1894s are rare and worth a considerable premium, perhaps as much as 1,000 percent. Guns with extra-cost options should be evaluated by an expert to determine proper value. Between 1894 and 1963, approximately 2,550,000 Model 1894s were sold.

NOTE: Fancy Sporting Rifles were also engraved at the customer's request. Check factory where possible and proceed with caution. Factory engraved Model 1894s are extremely valuable.

Model 1895

The Model 1895 was the first nondetachable box magazine rifle offered by Winchester. Built on a John M. Browning patent, this rifle was introduced by Winchester to meet the demand for a rifle that could handle the new high-power, smokeless hunting cartridges of the period. The Model 1895 was available in these calibers: .30-40 Krag, .38-72 Winchester, .40-72 Winchester, .303 British, .35 Winchester, .405 Government, 7.62 Russian, .30-03, and .30-06. The rifle gained fame as a favorite hunting rifle of Theodore Roosevelt. Because of its box magazine, the Model 1895 has a distinctive look like no other Winchester lever-action rifle.

The rifle was available in several different configurations:

1) Sporting Rifle, 28" or 24" (depending on caliber) round barrel, plain walnut straight-grip stock with plain forend. The first 5,000 rifles were manufactured with flat-sided receivers, and the balance of production were built with the receiver sides contoured. After serial-number 60000, a takedown version was available.

2) Fancy Sporting Rifle, 28" round barrel, fancy walnut checkered straight-grip stock and fancy walnut checkered forearm. Rifles with serial numbers below 5000 had flat sided frames.

3) Carbine, 22" round barrel, plain walnut straight-grip stock with military-style hand guard forend. Some carbines are furnished with saddle rings on left side of receiver. Beware of fakes!

4) Musket: Standard Musket, 28" round, plain walnut straight-grip stock with musket style forend with two barrel bands; U.S. Army N.R.A. Musket, 30" round barrel, Model 1901 Krag-Jorgensen rear sight, stock similar to the standard musket; N.R.A. Musket, Models 1903 and 1906, 24" round barrel with special buttplate; U.S. Army Musket, 28" round barrel chambered for the .30-40 Krag. Came equipped with or without knife bayonet; Russian Musket, similar to standard musket but fitted with clip guides in the top of the receiver and with bayonet. Approximately 294,000 Model 1895 Muskets were sold to the Imperial Russian Government between 1915 and 1916. The first 15,000 Russian Muskets had 8" knife bayonets, and the rest were fitted with 16" bayonets. Beware of fakes!

The Model 1895 was produced from 1895 to 1931 with about 426,000 sold.

SHARPS

Model 1849

A breechloading .44 caliber percussion rifle with a 30" barrel having a wooden cleaning rod mounted beneath it. The breech is activated by the trigger guard lever, and there is an automatic disk-type capping device on the right side of the receiver. The finish is blued and case colored. The stock is walnut with a brass patch box, buttplate, and forend cap. It is marked "Sharps Patent 1848." There were approximately 200 manufactured in 1849 and 1850 by the A.S. Nippes Company.

Model 1850

As above, with a Maynard priming mechanism mounted on the breech. Marked "Sharps Patent 1848" on the breech and the barrel "Manufactured by A.S. Nippes Mill Creek, Pa." The priming device marked "Maynard Patent 1845." There were approximately 200 manufactured in 1850. This model is also known as the 2nd Model Sharps.

Model 1851 Carbine

A single-shot breechloading percussion rifle in .36, .44, or .52 caliber with a 21.75" barrel and Maynard tape priming device. Blued and case hardened with a walnut stock and forearm held on by a single barrel band. The buttplate and barrel band are brass, and the military versions feature a brass patch box. The tang marked "C. Sharps Patent 1848," the barrel "Robbins & Lawrence," and the priming device "Edward Maynard Patentee 1845." Approximately 1,800 carbines and 180 rifles were manufactured by Robbins & Lawrence in Windsor, Vermont, in 1851.

Model 1852

Similar to the above, but with Sharps' Patent Pellet Primer. The barrel marked "Sharps Rifle Manufg. Co. Hartford, Conn." Blued, case hardened, brass furniture and a walnut stock. Manufactured in carbine, rifle, sporting rifle and shotgun form. Approximately 4,600 carbines and 600 rifles were made between 1853 and 1855.

Model 1853

As above, but without the spring retainer for the lever hinge being mounted in the forestock. Approximately 10,500 carbines and 3,000 rifles were made between 1854 and 1858.

Model 1855

As above, in .52 caliber and fitted with a Maynard tape primer that is marked "Edward Maynard Patentee 1845." Approximately 700 were made between 1855 and 1856.

Model 1855 U.S. Navy Rifle

As above, with a 28" barrel, full-length stock and bearing U.S. Navy inspection marks. Approximately 260 were made in 1855.

Model 1855 British Carbine

The Model 1855 with British inspection marks. Approximately 6,800 were made between 1855 and 1857.

SHARPS STRAIGHT BREECH MODELS

Similar to the above models, but with the breech opening cut on an almost vertical angle.

Model 1859 Carbine

Model 1863 Carbine

Model 1865 Carbine

Model 1859 Rifle

Model 1863 Rifle

Without bayonet lug.

Model 1865 Rifle (without bayonet lug)

Sporting Rifle

As above, with octagonal barrels, set triggers and finely figured walnut stocks. The Model 1853 Sporting rifle was built as a special order. About 32 were produced. The Model 1863 Sporting Rifle was also built on special order. About 16 were produced. No two of this model are alike. All reside in museums or collections. Beware of fakes!

Coffee-Mill Model

Some Sharps' carbines were fitted with coffee-mill style grinding devices set into their buttstocks. CAUTION: These arms are exceptionally rare and extreme caution should be exercised prior to purchase. Fakes exist.

Metallic Cartridge Conversions

In 1867 approximately 32,000 Model 1859, 1863 and 1865 Sharps were altered to .52-70 rimfire and centerfire caliber.

Model 1869

A .40-50 to .50-70 caliber model produced in a military form with 26", 28", or 30" barrels; as a carbine with 21" or 24" barrels and in a sporting version with various barrel lengths and a forend stock fitted with a pewter tip. Approximately 650 were made.

Model 1870 Springfield Altered

Chambered for .50-70 caliber and fitted with a 35.5" barrel with two barrel bands, walnut stock, case hardened lock and breechlock. Buttplate stamped "US." Also built for Army trials with 22" barrel converted to centerfire.

Model 1874

This model was manufactured in a variety of calibers, barrel lengths, and stock styles. The barrel markings are of three forms: initially, "Sharps Rifle Manufg. Co. Hartford, Conn."; then, "Sharps Rifle Co. Hartford, Conn."; and finally "Sharps Rifle Co. Bridgeport, Conn." As of 1876 "Old Reliable" was stamped on the barrels. This marking is usually found on Bridgeport-marked rifles only. The major styles of this model are listed.

Military Carbine

.50-70, 21" barrel (460 made).

Military Rifle

In .45-70 and .50-70 centerfire caliber with a 30" barrel and full-length forend secured by three barrel bands. Approximately 1,800 made.

Hunter's Rifle

In .40, .44, .45-70, and .50-70 caliber with 26", 28", or 30" round barrels having open sights. Approximately 600 were manufactured.

Business Rifle

In .40-70 and .45-75 Sharps caliber with a 26", 28", or 30" round barrel, adjustable sights and double-set triggers. Approximately 1,600 manufactured.

Sporting Rifle

Offered in a variety of calibers, barrel lengths, barrel weights, barrel styles and stock styles. Approximately 6,000 were manufactured.

Creedmoor Rifle

With a checkered pistol grip stock, vernier sights, combination wind gauge and spirit level front sight, set trigger and shotgun style butt. Approximately 150 were made.

Mid-Range Rifle

Similar to the above, with a crescent buttplate. Approximately 180 were made.

Long-Range Rifle

As above with a 34" octagonal barrel. Approximately 425 were manufactured.

Schuetzen Rifle

Similar to the above, with a checkered pistol grip stock and forend, a large Schuetzen style buttplate, double-set triggers and a vernier tang sight. Approximately 70 were manufactured. Beware of fakes!

Model 1877

Similar to the Model 1874, and in .45-70 caliber with a 34" or 36" barrel which is marked "Sharps Rifle Co. Bridgeport, Conn. Old Reliable." Approximately 100 were manufactured in 1877 and 1878. Beware of fakes!

Model 1878 Sharps-Borchardt

An internal hammer breechloading rifle manufactured from 1878 to approximately 1880. The frame marked "Borchardt Patent Sharps Rifle Co. Bridgeport Conn. U.S.A."

Military Rifle

Approximately 12,000 were made in .45-70 caliber with 32.25" barrels and full stocks secured by two barrel bands.

Sporting Rifle

Approximately 1,600 were made in .45-70 caliber with 30" round or octagonal barrels.

Hunter's Rifle

Approximately 60 were made in .40 caliber with 26" barrels and plain walnut stocks.

Business Rifle
Approximately 90 were made with 28" barrels in .40 caliber.

Officer's Rifle
Approximately 50 were made in .45-70 caliber with 32" barrels and checkered walnut stocks.

Express Rifle
Approximately 30 were made in .45-70 caliber with 26" barrels, set triggers and checkered walnut stocks.

Short-Range Rifle
Approximately 155 were made in .40 caliber with 26" barrels, vernier rear sights, wind gauge front sight and a checkered walnut stock.

Mid-Range Rifle
Similar to the above, with a 30" barrel. Approximately 250 were manufactured.

Long-Range Rifle
Similar to the above, with different sights. Approximately 230 were manufactured.

REMINGTON

1st Model Remington-Beals Revolver
A .31 caliber 5-shot percussion revolver with a 3" octagonal barrel. The cylinder turning mechanism is mounted on the left outside frame. Blued, case hardened, silver-plated, brass trigger guard and gutta-percha grips. The barrel marked, "F. Beal's Patent, June 24, '56 & May 26, '57" and the frame, "Remington's Ilion, N.Y." Approximately 5,000 were manufactured in 1857 and 1858.

2nd Model Remington-Beals Revolver
A spur trigger .31 caliber 5-shot percussion revolver with a 3" octagonal barrel. Blued, case hardened with a squared gutta-percha grip. The barrel marked, "Beals Patent 1856 & 57, Manufactured by Remingtons Ilion, N.Y." Approximately 1,000 were manufactured between 1858 and 1860.

3rd Model Remington-Beals Revolver
A .31 caliber 5-shot percussion revolver with a 4" octagonal barrel. A loading lever mounted beneath the barrel. Blued, case hardened with gutta-percha grips. The barrel marked, "Beals Pat. 1856, 57, 58 and also "Manufactured by Remingtons, Ilion, N.Y." Approximately 1,500 were manufactured in 1859 and 1860.

Remington-Rider Revolver
A double-action .31 caliber percussion revolver with a 3" barrel and 5-shot cylinder. Most of these revolvers were blued but a few were nickel-plated, case hardened with gutta-percha grips. This model is also encountered altered to .32 rimfire. The barrel marked, "Manufactured by Remingtons, Ilion, N.Y., Riders Pt. Aug. 17, 1858, May 3, 1859." Approximately 20,000 were manufactured between 1860 and 1873.

Remington-Beals Army Revolver

A .44 caliber percussion revolver with an 8" barrel and 6-shot cylinder. Blued, case hardened with walnut grips. The barrel marked "Beals Patent Sept. 14, 1858 Manufactured by Remington's Ilion, New York." Approximately 2,500 were manufactured between 1860 and 1862.

Remington-Beals Navy Revolver

Similar in appearance to Remington-Beals Army Revolver, but in .36 caliber with a 7.5" octagonal barrel. The first examples of this model were fitted with a loading lever that would not allow the cylinder pin to be completely removed. These examples are worth approximately 80 percent more than the standard model. Approximately 1,000 of these revolvers were purchased by the United States government and martially marked examples are worth approximately 40 percent more than the values listed below. Manufactured from 1860 to 1862 with a total production of approximately 15,000.

1861 Army Revolver

A .44 caliber percussion revolver with an 8" octagonal barrel and 6-shot cylinder. The loading lever is cut with a slot so that the cylinder pin can be drawn forward without the lever being lowered. Blued, case hardened with walnut grips. The barrel marked "Patented Dec. 17, 1861 Manufactured by Remington's, Ilion, N.Y." Some examples were converted to .46 caliber rimfire cartridge, and would be worth approximately 25 percent more than the original, martially marked, standard percussion model. Approximately 12,000 were manufactured in 1862. This model is also known as the "Old Army Model."

1861 Navy Revolver

As above, but .36 caliber with a 7.25" octagonal barrel. Blued, case hardened with walnut grips. This model is also found altered to .38 metallic cartridge. Cartridge examples are worth approximately 35 percent less than the percussion versions. Approximately 8,000 were manufactured in 1862.

New Model Army Revolver

A .44 caliber 6-shot percussion revolver with an 8" octagonal barrel. Blued, case hardened with walnut grips. The barrel marked "Patented Sept. 14, 1858 E. Remington & Sons, Ilion, New York, U.S.A. New Model." Approximately 132,000 were made between 1863 and 1873.

New Model Navy Revolver

As above, but .36 caliber with a 7.23" octagonal barrel. Approximately 22,000 were made between 1863 and 1875.

New Model Single-Action Belt Revolver

As above, but with a 6.5" barrel. Blued or nickel-plated, case hardened with walnut grips. This model is sometimes encountered altered to .38 cartridge. Cartridge examples are worth approximately 25 percent less than the values listed below. Approximately 3,000 were made between 1863 and 1873.

Remington-Rider Double-Action Belt Revolver

A double-action .36 caliber percussion revolver with a 6.5" octagonal barrel marked, "Manufactured by Remington's, Ilion, N.Y. Rider's Pt. Aug. 17, 1858, May 3, 1859." Blued or nickel-plated, case hardened with walnut grips. This model is also found altered to cartridge and such examples would be worth approximately 20 percent less than the values listed below. Several hundred of this model were made with fluted cylinders and are worth a premium of about 25 percent. Approximately 5,000 were made between 1863 and 1873.

New Model Police Revolver

A .36 caliber percussion revolver with octagonal barrels ranging from 3.5" to 6.5" and with a 5-shot cylinder. Blued or nickel-plated, case hardened with walnut grips. This model is also found altered to cartridge and such examples would be worth approximately 20 percent less than the values listed below. Approximately 18,000 were manufactured between 1863 and 1873.

New Model Pocket Revolver

A .31 caliber spur trigger percussion revolver with octagonal barrels ranging from 3" to 4.5" in length and a 5-shot cylinder. Blued or nickel-plated, case hardened, walnut grips. The barrel marked, "Patented Sept. 14, 1858, March 17, 1863 E. Remington & Sons, Ilion, New York U.S.A. New Model." Approximately 25,000 were manufactured between 1863 and 1873.

1st Version
Brass frame and trigger.

2nd Version
Iron frame, brass trigger.

3rd Version
Iron frame, iron trigger.

.32 Cartridge Conversion

Appendix 2

SELECTED RESOURCES

SOURCES FOR REPRODUCTION FIREARMS

American Derringer: The world's most powerful pocket pistols. Made in the U.S. www.amderringer.com

Armi Sport [di Chiappa Silvia]: Since 1958 "Armi Sport, the mark on the replicas of muzzle loading and breech loading historical weapons," both rifles and pistols. www.armisport.com, www.chiappafirearms.com or www.armichiappa.com

Brownells: A leading supplier of firearms accessories, gun parts and gunsmithing tools. www.brownells.com

Chaparral Firearms: "Not just a replica," Chaparral says, "but a tribute." Reproduction 19th century Winchesters made in Italy. www.chaparralfirearms.com

Cimarron Firearms: "Detailed copies" of firearms used taming the frontier in Texas and the American West. In business since 1984 and now in partnership with Uberti of Italy, Cimarron is a leader in cowboy action shooting. www.cimarron-firearms.com

Collector's Armoury: Source for reproductions, military collectibles and replica guns, featuring hundreds of Old West, Civil War, etc. gifts and collectibles. www.collectorsarmoury.com/ep5sf/

Colt: Colt's Manufacturing continues to offer pistols, revolvers, rifles and sparte parts. www.coltsfmg.com

Dixie Gun Works: Replica muzzleloading, cartridge firearms and accessories, parts and supplies. www.dixiegun.com

Henry Repeating Arms: Made-in-America rifles from 19th through 21st century. www.henryrepeating.com

Heritage Manufacturing: Importers of replica (and new) firearms and accessories. www.hertiagemfg.com

Navy Arms: Reproduction firearms from the 19th century. www.navyarms.com

Pedersoli [Davide Pedersoli]: Guns that faithfully duplicate models of the American tradition, European history and the independence wars of the Old and New Worlds. www.davide-pedersoli.com

Pietta (F.Lli Pietta): Founded in 1960, produces guns from U.S. mid-19th century, plus new shotgun line. www.pietta.it

Pioneer Arms: Double-barrel 12-gauge hammer shotgun for cowboy action shooting made in the style of the Old West in Poland. www.pioneer-pac.com; also manufacturer of throwing tomahawks, gun locks and other reproductions from the 17th, 18th and 19th century. www.pioneerarms.com

Shiloh Sharps: "...as with original Sharps, our rifles are not intended for the mass market." www.shilohrifle.com

Sturm, Ruger: Single- and double-action black powder revolvers for cowboy action shooting. www.ruger-firearms.com

Super Six: Builds Bison Bull Series six-shooters

Taylor's: Imports black powder 1840s-1892 revolvers, rifles and shotguns. www.taylorsfirearms.com

Thompson/Center: Manufacturer of new and old in the muzzleloading realm. www.tcarms.com

Traditions Performance Firearms: New and old black powder firearms and accessories. www.traditionsfirearms.com

Uberti [A. Uberti]: High quality late 19th century replica revolvers, black powder revolvers, rifles and miniatures. www.uberti.com

U.S. Fire Arms: Guns built in the U.S. in the classic style of the Old West. www.usfirearms.com

NATIONAL CLUBS & ASSOCIATIONS

Colt Collectors Association, P.O. Box 2241, Los Gatos, CA 95031-2241 www.coltcollectorsassoc.com. Founded in 1980 by avid collectors of Colt firearms and memorabilia for the purpose of promoting the collecting of all types of Colt firearms and memorabilia; to provide a means of exchanging knowledge among collectors; and to offer an annual show and meeting for members and guests with an emphasis on a convenient and quality location.

National Automatic Pistol Collector's Association, P.O. Box 15738, Tower Grove Station, St. Louis, MO 63163 www.napca.net Created in 1968 the purposes of this association are: to exchange information on all semi-automatic pistols; to assist and encourage new collectors; to exchange ideas; to assist authors writing new reference works; and to assist members in building their collections.

Remington Society of America, C/O RSA Treasurer Robert Kneppler, RBK Services, 718 Westcott St., Houston, TX 77007 www.remingtonsociety.com An organization dedicated to the collection and study of Remington firearms, ammunition and history. The first official meeting of two dozen dedicated collectors took place at the Winter Antique Arms Show in Las Vegas in January 1982.

Sharps Collector Association, P. O. Box 36674, Phoenix, AZ 85067-6674 www.sharpscollector.com The Sharps Collector Association was formed in 1993 to study the firearms of Christian Sharps and the Sharps Companies: Sharps Rifle Manufacturing Company, Sharps Rifle Company, C. Sharps & Company and Sharps and Hankins.

Smith & Wesson Collectors Association, Inc., C/O Michael G. Speers, Administrative Assistant, P.O. Box 357, Larned, KS 67550 www.theswca.org Formed officially in 1970, SWCA is the oldest specialized collector's association in the US. SWCA is dedicated to the collecting of all Smith & Wesson products from the antique firearms to modern arms currently produced by the company. The main purpose is the preservation of Smith & Wesson history.

The Vintagers: Order of Edwardian Gunners, 29 Pond Rd., Hawley, MA 01339 (413-339-5347 www.vintagers.org) The mission of this not-for-profit corporation is to provide an opportunity for the use, appreciation and collection of side-by-side shotguns and rifles.

Winchester Arms Collectors Association, Inc., 270 Hwy. 96 S/P.O. Box 367, Silsbee, TX 77656 (409-385-9768 www.winchestercollector.org) The Winchester Arms Collectors Association (WACA) is a non-profit corporation dedicated to the preservation of all Winchester produced and related items. Includes Henry Rifles.

AUCTION HOUSES

AuctionArms.com: Online auction for firearms and collectibles. www.auctionarms.com

GunBroker.com: Online auction, with on line firearms and accessory appraisals. www.gunbroker.com

Cowan's Auctions: 673 Wilmer Ave., Cincinnati, OH 45226 (513) 871-1670 www.cowanauctions.com

James D. Julia: P.O. Box 830 Rte. 201, Skowhegan Rd., Fairfield, ME 04937 (207) 453-7125 www.juliaauctions.com

Kull & Supica: Online firearms and accessory auction. www.armsbid.com (links to Jim Supica's http://armchairgunshow.com/.)

Rock Island Auction: 4507 49th Ave., Moline, IL 61265 (800) 238-8022 www.rockislandauction.com

ONLINE AND OF INTEREST

http://armsbid.com: The Kull & Supica Arms Auction. Jim Supica accepts consignments (913-492-3000 jim@armchairgunshow.com)

www.antiquegunlist.com: Antiquegunlist.com is the leading provider of antique firearms for sale to collectors who specialize in firearms. We provide antique gun prices and multiple pictures of each antique firearm we sell. (Also sells other categories such as coins, books, fishing collectibles, badges and gun parts.) Affiliated with Ed Cox, Box 2197, Fernley, NV 89408 (557-575-6205 ed@coltparts.com)

www.armchairgunshow.com: Fine firearms for sale from Jim Supica's Old Town Station, Ltd. This site associated with http://armsbid.com and www.downrange.tv with Michael Bane (620-374-3079 office@downrange.tv).

www.collectorsfirearms.com: Collector's Firearms, 3301 Fondren Suite O, Houston, TX 77063 (713-781-1960/877-214-9327) Large collection of militaria, uniforms, weapons, and memorabilia of all types. We stock reference books on these and other subjects. We go beyond the purely collectable by having all kinds of shootable firearms, both antique and modern in our store. More than 5,000 guns in stock at any one time and 2,000 books.

www.coltparts.com: We have Colt gun parts for pre 1898 models. Also features fine antique guns, accoutrements and Old West memorabilia. Ed Cox, Box 2197, Fernley, NV 89408 (557-575-6205 ed@coltparts.com). Affiliated with John Kopec Publications www.coltparts.com/johnkopec.html (1366 Carla Circle, Redding, CA 96003 530-222-4440) and Colt cavalry and artillery revolver authentication service.)

www.flayderman.com: N. Flayderman & Co., Historic Antique Arms & Militaria, P.O. Box 2446, Ft. Lauderdale, FL 33303 (954-761-8855) Established in 1952, Flayderman is recognized as one of the best known names in the antique arms and militaria fields. Their slogan is "You Can Order With Confidence...Our Reputation is Our Guarantee." Although they no longer issue catalogs, they remain active and continue to list and describe interesting and rare items via their web page.

www.historicalguns.net/www.michaelsimens.com: Michael Simens, 5900 Som Center Rd., Bldg. 12, Suite 275, Willoughby, OH 44094 (216-541-4111 msimens@adelphia.net) Pre-1898 antique guns, weapons and artifacts; U.S. Civil War swords and Colt percussion specialists.

www.incavoappraisals.com: 105 E Vallette Street, Suite 1336, Elmhurst, IL 60126 (630-359-9013 thomas.guerin@incavoappraisals.com) Experienced consultants personally determine the fair market value of firearms and provide appraisal letters to protect a firearms investment with adequate insurance. More than 25 years experience buying and selling firearms of all types – Revolutionary War flint-lock rifles to trap and skeet shotguns to modern handguns and rifles.

www.krause.com: Krause Publications, 700 E State St., Iola, WI 54990 The world's largest publisher of leisure-time magazines and books.

www.oldwestgunsmith.com: Site of David R. Chicoine, author, gunsmith, gun appraiser, dealer, restoration specialist. The Smith & Wesson factory has been referring its customers with older and antique S&W's to David since about 1976. In recent years, David has been joined in the gunsmithing business by his son, David T. Chicoine. DRC has been working on Smith & Wesson revolvers since he was a teenager in the 1960s when he began tinkering with police friend's revolvers in New York. Later, starting in about 1974 in southern NY, operating as Liberty Antique Sixgun Parts he has kept an inventory of obsolete-antique Smith & Wesson parts and offered gunsmithing services for antique S&W's. David then moved his family to southeastern Connecticut and operated as Liberty Antique Gunworks offering repair serevices for all older firearms for several years. Moving to Maine in 1983, he spent the next 17 years gunsmithing in northeastern Maine on the Atlantic coast, we have been in sunny North Carolina since 2000.

www.singleshotexchange.com: Single Shot Exchange, P. O. Box 1055, York, SC 29745 (803) 628-5326 The Single Shot Exchange magazine was started in 1991, and has grown to become today's definitive periodical for shooters and collectors. Styled after similar publications from the 1850's through the early 1900's, excellent articles written for today are enhanced by catalog plates or photos and tintypes from earlier eras. Single Shot Exchange puts you in touch with collectors, shooters, suppliers, and dealers on a national and international basis - and is a must-have for anyone interested in antique and classic firearms. In addition to informative and entertaining content, each issue contains new advertisements from hundreds of individuals with fine high-quality antique and classic arms for sale. National lists of upcoming matches are given, too. Equally important are the many outstanding commercial advertisers.

www.vincaponi.com: Vin Caponi Historic Antiques, 10 Broadway, Malverne, NY 11565 (516-593-3516) A family business buying and selling fine antiques since 1965. "Civil War military to antique military and toys. Our collection of Colt firearms and accessories, revolvers, pistols, carbines, accoutrements, photography, edged weapons and swords are of the highest quality. As taught by my father before me, we sell original quality items that are backed by our family guarantee."

INTERNET RESOURCES

Antique & Collectable Firearms & Militaria Headquarters: http://oldguns.net/ Appraisals, classic and modern firearms, accessories, edged weapons, militaria, books, related items.

Antique Firearm Network: http://www.americanselfdefense.com/links/antiquefirearms.html Information on antique and vintage firearms.

AntiqueGuns.com: www.antiqueguns.com Antique firearms, swords and collectibles.

Arms & Armor Inc.: www.armor.com/ Medieval arms and armor.

Cartridge Identification Bibliography: www.digitalpresence.com/histarch/cartridg.html, www.recguns.com/Sources/VIIE1.html (both by Michael Pfeiffer) and http://cartridgecollectors.org/bibliography.htm Citations for cartridge identification.

Collector Online Club Directory: www.collectoronline.com/cgi-bin/clubs.cgi?groupKey=7 Directory of clubs related to antiques and collectibles.

US Army Museum Directory: www.history.army.mil/Museums/AMS-Directory/index.htm Directory of US Army museums.

MUSEUMS AND FIREARMS/ARMAMENTS INFORMATION

Air Force Armament Museum: 100 Museum Dr., Eglin Air Force Base, FL 32542 (904) 882-4062 www.afarmamentmuseum.com Collection includes armaments, gun vault, and related items; exhibits.

The Alamo: 300 Alamo Plaza, San Antonio, TX 78205 (210) 225-1391 www.thealamo.org Collection includes rifles, pistols, cannon, knives, spurs and related items; exhibits; educational programs.

American Historical Foundation Museum: 1142 West Grace St., Richmond, VA 23220 (804) 353-1812 www.ahfrichmond.com/museum.html Collection includes militaria, military knives and bayonets; library; exhibits; educational programs. Sales of replicas and collectibles.

American Institute for Conservation of Historic & Artistic Works (AIC): 1717 K St., NW, Suite 200, Washington, DC 20006 (202) 452-9545 http://aic.stanford.edu/ Provides referrals for conservators.

American Military Heritage Foundation Museum: 1215 S Franklin Rd., Indianapolis, IN 46229 (317) 335-2889 www.amhf.org Dedicated to preserving, in flying condition, vintage military aircraft.

American Military Museum: 40 Pinckney St., Charleston, SC 29401 (803) 723-9620 www.americanmilitarymuseum.org Collection includes weapons and related items; exhibits.

American Police Center and Museum: 1717 South State St., Chicago, IL 60616 (312) 431-0005 Collection includes weapons and other police artifacts; library; educational programs; exhibits.

American Society of Arms Collectors: Membership by Invitation Only http://americansocietyofarmscollectors.org/ Advanced arms collectors, researchers, authors & museum directors interested in antique arms and weapons.

American Society of Military History Military Museum: 1918 North Rosemead Blvd. South El Monte, CA (626) 442-1776 http://hometown.aol.com/tankland/museum.htm To preserve and restore examples of American military equipment with exhibits from all branches of the U.S. Armed Forces.

Antietam National Battlefield: P.O. Box 158, Sharpsburg, MD 21782 (301) 432-5124 www.nps.gov/anti/index.htm Collection includes Civil War weapons and related items; library; exhibits; educational programs.

Berman Museum of World History: 840 Museum Dr., Anniston, AL 36206 (256) 237-6261 www.bermanmuseum.org Collection includes firearms from around the world.

Buffalo Bill Historical Center: 720 Sheridan Ave., Cody, WY 82414 (307) 587-4771 www.bbhc.org Center houses five museums including the Cody Firearms Museum with its comprehensive assemblage of American firearms.

Chickamauga-Chattanooga National Military Park: US 27 South, P.O. Box 2128, Fort Oglethorpe, GA 30742 (706) 866-9241 www.nps.gov/chch/ Collection includes Civil War relics and the Fuller gun collection of American military shoulder arms; library.

Cleveland Police Historical Society, Inc. and Museum: 1300 Ontario St., Cleveland, OH 44113 (216) 623-5055 www.clevelandpolicemuseum.org Collection includes Cleveland Police Department artifacts from 1866 to the present including firearms; programs.

Colonial National Historical Park: Jamestown & Yorktown, Colonial Parkway, P.O. Box 210, Yorktown, VA 23690 (804) 898-3400 www.nps.gov/colo/ Collection includes 17th and 18th century arms and artifacts; library; exhibits; educational programs.

Columbus Chapel, Boal Mansion Museum: Business Route 322, P.O. Box 116, Boalsburg, PA 16827 (814) 466-6210 www.boalmuseum.com Collection includes weapons from colonial period to WWI and related items; library; exhibits; educational programs.

The Company of Military Historians (Headquarters and Museum): N. Main St., Westbrook, CT 06498 (203) 399-9460 http://www.military-historians.org/ Military collection from 1775 to the present; library; exhibits; educational programs.

Confederate Museum: Alexander St., Crawfordville, GA 30631 (706) 456-2221 Collection includes Civil War arms and memorabilia; exhibits.

Confederate Museum: 929 Camp St., New Orleans, LA 70130 (504) 523-4522 www.confederatemuseum.com Collection includes Civil War weapons and related items; exhibits.

Cowpens National Battlefield: P.O. Box 308, Chesnee, SC 29323 (864) 461-2828 www.nps.gov/cowp/ Collection includes Revolutionary War period weapons and records.

Crockett County Museum: Courthouse Annex, 404 Eleventh St., Ozona, TX 76943 (915) 392-2837 Collection includes guns and early pioneer items; library; educational programs.

Dane G. Hansen Memorial Museum: 110 West Main St., Logan, KS 67646 (913) 689-4846 www.hansenmuseum.org/ Collection includes guns, coins and Oriental art; exhibits.

Drum Barracks Civil War Museum: 1052 Banning Blvd., Wilmington, CA 90744 (310) 548-7509 www.drumbarracks.org Collection includes Civil War firearms and related items; library; exhibits; educational programs.

The Exchange Hotel Civil War Museum: 400 South Main St., Gordonsville, VA 22942 (540) 832-2944 www.hgiexchange.org Collection includes Civil War weapons and related items; library; exhibits; educational programs.

Favell Museum of Western Art and Indian Artifacts: 125 West Main St., Klamath Falls, OR 97601 (541) 882-9996 www.favellmuseum.org Collection includes mini firearms and guns; exhibits; educational programs.

Fort Bliss Museum, ATSA-MM: Pleasonton & Sheridan Roads, Fort Bliss, TX 79916 (915) 568-4518 www.bliss.army.mil/Museum/fort_bliss_museum.htm Military and civilian firearms and related items; library; exhibits.

Fort Davis National Historic Site: Highway 17-118, Fort Davis, TX 79734 (915) 426-3224 www.nps.gov/foda/ Late 19th century military and civilian weapons and related items; library; exhibits.

Fort de Chartres State Historic Site & Peithmann Museum: 1350 State Route 155, Prairie du Rocher, IL 62277 (618) 284-7230 Weapons and related items; library; exhibits; educational programs.

Fort Frederick State Park: 11100 Fort Frederick Rd., Big Pool, MD 21711 (301) 842-2155 http://www.dnr.state.md.us/publiclands/western/FortFrederick.html Early firearms and Civil War rifles and related items; exhibits.

Fort George G. Meade Museum: 4674 Griffin Avenue, ANME-OPM, Fort Meade, MD 20755 (410) 677-6966/7054 http://www.ftmeade.army.mil/Museum/Index.htm Weapons and equipment from the Revolutionary War to the present; library; exhibits.

Fort Gibson Historic Site: 110 East Ash, Hwy. 80, Fort Gibson, OK 74437 (918) 478-2669 www.fortgibson.com/historical_sites.htm Weapons and related items; exhibits.

Fort Harker Museum: 309 West Ohio St., Kanopolis, KS 67454 (913) 472-5733 Guns and memorabilia from 1870 to the present; exhibits.

Fort Hartsuff State Historical Park: RR1, Box 37, Burwell, NE 68823 (308) 346-4715 Firearms and military guns; exhibits.

Fort Kearney Museum: 131 South Central Ave., Kearney, NE 68847 (308) 234-5200 www.trailsandgrasslands.org/kearny.html Pioneer arms and related items; exhibits.

Fort Laramie National Historic Site: P.O. Box 86, Fort Laramie, WY 82212 (307) 837-2221 www.nps.gov/fola/ Collection includes 19th century small arms and weapons and related items; library; exhibits; educational programs.

Fort Lewis Military Museum: Building 4320, Fort Lewis, WA 98433 (206) 967-7206 www.lewis.army.mil/DPTMS/POMFI/museum.htm Collection includes historical military artifacts of the Northwest from Lewis & Clark to the present (includes weapons); exhibits.

Fort MacArthur Museum: 3601 South Gaffey St. at Battery Osgood-Farley (P.O. Box 268), San Pedro, CA 90731 (310) 548-2631 www.ftmac.org Collection includes artillery and military items; exhibits.

Fort Morgan Museum: 51 Hwy. 180 W, Gulf Shores, AL 36542 (334) 540-7125 www.ftmorganmus.org/ Weapons from the Civil War to the present; exhibits.

Fort Ontario State Historical Site: One East 74th St. (One 4th St.), Oswego, NY 13126 (315) 343-4711 www.fortontario.com/ Collection includes firearms and related items; library; exhibits; educational programs.

Fort Pike State Commemorative Area: Route 6, Box 194, New Orleans, LA 70129 (504) 662-5703 Armaments from 1812-1865 and related items; exhibits.

Fort Sam Houston Museum: 1207 Stanley Rd., MCGA-PTM-M, Fort Sam Houston, TX 78234 (512) 221-1886 http://ameddregiment.amedd.army.mil/fshmuse/fshmusemain.htm Collection includes weapons from 1835 to the present and related items; library; exhibits; educational programs.

Fort Sill Museum: 437 Quanah Rd., Fort Sill, OK 73503 (405) 351-5123 http://sill-www.army.mil/ Army field artillery, military ordnance and related items; library; exhibits; educational programs.

Fort Stanwix National Monument: 112 East Park St., Rome, NY 13440 (315) 336-2090 www.nps.gov/fost/ Arms and accoutrements from the French War, Indian War and American Revolutionary War; library; exhibits.

Fort Ticonderoga: Fort Road, Ticonderoga, NY 12883 (518) 585-2821 www.fort-ticonderoga.org/ 18th century guns and swords; library; exhibits; educational programs.

Fort Verde State Historic Park: 125 East Holloman, Camp Verde, AZ 86322 (520) 567-3275 www.pr.state.az.us/Parks/parkhtml/fortverde.htm Guns from 1871-1890 and related items; library; exhibits.

Gathland State Park: c/o South Mountain Recreation Area, 21843 National Pike, Boonsboro, MD 21713 (301) 791-4767 www.dnr.state.md.us/publiclands/western/gathland.html Collection includes Civil War guns.

Gen. Douglas L. McBride Museum: New Mexico Military Institute, 101 West College Blvd., Roswell, NM 88201 (505) 624-8820 www.nmmi.cc.nm.us/index.htm Collection includes Civil War to the present small weapons and related items; library; exhibits.

Guilford Courthouse National Military Park: 2332 New Garden Rd., Greensboro, NC 27410 (910) 288-1776 www.nps.gov/guco/ Collection includes Revolutionary War weapons and related objects; library; exhibits.

Harold B. Simpson Confederate Research Center & Audie L. Murphy Gun Museum: P.O. Box 619, Hillsboro, TX 76645 (817) 582-2555 http://gen.1starnet.com/civilwar/crcmain.htm Collection includes Civil War guns and related items; library; exhibits.

Higgins Armory Museum: 100 Barber Ave., Worcester, MA 01606 (508) 853-6015 www.higgins.org/ Collection includes ancient, medieval and renaissance arms, armor and related material culture; library; exhibits; educational programs.

Historic Fort Stockton: 300 E Third, Fort Stockton, TX 79735 (915) 336-2400 Collection includes historic weapons and related items; library; educational programs.

Houston Police Museum: 17000 Aldine Westfield Rd., Houston, TX 79914 (713) 230-2361 Collection includes police artifacts from 1841 to the present including weapons; library; educational programs; exhibits.

International Association of Museums of Arms and Military History (IAMAM)

Musée d'Armes de Liège: Quai de Maestricht 8, B-4000 Liège, Belgium Information on armaments and related items.

J.M. Davis Arms and Historical Museum: 333 N Lynn Riggs Blvd., Claremore, OK 74018 (918) 341-5707 www.state.ok.us/~jmdavis/index.html Collection includes firearms, swords and knives, and related items; library; educational programs.

Kennesaw Mountain National Battlefield Park: 900 Kennesaw Mountain Dr., Kennesaw, GA 30152 (770) 427-4686 www.state.ok.us/~jmdavis/index.html Collection includes Civil War weapons and uniforms; library.

LaPorte, Indiana, Historical Society Museum: 2405 Indiana Ave., LaPorte, IN 46350 (219) 324-6767 www.laportecountyhistory.com Contains W.A. Jones collection of ancient weapons and thousands of historic firearms with complementary exhibits.

Medal of Honor Museum: 400 Georgia Ave., Chattanooga, TN 37403 (423) 267-1737 www.mohm.org/ Collection includes weapons from 1776 to the present; photo archives; exhibits.

Metropolitan Museum of Art: 1000 Fifth Ave., New York, NY 10028 (212) 535-7710 www.metmuseum.org Collections include vast array of armor, edged weapons and firearms including full suits of Japanese armor.

Military Museum of Southern New England: 125 Park Ave., Danbury, CT 06810 (203) 790-9277 www.usmilitarymuseum.org/ Collection includes weapons and other related items; restoration of military vehicles and weapons; exhibits.

Military Police Corps Museum: Building 3182, Fort McClellan, AL 36205 (205) 848-3522 www.wood.army.mil/usamps/history/ Collection includes military police corps weapons and memorabilia; library; exhibits.

Miniature Arms Collectors and Makers Society: c/o William Adrian, 22W071 Stratford Ct., Glen Ellyn, IL 60137 (800) 847-6788 www.miniaturearms.com/ Collecting, making, promoting knowledge, studying, preserving, and disseminating information on miniature arms collecting and making.

Miracle of America Museum: 58176 Hwy. 93, Polson, MT 59860, (406) 883-6804 www.miracleofamericamuseum.org/ Collection includes Civil War to the present guns and militaria; library; exhibits; educational programs.

Moores Creek National Battlefield: 200 Moores Creek Dr., Currie, NC 28435 (910) 283-5591 www.nps.gov/mocr/ Collection includes weapons and related items; library; exhibits.

Morristown National Historical Park: Washington Place, Morristown, NJ 07960 (201) 539-2016 www.nps.gov/morr/index.htm Collection includes 18th century military weapons and equipment; library; exhibits; educational programs.

Museum of Southern History: 2740 FM 359, Richmond, TX 77406 (713) 342-8787 www.museumofsouthernhistory.org/ Collection includes Civil War period weapons and related artifacts; library; exhibits.

National Firearms Museum: 11250 Waples Mill Rd., Fairfax, VA 22030 (703) 267-1600 www.nationalfirearmsmuseum.org/default.asp Collection includes antique and modern firearms; library; exhibits.

National Infantry Museum: U.S. Army Infantry Center, Building 396, Baltzell Ave., Fort Benning, GA 31905 (706) 545-6762 www.benningmwr.com/museum31905.htm Collection includes weapons, collection of firearms including experimental US items, and other related items; library; exhibitions.

Harpers Ferry Armory and Arsenal: Harpers Ferry, WV 25425 (304) 535-6139. Collection includes weapons and related items at various holding across the U.S.

The Navy Museum: Washington Navy Yard, 901 M St. SE, Washington, DC 20374 (202) 433-4882 www.history.navy.mil/branches/nhcorg8.htm Collection includes 19th-20th century weapons and related items; library; exhibits; educational programs.

Ogden Union Station: 2501 Wall Ave., Ogden, UT 84401 (801) 393-9882 www.theunionstation.org Includes the Browning Firearms Museum, celebrating the genius of John M. Browning (1855-1926).

Old Guard Museum: Building 249, Sheridan Ave., Fort Myer, VA 22211 (703) 696-6670/4168 www.army.mil/oldguard/Museum/togm-web/index.htm Collection includes military weapons, uniforms, and related items from 1784 to the present; library; exhibits.

Old Stone House Museum: 22 Chestnut St., Windsor, NY 13865 (607) 655-1443/1491 http://Old Stone House Museum.org Collection includes Civil War weapons and related items; library; exhibits.

Presidio Museum: Golden Gate National Recreation Area, Building 2, Presidio of San Francisco, San Francisco, CA 94129 (415) 561-4331 www.nps.gov/goga/ Collection includes 18th - 20th century weaponry and related items; library; exhibits.

Puget Sound Coast Artillery Museum at Fort Worden: Building 201, Fort Worden State Park, 200 Battery Way, Port Townsend, WA 98368 (360) 385-3295 www.centrum.org/fortworden/coast_artillery_museum/index.html Collection includes military rifle collection from 26 countries and related items; library; exhibits.

Remington Firearms Museum & Country Store: 14 Hoefler Ave., Ilion, NY 13357 (315) 895-3200 Collection includes Remington firearms and artifacts from the 1820s to the present; exhibits.

Rock Island Arsenal Museum: Rock Island Arsenal, SIORICFM, Rock Island, IL 61299 (309) 782-5021 www.ria.army.mil/ Collection includes weapons and equipment.

Rockwell Museum: 111 Cedar St., Corning, NY 14830 (607) 937-5386 www.rockwellmuseum.org/flash/index.html Collection includes firearms; library; exhibits; educational programs.

Rosehill Cemetery and Civil War Museum: 5800 N Ravenswood, Chicago, IL 60660 (312) 561-5940 www.waymarking.com/waymarks/WMHYV Collection includes firearms, infantry weaponry, artillery cannon and related items; library; exhibits; educational programs.

Royal Hamilton Light Infantry Heritage Museum: John W. Foote VC Armoury, 200 James St. N, Hamilton, ON Canada L8R 2L1 (905) 528-2945 www.rhli.ca/museum/museum.html Preservation, interpretation and acquisition of civilian and military artifacts of the area.

Sackets Harbor Battlefield State Historic Site: 505 West Washington Street, PO Box 27, Sackets Harbor, NY 13685 (315) 646-3634 www.nysparks.state.ny.us/sites/info.asp?siteID=25 Collection includes weapons and related items from the War of 1812; library; exhibits; educational programs.

Saunders Memorial Museum: 113-15 E Madison St., Berryville, AR 72616 (501) 423-2563 Collection includes guns; exhibits.

Smithsonian Institution: National Museum of American History, Dept. of the History of Science and Technology, Division of Armed Forces History, AHB 4013, MRC 620, Washington, DC 20560 (202) 357-1883

www.si.edu/Encyclopedia_SI/History_and_Culture/Military_History.htm
Large collection of firearms; information on care.

Society of American Bayonet Collectors: P.O. Box 234, East Islip, NY 11730 Study, collection and preservation of antique and modern bayonets and related accoutrements.

Soldiers' Memorial Military Museum: 1315 Chestnut St., St. Louis, MO 63103 (314) 622-4550 http://stlouis.missouri.org/government/sol-mem.html Collection includes weapons and related items; exhibits.

Springfield Armory National Historic Site: One Armory Square, Springfield, MA 01105 (413) 734-8551 www.nps.gov/spar/ Collection includes military small arms, Springfield firearms from 1790-1969 including experimental and prototypes, Civil War rifle-muskets, hand guns, machine guns, and related items; library education center; exhibits.

Texas Ranger Hall of Fame & Museum: Fort Fisher Park, Interstate 35 & the Brazos River, Waco, TX 76702 (817) 750-8631 www.texas-ranger.org/ Collection includes Texas Ranger firearms and memorabilia; library; exhibits.

3rd Calvary Museum: Building 2160, AFZC-DT-MM, Fort Carson, CO 80913 (719) 526-3674 www.6thcavalrytroopb.com/ Collection includes weapons and related items from 1846 to the present; library; exhibits.

US Army Center of Military History – Museum Division: 1099 14th St. NW, Washington, DC 20005-3402 (202) 761-5373 www.history.army.mil/ Large military collection; exhibits; educational programs.

U.S. Army Ordnance Museum: c/o US Army Ordnance Center & School, Aberdeen, MD 21005 (410) 278-3602/3696 www.ordmusfound.org/ Collection include ordnance equipment from many countries and wars, small arms from the 16th century to the present and related items; library; exhibits.

US Army Quartermaster Museum: Attn: ATSM-QMG-M, Fort Lee, VA 23801 (804) 734-4203 www.qmmuseum.lee.army.mil/ Collection includes weapons and related items; exhibits.

US Army Signal Corps and Fort Gordon Museum: Building 36305, Fort Gordon, GA 30905 (706) 791-2818/3856 www.gordon.army.mil/ocos/Museum/ Collection includes weapons, swords and other related items; library; exhibits; educational programs.

US Marine Corps Air-Ground Museum: 2014 Anderson Ave., Quantico, VA 22134 (703) 784-2606 www.aero-web.org/museums/va/usmcagm.htm Collection includes weapons and related items; exhibits.

U.S. Marine Corps Museum: Marine Corps Historical Center, Washington Navy Yard, Building 58, 901 M St. SE, Washington, DC 20374 (202) 433-3534/2484 www.usmcmuseum.org/index.asp Collection includes weapons and related items; library; exhibits.

Varnum Memorial Armory & Military Museum: 6 Main St., East Greenwich, RI 02818 (401) 884-4110 www.varnumcontinentals.org Collection includes armament and military artifacts from the 16th-20th centuries.

Virginia War Museum: 9285 Warwick Blvd., Huntington Park, Newport News, VA 23607 (757) 247-8523 www.warmuseum.org/ Collection includes weapons and related items from 1776 to the present; library; exhibits.

Warren Rifles Confederate Museum: 95 Chester St., Front Royal, VA 22630 (703) 636-6982 http://users.erols.com/va-udc/museum.html Collection includes War between the States relics - guns, uniforms, swords, and other related items; library; exhibits.

Washington's Headquarters State Historic Site: 84 Liberty St., Newburgh, NY 12550 (914) 562-1195 www.nysparks.state.ny.us/sites/info.asp?siteID=32 Collection includes firearms of the American Revolutionary War and related items; archives; exhibits; educational programs.

Watervliet Arsenal Museum: Watervliet Arsenal, Route 32, Watervliet, NY 12189-4050 (518) 266-5805 http://www.wva.army.mil/MUSE-UM.HTM Collection includes military materials and equipment from the 1700s to the present; library; exhibits.

Woolaroc Museum: State Highway 123, Route 3, Box 2100, Bartlesville, OK 74003 (918) 336-0307 www.woolaroc.org/ Collection includes guns and related items; exhibitions; educational programs.

CHECKLIST FOR POTENTIAL FAKE OR ALTERED GUNS

Note: The following checklist is not infallible but does include points that merit close examination. When in doubt, consult an appropriate reference work or competent authority before purchasing!

FINISH:

☐ Does bluing/nickel still exist in protected areas (e.g., underneath wood; where barrel meets receiver)? If not, gun may have been cleaned or may be an aged reproduction.

☐ Is there pitting underneath the surface finish? If so, this indicates a re-finish/restoration.

☐ Nickel finish: Does it fill in letterings/markings, making them look muddy and indistinct? If so, this may indicate a re-finish.

☐ Is finish more or less evenly worn? If not, some parts may have been replaced.

☐ Is the condition of the external finish consistent with the condition of the stocks/grips and bore? If not, the gun may have ben re-finished, or new grips added.

LETTERING/MARKINGS:

☐ Are edges sharp and clear? Are they TOO sharp and clear? If markings have blurred or indistinct edges, is it because of honest wear or has the metal been buffed? (Buffing tends to produce "smeared" markings.)

☐ Is the metal at the bottom of the markings bright? Does it match the rest of the exterior metal finish? Too-bright lettering may indicate restamping.

☐ Do serial numbers match? Are they correct for the claimed vintage? (Note: Beware of so-called "low serial number" guns. One-, two-, or three-digit numbers are often assembly numbers, not serial numbers, especially on 19th-century European guns.)

☐ Are markings correct for period? (Pre-1900 lettering is generally, but not always, characterized by serifs: small perpendicular lines found at the base and crossbars of the individual letters, as in: **COLT**.

STOCKS/GRIPS:

☐ Do they fit flush with metal surfaces? Large, irregular gaps may indicate replaced wood. Uniform shrinkage, however, is common in antique guns.

☐ Are there splits/repairs/splices?

☐ Too smooth? Too shiny? If so, it may indicate sanding or refinishing.

☐ Hard rubber: Should not be too shiny. As hard rubber ages, resins leech from the material, causing a dull appearance.

☐ Is appearance consistent with bore and external finish?

MECHANICAL:

☐ Do all parts fit properly? (Revolvers: Do bores of cylinders match barrel bore?) If not, suspect replacement parts.

☐ Are metal edges sharp or rounded? Rounded edges may indicate buffing/re-finishing.

☐ Is condition of bore consistent with external appearance? If not, suspect re-finishing.

☐ Is caliber/bore consistent with known examples? Reproductions are often chambered for readily-available modern cartridges and round ball sizes.

☐ Screws: American- and British-made vintage guns should have screws with standard thread pitch. Guns made in continental Europe (including modern reproductions) usually have metric threads. A common thread gauge can detect the difference.

☐ Fired vs. Unfired: Guns that have been fired will usually bear some signs of leading (i.e., lead deposits) or powder residue. Use a clean cotton swab to check for powder residue. Check the face of the bolt (rifles) and cylinder (revolvers). In semi-auto pistols and shotguns, check the bolt and frame for wear. If present, it shows the action has at least been cycled. In revolvers, check for a faint line passing through the bolt cutouts on the cylinder. Such a line indicates that the cylinder has been turned.

More Firearms Expertise and Advice

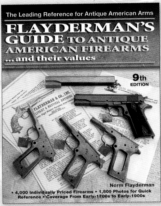
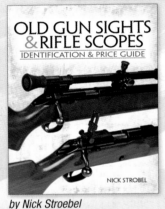
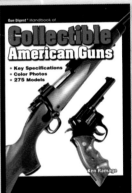

☐ Are markings correct for period? (Pre-1900 lettering is generally, but not always, characterized by serifs: small perpendicular lines found at the base and crossbars of the individual letters, as in: **COLT**.

STOCKS/GRIPS:

☐ Do they fit flush with metal surfaces? Large, irregular gaps may indicate replaced wood. Uniform shrinkage, however, is common in antique guns.

☐ Are there splits/repairs/splices?

☐ Too smooth? Too shiny? If so, it may indicate sanding or re-finishing.

☐ Hard rubber: Should not be too shiny. As hard rubber ages, resins leech from the material, causing a dull appearance.

☐ Is appearance consistent with bore and external finish?

MECHANICAL:

☐ Do all parts fit properly? (Revolvers: Do bores of cylinders match barrel bore?) If not, suspect replacement parts.

☐ Are metal edges sharp or rounded? Rounded edges may indicate buffing/re-finishing.

☐ Is condition of bore consistent with external appearance? If not, suspect re-finishing.

☐ Is caliber/bore consistent with known examples? Reproductions are often chambered for readily-available modern cartridges and round ball sizes.

☐ Screws: American- and British-made vintage guns should have screws with standard thread pitch. Guns made in continental Europe (including modern reproductions) usually have metric threads. A common thread gauge can detect the difference.

☐ Fired vs. Unfired: Guns that have been fired will usually bear some signs of leading (i.e., lead deposits) or powder residue. Use a clean cotton swab to check for powder residue. Check the face of the bolt (rifles) and cylinder (revolvers). In semi-auto pistols and shotguns, check the bolt and frame for wear. If present, it shows the action has at least been cycled. In revolvers, check for a faint line passing through the bolt cut-outs on the cylinder. Such a line indicates that the cylinder has been turned.

More Firearms Expertise and Advice

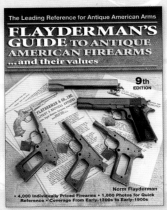

by Norm Flayderman
Flayderman's is where it's at for checking updated collector values of all your antique arms, while you brush up on the characteristics of vintage firearms manufactured between the colonial era and 1900.
Softcover • 8-1/4 x 10-7/8 • 752 pages
1900 b&w photos • 16-page color section
Item# Z0620 • $39.99

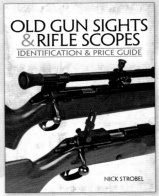

by Nick Stroebel
Sights and scopes in one authoritative reference – it doesn't get much better than this. Whether a collector or a shooter you're sure to appreciate the market pricing, and identifying photos of devices manufactured between the mid-1880s through 1985.
Softcover • 8-1/4 x 10-7/8
584 pages • 650 b&w photos
100 color photos
Item# Z2346 • $34.99

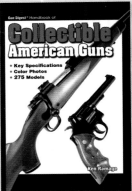

Edited by Ken Ramage
Unique and easy-to-carry, this book features 275 of the most collectible modern American firearms ever made. Collection includes the Colt 1911, Savage Model 99 Rifle, Winchester Model 70 Rifle and more.
Softcover • 6 x 9 • 304 pages
250 color photos
Item# Z0784 • $24.99

by Joseph Cornell
Immerse yourself in expertly analyzed prices, 500 superb color photos, and technical details for Winchester rifles and shotguns, manufactured between 1866 and the present.
Softcover • 8-1/4 x 10-7/8
288 pages • 350 color photos
Item# Z0932 • $29.99